Spirit of Freedom

Living FREE vs. FREE Living

> *"Those who desire to give up freedom to gain security, will not have, nor do they deserve, either one."*
> *— Benjamin Franklin*

Rod Miller with
Thomas Young, PhD.

First Printing Date: June, 2013
Revised Edition: July, 2013

ISBN: 1479223395
ISBN 13: 9781479223398
Library of Congress Control Number: 2012916857
CreateSpace, North Charleston, SC

Printed in the United States of America

Author's Note

This book is a compilation of essays and commentary covering political and economic history and what can be expected the future.

Individualism and collectivism are forever a concern in society. The purpose of this book is to contrast the subtle and not so subtle differences.

There are people whose accomplishments in life merit substantial recognition and their 'smarter than me' thoughts are generously sprinkled throughout as essays and quotes. In a sense, this book is a hybrid anthology.

Most essays were first published in 1952 or earlier. The accepted spelling and grammar used in those times has been left untouched.

Now, sixty years later, our intent is to enable the reader to compare a variety of current conditions to those of past generations. Those clues from history reveal a predictable future.

The images found on the Internet and included herein are understood to be in the public domain.

The Internet is a dynamic resource and any Internet addresses or links contained herein may change after publication and may not be valid.

This soft cover book is printed in black and white. Color printing is much more expensive so illustrations referring to colors may be more challenging to the reader. The electronic book version is published in full color for reasons of economy, clarity and better communication of the ideas presented.

The customary INDEX has been replaced with an INDEX OF CONTENTS. Technological advances are replacing the INDEX with an easy to use SEARCH capability in digital versions of this book.

Brief biographies of each author may be found at end of the book.

Dedication

This book is dedicated to America's service men and women and memorializes my brother, Robert Charles Miller.

ROBERT C. MILLER (1939-2010)

Bob smoked cigarettes since age 14 and lived to regret it.
The moral is obvious.
SEMPER FI, Brother

Acknowledgments

All of us have been influenced by people who made special contributions to enhance our lives.

My best friend, Faith Joy Heckenberg encouraged me to compile and write this book. Her gentle persuasion assured me that others would benefit from my life's experiences.

My high school history teacher, Mrs. Myrtle Higley, introduced me to the wisdom and brilliance embodied in the Constitution of the United States giving me a sense of history and its importance.

In 1967, Edward P. Prescott, Sanford B. Noll and Eugene V. True introduced me to the real world of business as seen from the top down. Their patience and understanding helped a budding entrepreneur enter the world of financial opportunity proving to me, first hand, that even the poorest of the poor can climb the ladder of success in America.

Thomas Young, Ph.D. is co-author of *Spirit of Freedom*. Dr. Young authored charts, graphs and valuable recent insight about the present day economic veracity of essays written long ago.

Last and most important of all, I am most thankful to my children, Chuck, Shelly, Erika and Winfield Scott "Buck" Miller, all of whom have made me proud to be their father.

Index of Contents

Preface

"Man is an individual being. Man is also a social being. His material success even his existence depends on the progress of others. Yet, man's fortunes and existence depend also on himself. In some respects he is tied to others, but in most respects he must be freed from others.

Defining this relationship between man and his fellow-men, discovering precisely where man should act socially and where he should act individually, has been a challenge throughout the ages. And the solution, if it has been found, is not well known in our times.

Today, all over the world in America as elsewhere the social side of man is being emphasized to the detriment of man's individual side. Nothing on this earth but understanding and the clear explanation of such understanding can erase this twentieth-century catastrophe."

... LEONARD E. READ 1952

Today, sixty years later in 2012, we face the same dilemma and this book is meant to clarify and simplify commonly discussed issues.

Anyone who wants a clearer understanding of business and government and how they relate to each other in terms of politics and economics history should carefully read this book. The moral side of living is also addressed as it relates to the way business is or should be conducted.

John P. Kotter, Professor at Harvard Business School says, ***"Without credible communication and a lot of it, the hearts and minds of others are never captured."***

And so it is with this book ... there will always be a need to remind Americans of their unique position in the history of the world. Toward that end, a regular stream of traditional and meaningful cartoons, credible audios, videos and books in any format all help to keep ignorance from creeping into our lives. So, from time to time, we must re-visit that which has made America great, hence the purpose of this book.

Charles Darwin once observed, *"Ignorance more frequently begets confidence than does knowledge."*

Superficial knowledge is dangerous to us all because the willfully delusional among us are easy prey for the sales pitches and empty promises of politicians and their benefactors. In football, it is said that the best offense is a good defense. The same is true with liberty ... it must be defended well because it is always under attack.

This book contrasts ideas about Liberty, Freedom and Individualism *versus* Power, Force and Collectivism (Statism). The words are used and set in opposition to emphasize the differences because labels can be confusing as well as intentionally misleading.

FREE living always sounds great until one examines the overall cost. As is usually the case, there is no such thing as a free lunch. Everything in life has a price tag and we should evaluate every 'purchase' as carefully as we do as when we guard pennies at Wal-Mart.

In 2012, **Conservatives** (those favoring a political and social philosophy of individual rights and liberties focused on retaining traditional social institutions inclusive of liberty, freedom and individualism) and **Liberals** (those favoring a political philosophy or worldview focused on equality through power, force and collectivism) find themselves sitting at opposite ends of the see-saw. This book is intended to help those in the middle make up their minds.

The lifestyles that *can* result from a free enterprise system *versus* the lifestyles that *do* result under the varieties of collectivism are critically important. Understanding the consequences associated with the two distinct alternatives can be life altering in the extreme.

According to William James, *"If you can change your mind, you can change your life."*

Approaching this book with an open mind just might change your life.

Introduction

*"In a sense there have always and ever been only two political philosophies:
liberty and power. Either people should be free to live their lives as they see
fit, as long as they respect the equal rights of others, or some people should
be able to use force to make other people act in ways they wouldn't choose."*

... DAVID BOAZ

When a legal document is written, lawyers usually include definitions to
precisely describe what is meant when words and/or phrases in a document
have conflicting meanings. The following definitions fit the theme of this
book quite well:

Living FREE refers to Liberty (Freedom) or Individualism, which is
the political philosophy or ideology stressing independence and self-reliance.
Individualists choose to realize their goals and desires on their own terms
without external interference from government or others.

FREE Living refers to Power (Force) or Collectivism, which stresses
human interdependence based on a group or common interest collective.
The importance of separate individuals is subservient to the interests of the
group with an emphasis on community and society with priority given to
group goals over individual goals.

Understanding the differences between these concepts can be found by
taking a look at the animal world and comparing it to the human existence.
Think about it, humans are the only animals who think life should be fair
and equal. Other living beings thrive on competition alone.

Animals can live in the wild or their freedom can be restrained as in
a zoo. In a zoo, the animals get FREE food and shelter, but no freedom.
Similarly, humans can live as free individuals or they can live constrained

by exchanging their freedom for FREE food, clothing and shelter. FREE in the extreme can mean slavery in the human world.

INDIVIDUALISM is FREEDOM (LIBERTY)

The level of comfort, success and dignity achieved by any living thing is directly proportional to its degree of individual freedom.

The enrichment of one's ability through education, hard work and common sense combined with luck and timing can produce great wealth for those who persist through success and failure. Energized by the prospects of wealth, capitalism rewards successful risk takers.

Some people choose to organize into self-serving groups and use political clout to achieve ends that do not necessarily benefit the entire population. When people buy into socialist behavior they deprive themselves of the chance to test their mettle against their peers in life. The challenge for each individual is to find a way to strive and succeed and overcome difficult circumstances. In an economic sense, capitalism is survival of the fittest for humans.

Nature brings people into the world one at a time. Even twins (or more) are not holding hands as they are born. We all come into this world serially, one by one, as individuals. Early on, children learn to be cautious. Eventually, they incorporate fear into themselves and all too often they do not learn how to overcome that fear.

Some fear is rational and some is not. Dealing with fear is part of what we hope you will take from this book. This alone will help you to deal with the inconsistencies or disagreements you may have based on how you presently view the subject matter. Overcoming fear is the first step toward an open mind.

From the earliest days of America and on to the present day, Americans need to be reminded about their heritage and how events can alter the future to the detriment of their way of life.

Free Enterprise (Liberty)

Per Wikipedia: "Capitalism is an economic system in which the means of production are owned by private persons, and operated for profit and where investments, distribution, income, production and pricing of goods and services are predominantly determined through the operation of a free market.

Capitalism is usually considered to involve the right of individuals and corporations to trade, using money, in goods, services (including finance), labor and land.

Ideally, capitalist systems are governed by the free price system set by the law of supply and demand rather than government regulation, though this does not exclude government defining and enforcing the basic rules of the market."

Those who permit the smallest losses of freedom will eventually be restrained by those in the majority. The insidious, satanic forces that seek to rule the lives of others must be contained to preserve freedom. Like the symptoms of an infection, threats to freedom must be treated. If not, history proves that government slavery is inevitable.

The wealthy and politically connected in ANY society are ALWAYS treated better. In reality, there is NO political system that provides equal "redistribution" and humans are the ONLY animals who seek fairness in life ... and we humans are supposed to be the intelligent ones?

The late Adrian Pierce Rogers, a Southern Baptist preacher who served two terms as president of the Southern Baptist Convention from 1979 to 1988 is quoted:

> *"You cannot legislate the poor into freedom by legislating the wealthy out of freedom. When half of the people get an idea that they do not have to work because the other half is going to take care of them, and when the other half gets the idea that it does no good to work because somebody else is going to get what they work for, that my dear friend, is about the end of any nation. You cannot multiply wealth by dividing it."*
>
> ... ADRIAN PIERCE ROGERS

An **incentive** is something that motivates an individual to perform well. Common sense tells us that when greater rewards are possible, greater dedication is devoted to the effort required to achieve those rewards.

It stands to reason that the amount taken from the wealthy and distributed to those of lesser means directly affects the amount of time, effort and investment the wealthy will devote to creating more wealth. A healthy economy runs best when everybody's oars are in the water.

Our contention is that free enterprise capitalism emphasizes the worth of the individual and maximizes the potential of every person. The challenge of management is to plan, organize and control the teamwork needed to make the product or service being offered the most successful it can be in the marketplace.

Of course, marketplace competition is inevitable, but success is guaranteed to those who do one thing better than anybody else making it virtually impossible to fail.

SOCIALISM is POWER (FORCE)

Socialist systems impose strict rules monitored and controlled by a centralized government. Individual freedom is restricted.

Marxism, Communism, Fascism, Nazism, monarchism and other isms all too frequently result in oppression by despotic dictators or corrupt regimes. The power of centralized control enables politicians to decide the quality of life of the people they control. Throughout history entire societies have unwittingly lost their freedom and lives to power hungry politicians.

Humans make bad choices by giving up their freedom and potential in exchange for empty promises. Eventually the will to strive and succeed is crushed by 'leaders' who take advantage of their power and the trust invested in them by the people.

Humans also seek parity in life and lobby for laws to gain unfair advantage. Is it morally acceptable to group together the have-nots against the haves to take their wealth through political chicanery and majority rule? To the extent they punish individual rights and liberties, morally unjust laws are the path to economic suicide.

When humans reason that everyone has a right to see a real live tiger, is it moral to take freedom away from the tiger to make that happen? Think about it from the tigers' point of view? Animals fight attempts to take their freedom which leads us to question: Will humans lose their freedom if they tolerate laws that chip away at their individual rights?

Socialist Systems (Power)

Per Wikipedia: "Socialism is an economic system in which the means of production are either state owned or commonly owned ... or a political philosophy advocating such a system."

In a Marxist or labor-movement definition of the term, socialism is a stage of society in Marxist theory transitional between capitalism and communism and distinguished by unequal distribution of goods and pay according to work done with the goal of creating a socio-economic system in which property and the distribution of wealth are subject to control by the community.

This control may be exercised on behalf of the state, through a market, or through popular collectives such as workers' councils and cooperatives. As an economic system, socialism is often characterized by state, cooperative, or worker ownership of the means of production, goals which have been attributed to, and claimed by, a number of political parties and governments."

Socialism wastes an individual's potential because it crushes personal incentive and rewards the weak, the lazy and the incompetent.

Socialism destroys one's will to strive and succeed and ultimately, the personal dignity that comes with achievement. Quality of life means more than just good health ... it means the freedom to control your own destiny.

Power is controlling the lives of others. Slavery, detention, or oppression is power and a threat to personal liberty. There will always be power seekers trying to take freedom away and history is replete with stories to prove just that.

Our individual right to live without restraint is in jeopardy and we must never permit ourselves to become government slaves.

Our world is built on differences of opinion. Once again, one should understand what one is disagreeing with. Can you imagine what life would be like if everyone had the same thoughts and opinions? Success and failure is the Miracle-Gro® food of life that makes society stronger. Competition makes us better people, fosters better businesses and ultimately, enhances the lives of our families. If future generations understand the importance of individual liberty and free enterprise, they too can better enrich themselves and their families.

Today, survival of the American lifestyle is at stake. Common sense suggests it is unwise for families to entrust their liberty to those who abuse that trust. Those who seek to understand the differences between free enterprise and socialism will be richly rewarded as they recognize encroachment on individual freedom and fight to retain their personal freedom.

Since the founding days of America, challenges to liberty and economic well-being is a continuing threat to the American way of life. From a historical perspective, the insidious encroachment of those seeking to control others is an ongoing battle for those who cherish personal liberty.

Some political groups and political parties tend to identify themselves with misleading names. Frequently, the identification name is claimed in ways that tend to cover up traditional meanings. Individualism and collectivism are often buried in a plethora of names, some of which have little or no connection to the aims and objectives of the organization. Common sense suggests it is wise to 'dig in' and ferret out the details.

In keeping with the idea of getting to the underlying aims of any given group in current times and to set a political and economic philosophy in light of today's prevailing descriptions, the extremes of individualism and collectivism can best be termed conservatism and liberalism.

Once we come to grips with our individual and personal outlook or worldview of how society should be, we can better select how we can best achieve that which is most appealing to us. There is nothing wrong with being motivated by our own self interests so long as they are moral and legal. Toward the end of this book you will find explicit analysis of related moral and legal questions.

There has never been a time in the history of the human race where there have been more wealthy people than poor people. Maybe not fair, but that is just the way it is and how it will always be. We need to understand and accept that reality completely.

All things are possible with imagination

Years ago, in the late fifties as I recall, I viewed one of those old, grainy, 16 mm black and white motivational movies. The initial scene has stuck with me all these years and now is a good time to share it with you because it ties into the 'theme' of the book and further ties into understanding our fear and succeeding in a free market economy.

The film begins with a large, ornate open lectern placed in the center of a stage with the customary stage drapes hanging in the background. If you were to remake that motivational movie and if he were alive today, William Conrad, the actor who played the TV Private eye, Frank Cannon, would be the player of choice, round belly, mustache and all.

Joe Powell, the speaker, roundish in face and girth takes his place behind the lectern and in a deep raspy voice begins speaking. He started by asking us to think about the word **IMAGINATION**.

Powell then asked us to think about the ancient Persians whose wildest imagination included the enticing vision of a magic carpet on which one could ride. Of course, the Persians of two thousand years ago did not know how to make a flying magic carpet. A magic carpet was simply the product of their wildest imagination.

Powell then reached under the open lectern and held up a model four engine, propeller-driven airliner famously known as the Lockheed Constellation ("Connie") as I recall, then asked who in their right mind would want to ride on a magic carpet with all the foul weather, wind and rain blowing in their faces, no stewardesses (that was the accepted word at the time) to serve up food and drinks, no coast to coast movies, pillows and blankets or any of the comforts air travelers had come to expect.

Mankind continually *EXCEEDS* his wildest imagination, Powell concluded. The motivational message of the rest of Powell's film that followed escapes me at the moment, but the word IMAGINATION has never left me.

One has only to think back a century or so to imagine how things must have been without radios, television, airplanes, home appliances such as dishwashers, washers and dryers, microwaves, movies, telephones, computers, video games, miracle drugs, surgical robots, cars and NASCAR.

As a boy, I recall cartoon character Dick Tracy communicating by wrist watch. It was amazing then, but reality now. I am still amused when I think of a fellow I sat next to at the local T.G.I. Friday's Restaurant some 15 years ago. He delighted in using his wrist watch to change the TV channels ... drove the employee's crazy.

Indeed, the future holds more surprises and the how and when those surprises come to be are largely dependent on the political and economic systems in place that will best foster creativity and entrepreneurship.

In **Think and Grow Rich** (1937), Napoleon Hill famously said, *"What the mind of man can conceive and believe, it can achieve."*

With the possible exception of the wheel, the future promises to reveal new discoveries that will trivialize all the progress human kind has made since the beginning of time or at least back to when man first walked on two legs instead of four.

Many years ago, I recall mentioning to a friend as we looked up at a full moon in the night sky, "Someday, people will live on the moon." He scoffed and advised me that the atmosphere is too thin, gravity is too weak and there is no food. He was certain life would not be sustainable. Recalling Joe Powell, I reminded my friend that the imagination of the human race exceeds the obvious and somehow we would make it happen and besides, *it had already been done*!

Our astronauts ate and drank, walked around and for a short time actually lived on the moon. It is just a matter of erecting structures that function like a large space suit so we can accommodate as many people as thought necessary.

Since the moon landing event we have a space station outside the pull of Earth's gravity. I think of the space station as like a bus stop on the route to the moon and other parts of the universe. It is only a matter of time until life on the moon and elsewhere becomes reality.

When I finished with high school with all the hopes and dreams of what could be, I thought it would be worth having a memorable quote attributed to me should I ever become famous. I came up with this: "The destiny of the human race is to colonize the universe."

So it is with this book. One must see things as they are, yet imagine what else the future can be and what it might bring … both good and bad. The choices of our times will dictate the course of our lives and the lives of our children, their children and those who follow.

Especially scary for the future is something called Agenda 21. For those who can visualize how change solutions can be worse than the problems, learn all you can about Agenda 21 which is a comprehensive plan of action to be taken globally, nationally and locally by organizations of the United

Nations System, Governments, and Major Groups in every area in which human impacts on the environment.

Agenda 21, the Rio Declaration on Environment and Development, and the Statement of principles for the Sustainable Management of Forests were adopted by more than 178 Governments at the United Nations Conference on Environment and Development (UNCED) held in Rio de Janeiro, Brazil, 3 to 14 June 1992.

The Commission on Sustainable Development (CSD) was created in December 1992 to ensure effective follow-up of UNCED, to monitor and report on implementation of the agreements at the local, national, regional and international levels. It was agreed that a five year review of Earth Summit progress would be made in 1997 by the United Nations General Assembly meeting in special session.

The full implementation of Agenda 21, the Programme for Further Implementation of Agenda 21 and the Commitments to the Rio principles, were strongly reaffirmed at the World Summit on Sustainable Development (WSSD) held in Johannesburg, South Africa from 26 August to 4 September 2002.

The history of the world records many instances of brutality and genocide perpetrated by all-powerful dictators. History repeats itself and the prospect of genocide in the future is a certainty. Someday there most certainly will be another Josef Stalin, Adolph Hitler or Pol Pot whose thirst for power will lead them to horrific crimes. The prospect of dealing with more than the 5.6 billion desperately poor of the world is sure to lead some madman (or woman) to 'solve the problem' for the 'good of all the people.'

With a world population now over seven billion people, sustainability of the human race is on the minds of world leaders. The short range, pessimistic view is survival on Earth. The optimistic view is that space travel will permit settlements off (or under) the face of the Earth.

The United Nations and its Agenda 21 must be closely watched lest Americans fall prey to those who would enslave us. Political forces in America are beyond the flirting stage with the objective of ceding American sovereignty to the UN. If such a development happens, the politicians will have effectively negated individual rights and liberties as we know them. If Star Wars looked farfetched, Agenda 21 is surely near fetched.

The reason for bringing Agenda 21 into this discussion is to alert the reader about the purpose of this book and how it can relate to the future.

History is the study of change. History repeats itself. Agenda 21 is now and too close in the immediate future to ignore.

Responding to the concerns about Agenda 21 is another book that needs to be written so let us get on with this book in which we hope to present ideas about survival of the individual in an increasingly complex and challenging world.

Earlier, we suggested this book would deal with the past, present and future. Of course there is significant overlap and we have not taken care to specifically place dates on most observations. Part of the reasoning is to challenge some deep readers to find observations only to surprise themselves to find a situation being argued today was in fact the same discussion that was being held fifty, sixty or more years ago.

Eternal vigilance is a term used to warn citizens to never take their liberty for granted. We must always know and be ever mindful that change is a certainty and change does not always produce predicted results. The world is closing in and those who are best prepared to handle change have the best chance to enjoy the quality of life that only individual freedom can provide. The opportunity of freedom works for every person and it does so without prejudice. The poor, especially, have a shot at the American Dream ... without freedom, their hopes are extremely limited. Without freedom, the American Dream becomes a nightmare.

Now let us fast forward American History from the days of the American Revolution up to 1952 when major essay chapters in this book were published. Some 1952 essay chapters are earlier and some are more recent, but we present them to show how the age old struggle between good and evil (Freedom vs. Power) continues to the present, 2012, and likely will continue.

Politics, Economics, Education and Government are inter-related. How well they all mesh determines collective success. As I see it, local, state and national government and their related entities is overhead. It all has to be paid for and sustained through taxes. Large and small businesses comprise the necessary economic engine required to produce the economic activity that will cover overhead and hopefully generate a **profit**.

In short, I see business and industry as **profit** and government as **overhead**. A healthy economy calls for successful businesses. How else will a prosperous society cover its obligation to the people? How can anyone reasonably advocate for adding the cost of government to a business and expect that business to better compete in global markets?

What business are you in?

Peter Drucker is credited with first asking that poignant question. Back in the late 1950s as I began to advocate for free enterprise, I found a long cherished example of the "What business are you in?" That question and an experience back then pre-dated Peter Drucker once again proving that history repeats itself. And I picked up the thought from others that preceded me.

Seems a lot of folks get credit for other people's thoughts and ideas and the same holds true with famous quotations. The person of fame frequently gets credit for repeating some other person's thoughts. Politicians have speech writers, comedians are forever lifting jokes and I am not without guilt since much of what is here is not original by me. I take in a lot of information drop it in my imaginary funnel, think it over and out drops what seems at the time to be a revelation.

All too often when I share one of those thoughts, someone will tell me, "Oh, I bought something like that a couple of years ago and it didn't work." Other times people mock me, giggle or both ... usually all in good fun. Sometimes my listeners think I am brilliant until I ask someone else their opinion only to be told why the idea is a loser.

So a good lesson here is to not get carried away with people who like or dislike your ideas. All too often they simply do not want to hurt your feelings and like most politicians will tell you what you want to hear. Due diligence is your friend. Learn to embrace it and lead your own passionate and thorough investigations doing it without prejudice. And don't be afraid to look at your own ideas and reject them when a fair and impartial analysis tells you what you do not want to hear. It can be fun to argue with yourself ... just not wise to have uninvited others listen in if you do it aloud.

Anyway, my first recollection of the question "What business are you in?" came in the 1950's when I was first alerted to the reasons for the eventual failure of railroads. When frustrated by anyone who had difficulty grasping some simple free enterprise concepts, I would change the subject and ask, "Have you been to the airport lately?" No matter the answer, I would ask, "Did you see any Penn Central airliners?" Invariably the response would be that Penn Central was in the railroad business. My reply was, aha, they thought so too and that is why they failed. They did not take advantage of new technologies that came to be in the business that they were in – transportation. Railroad companies completely missed the early days of aviation because they did not adapt to the changes affecting their basic business mission.

Can you recall seeing the old black and white movies from the twenties and thirties where a row of telephone operators worked feverishly taking calls and then plugging a hard wire connection into the proper socket to connect the call to the receiving party? Well, early in the 1960's, I recall giving a speech and cited the communications industry as an example of hanging on to old ideas and technologies thus depriving people of faster, cheaper services. I suggested that prior to the 1950's communication workers unions fought the telephone companies in their efforts to automate the calling process. The unions had bitterly complained about the loss of operator's jobs and fought to keep phone companies from upgrading their equipment.

Anyway, I had read about the situation and followed it in the papers. The message was incorporated it into my talk about the business because I had read somewhere that if automated telephone call handling had not come into use when it did, every single female high school graduate in the country would have had to work as a telephone operator. (For the sake of clarification, in those days telephone operator's jobs were deemed 'women's work and that is not an issue for discussion now).

After finishing that early sixties speech, a local telephone company executive came up to inform me about the truth of my comments. He said his management team had been seriously concerned at that time about what they could do to handle management of the projected call volume should the union problem not be resolved. He further stated that his company came ever so close to utter chaos and had the phone companies lost that battle with the unions, indeed as late as the early 1950's, every female graduate *would* have been needed to handle the volume of calls.

The speed, accuracy and flexibility of call automation would have been denied if the unions had their way. Can you imagine how many operators would be needed just to handle the cell phone calls of today?

Once again, the obvious lessons of history are being repeated before our very eyes and largely ignored by newspapers (and even television). They think they are in the "newspaper business" but in reality they are in the business of providing information. So engrossed in the rush to meet deadlines and publish written communication, they fail to see technology taking over and replacing their domain ... with domains (pun) of another kind.

Newspapers are rooted in protection of the status quo when they should be embracing the latest methods of communication. They bemoan their inability to compete and attack the credibility of the Internet as a news purveyor. Much like a frog coming to its demise while sitting in a slowly coming to a boil pot of water, newspapers are going the way of the railroads. They just didn't see change coming. As I write this, the media are wringing their collective hands trying to figure out how they can profit from the new methods of communication ... all while dumping money into the very technologies that are eating their market.

Some of the very best advice I ever heard was from a Harvard MBA who said I did not have to spend the money to go to Harvard if I followed one simple rule that his professors emphasized: "If you want to succeed in business, do one thing better than anyone else and you cannot fail." I suppose that thought can apply to most anyone's life's work ... doesn't have to be a for profit business. Non-profits present special challenges and profits for the souls of those who enjoy giving of themselves.

How about government? It seems to me that the larger the government, the more confused it becomes as to its proper role. A local government has problems on its doorstep and can see the problem and address the solution directly. State governments are more complex, but still close enough to its citizenry to handle larger common interest problems. For example, too many prisoners with a multitude of offenses from minor to extreme may necessitate a facility with greater security and oversight. The state must address this as a collective issue according to the laws of their state.

Now the federal government is another story. Over the past several decades, the United States has lost its focus. It no longer does one thing best. Its primary mission is to protect the citizens. Their view should be a world view which is no small task to say the least, but why do they insist on stepping on the toes of their own citizens? How do the branches find time away from their day jobs to participate in matters other than simple oversight and protection of its citizens? Surely the states can enforce their own constitutions within the framework of our own United States Constitution. Who needs more government than that?

The power personalities that make up the Washington DC community are out of control. The pettiness of politics has them looking at America in terms akin to trying to find the last visible round spot in a slowly diminishing mass of concentric circles. Have you ever looked into mirrors in front and behind you trying to see 'how far' in you can go? Same deal ... just as distant objects become blurred (Myopia in medical terms) too many people of power are near sighted and oblivious to issues that are not within their control or realm.

No matter how much people demean Richard Nixon his comprehension about the big picture is questioned only by those who would find fault with Mother Teresa. Nixon could see beyond the pettiness. He had a world view. Think of it this way. Japan had Godzilla. Picture the terrible fright and despair of the people in those Godzilla movies. Well the western world is in the same predicament only our terrifying enemy is not a Godzilla. One could escape from Godzilla, but our path is blocked from all sides should our enemy prevail. So just who is our enemy? Well, if you believe America is good, then the enemy must be evil. So as President Richard Nixon saw it, we are in a classic battle between good and evil ... everywhere in the world.

Just who and what is evil? Our way of life as a free people governed by the rule of law is good. Those whose governments oppress their people with total government control are evil. So begs the question: Is the United States Government fully focused on attending to the task of citizen protection or are they overstepping their bounds? Like the old railroad barons, many of our politicians seem NOT to be focused on being in the governing business and protecting the people. Is the national government missing the big picture ... fighting evil? In golf, we call it taking your eye off the ball. Government meddling in the affairs of business is a dangerous and costly exercise.

The enrichment of one's ability through education, hard work and common sense combined with luck and timing **can** produce great wealth for those who persist through success and failure. Energized by the prospects of wealth, capitalism rewards the successful risk takers.

The American Free Enterprise System or capitalism gives every minnow the chance to grow into a shark. It's the American way. capitalism gives poor people a way to 'catch up' while socialism preserves the status quo at a lesser level of human comfort.

The American Free Enterprise Economic System consists of a free-price system where supply and demand are allowed to reach their point of equilibrium without intervention by the government. Productive enterprises are privately owned, and the role of the state is limited to protecting the rights to life, liberty, and property.

When people buy into socialist behavior they deprive themselves of the chance to test their mettle against their peers in life. The challenge is to find a way to strive and succeed and overcome difficult circumstances.

Along the way, free enterprise capitalism takes care of people by providing jobs that enable lifestyles commensurate with the capabilities of an individual. **Too, we believe the best capitalism is legally fair and equal, properly regulated to assure competitive balance and populated by persons of impeccable character.**

"We are what we repeatedly do; excellence, then, is not an act but a habit." – Aristotle, BC 384-322, Philosopher

On the subject of impeccable character, here are some random and supportive considerations and thoughts about individual values that are too important to exclude. The value of these thoughts properly applied will enhance your life:

1. I (we) believe in the importance of human values such as Honesty, Good Character, Self-Discipline, Open-mindedness, Persistence, Citizenship, Perspective, Integrity, Moral Courage, Generosity, Self-Discipline, Optimism, Gratitude, Kindness, Empathy, Humor, Humility, Valor, Leadership, Love, Industriousness, Spirituality, Knowledge, Wisdom and a Love of Learning comprise many of the building blocks of a stable society. Often religion is the glue that holds it all together.

2. I (we) particularly like this Wikipedia definition: "Spirituality is belief in an ultimate or an alleged immaterial reality; an inner path enabling a person to discover the essence of his/her being; or the "deepest values and meanings by which people live" ... Spirituality is often experienced as a source of inspiration or orientation in life.

3. Finding one's inner self often contributes to economic success. Some of the most successful business people I know are grounded in living their religions. Going it alone is okay too ... so long as one is grounded in positive human values.

4. When a person loses his or her moral compass, what is wrong with following the positive and worthy teachings of Moses, Jesus Christ, Mahatma Gandhi, The Buddha, Martin Luther and important others in the meantime? In the absence of a deity-based moral code, atheists can adopt a set of ethics common to society, so belief in God is not a requirement for ethical behavior or an enjoyable life.

5. "Whether you believe in God or not does not matter so much, whether you believe in Buddha or not does not matter so much: as a Buddhist whether you believe in reincarnation or not does not matter so much. You must lead a good life. And a good life does not mean just good food, good clothes (and) good shelter. These are not sufficient. A good motivation is what is needed: compassion, without dogmatism, without complicated philosophy, just understanding that others are human brothers and sisters and respecting their rights and human dignity." – Dalai Lama XIV

THE THREE UNIVERSAL TRUTHS from the BASIC TEACHINGS OF THE BUDDHA:

1. **Nothing is lost in the universe**

   The first truth is that nothing is lost in the universe. Matter turns into energy, energy turns into matter. A dead leaf turns into soil, a seed sprouts and becomes a new plant. Old solar systems disintegrate and turn into cosmic rays.

   We are the same as plants, as trees, as other people, as the rain that falls. We consist of that which is around us we are the same as everything. If we destroy something around us, we destroy ourselves. If we cheat another, we cheat ourselves.

2. **Everything Changes**

   The second universal truth of the Buddha is that everything is continuously changing. Life is like a river flowing on and on, ever-changing. Sometimes it flows slowly and sometimes swiftly. It is smooth and gentle in some places, but later on snags and rocks crop up out of nowhere. As soon as we think we are safe, something unexpected happens.

3. **Law of Cause and Effect**

   The third universal truth explained by the Buddha is that there are continuous changes due to the law of cause and effect. This is the same law of cause and effect found in every modern science textbook. In this way, science and Buddhism are alike.

The law of cause and effect is known as karma. Nothing ever happens to us unless we deserve it. We receive exactly what we earn, whether it is good or bad. We are the way we are now due to the things we have done in the past. Our thoughts and actions determine the kind of life we can have. If we do good things, in the future good things will happen to us. If we do bad things, in the future bad things will happen to us. Every moment we create new karma by what we say, do, and think. If we understand this, we do not need to fear karma. It becomes our friend. It teaches us to create a bright future.

Following this line of thought is not too difficult. "What goes around comes around" is an oft used expression akin to karma. "You get in proportion to what you give" and "cast your bread upon the waters and it shall be returned to you" are other commonly used variations, but it all comes down to karma.

From a biblical perspective, Ecclesiastes 11:1 explains, "Cast thy bread upon the waters: for thou shalt find it after many days. Give a portion to seven, and also to eight; for thou knowest not what evil shall be upon the earth." In other words, put out good, help others, and it will be returned to you.

Ecclesiastes 11:4 says, "He that observes the wind shall not sow; and he that regards the clouds shall not reap." In other words, those who are so preoccupied with their current circumstances will not put forth the effort to sow or to reap. The fact that they cannot see how they're going to benefit will discourage them. So they'll do nothing and seek sustenance in the wealth of those who give charity. And for some, the temptation to extract "charity" through extortion, blackmail, majority rule laws and outright theft seems a justifiable recourse. In the end, karma will prevail.

In any instance, the business of living pretty much boils down to one getting out of life what one puts into it. One's personal integrity speaks volumes about a person.

According to Wikipedia, "Integrity is a concept of consistency of actions, values, methods, measures, principles, expectations, and outcomes. In ethics, integrity is regarded as the honesty and truthfulness or accuracy of one's actions. Integrity can be regarded as the opposite of hypocrisy in that it regards internal consistency as a virtue, and suggests that parties holding apparently conflicting values should account for the discrepancy or alter their beliefs."

Earlier, we suggested this book would deal with the past, present and future. What may seem to be out-dated is often quite relevant because the issue being argued today is in fact the same topic that was being discussed fifty, sixty or more years ago.

The following chapter essays are intended to pinpoint important differences between significant economic and political matters. In a sense, economic history is static in that the common sense solutions of yesteryear are usually as valid today as they were then.

If you recall the earlier reference to William James, *"If you can change your mind, you can change your life."* this is a good time to think seriously about that. Now is the time to let go of pre-conceived notions about politics and pursue truth on your own terms. Common sense, logic and an open mind can, if fact, change your life.

Getting to know and understand *both* sides of every issue makes for an educated person. So take a chance. Dig into the following chapters for old perspectives that may be quite new to you. Let us start by dealing with and conquering fear.

> *"You gain strength, courage, and confidence by every experience in which you really stop to look fear in the face. You must do the thing which you think you cannot do."*
>
> … ELEANOR ROOSEVELT

FEAR – DON'T LET IT CONTROL YOU!

Fear. What is it? Can you touch it? Can you hold it? Can you show it to another person? I can almost hear you from where I am sitting. No, no, no. Okay then, so you can't touch it, you can't hold it, and you can't show it to another person. The question then is, why? Why do we have fear? Fear is nothing more than an emotion or a feeling that we hold in our mind. We fear either the emotional or physical pain something may cause. The problem is these emotions and feeling affect the way we live our lives. We fear doing certain things because we think we might fail. This may be due to past failures we have actually experienced or it may be due to failures we fear we might experience.

I urge you to remember and live by the following motto. Fear stands for,

False
Evidence that
Appears
Real

Most of the time what we fear, we have never even experienced! Isn't that crazy? You see, your mind has a hard time determining whether you've actually experienced the failure or just imagined it. Either way, you feel the physiological symptoms of the fear; such as an upset stomach.

Often, because we can imagine some sort of failure, we believe it will come true, and then we don't even try! And that is what makes a failure; a person who is afraid to try because they fear the potential of a negative outcome. If you don't at least try, you can never succeed.

"I have been through some terrible things in my life, some of which actually happened."

... MARK TWAIN

The question now becomes who defines what 'failure' and 'success' is? You do right? Either you create the definition yourself or you accept someone else's definition. Is it true then that some people create more difficult definitions of success and failure for themselves than others do? You bet it is! Who do you think leads a more successful life, Alex who defines success as, everyday that I wake up and I'm not six feet under, is a great day. Or Jeff, who defines success as, I have to be earning at least million dollars a year before I am successful.

You guessed right again. Alex. You see, Alex has created her definition of what success means and that definition is relatively easy to achieve! Therefore, in her mind, she is successful every day. Whereas Jeff, as per his own definition, cannot be successful until he is earning one million dollars a year. What are the chances that most of the 'Jeff's' in the world feel like failures on a daily basis because they are not yet earning one million dollars a year? Now don't get me wrong. I'm not saying that you should not set high standards and goals for yourself. What I am saying is that you have to be careful that you 'happily achieve, rather than achieve to be happy'.

The more difficult your definition of success is to attain, the more fear you will attach to it. Don't let your own definitions limit you or even worse, the definitions of others. Create your own definitions to make it harder to feel like a failure and easier to feel like a success. That way you will attach less fear to what you want in life. What would you attempt to do if you knew you could not fail? Image what you can do in your life with that type of belief system. Try thinking of every 'failure' as a success. That is, every time you 'fail' at something, you have really succeeded because you have learned what does not work. Therefore, you are closer to succeeding the next time you try. Remember that the past does not equal the future. Yesterday's failure does not equal your future outcomes. Just because you may have failed yesterday, or even five minutes ago, it doesn't mean you are going to fail again. Just learn from what you did wrong and change your approach. Don't fear the past. The past is what has taught you how to succeed in the future. Be fearless!

May be reprinted with the following attachment: Copyright (c) 1999 Glen Hopkins

> *"What you and I have in common with each other and with everyone else on this planet is a need to mutually protect one another's individuality. All political systems thrive on collectivism, but liberty is dependent upon a shared love and respect for the inviolability of one another."*
>
> ... BUTLER SHAFFER

THE FEAR OF INDIVIDUALISM

One of America's most important gifts to the world was the political philosophy of individualism. The central tenet of this idea is that every human being is important, especially from the point of view of law and politics, as a sovereign individual, not living by the permission of the government or some master or lord. That is the basic idea underpinning not only the democratic process, the First Amendment of the U.S. Constitution, and the various prohibitions addressed to the government concerning how to treat the citizenry, but the free market economic system as well.

Individualism and Capitalism

The free market system or capitalism is founded on the doctrine that each person has a basic right to private property in his or her labor and what he or she creates and earns freely and honestly. The economic idea of freedom of trade - in labor, skill, goods, services, etc. - rests squarely on individualism. No one is anyone else's master or servant, No involuntary servitude except as punishment for crime is permitted. Thus everyone has the basic right to engage in free trade - as in any other kind of peaceful action, even when his or her particular decision may not be the wisest or even morally exemplary.

In an individualist society the law upholds the idea that everyone is free to choose to associate with others on his or her own terms - whether for economic, artistic, religious, or romantic purposes. Not that all the choices people make will be good. Not that those individuals are infallible. Not that they cannot abuse their freedoms. All of that is granted. But none of that justifies making others their masters, however smart those others may be. To quote Abraham Lincoln, "No man is good enough to govern another man, without that other's consent."

But today the political philosophy under the most severe attack in many intellectual circles is individualism. From leftover Marxists to newly emergent communitarians, and all the way to democratic pragmatists - in the fields of political economy, sociology, and philosophy - everyone is bad-mouthing individualism. It picked up several years ago with the publication of Robert N. Bellah's book Habits of the Heart, Individualism and Commitment in American Life, and continues with innumerable related efforts, including the launching of the journal The Responsive Community and the publication of a new book by Bellah, The Good Society, as well as Amitai Etzioni's just-published The Spirit of Community.

These and many other efforts constitute a concerted attack against the individual and his rights. Perhaps predictably, the efforts involve gross distortions of what individualism actually is. It is supposed to foster disloyalty to family, friends, and country. It is supposedly hedonistic and instills anti-social sentiments in people. It is allegedly purely materialistic, lacking any spiritual and cultural values.

But such distortion is accomplished by focusing selectively on a very limited area of individualist philosophy, one employed mostly in technical economic analysis and serving merely as a model by which to understand strictly commercial events in free market economies. An exclusively economic conception of the human individual is admittedly barren - it treats everyone as nothing other than a bundle of desires. But this is not very different from the way every science employs models, taking a very simple idea to make sense of a limited area of the world.

Individualism, True versus False

The anti-individualists do not look at individualism as it is developed by social thinkers such as Frank Chodorov, F. A. Hayek, or Ayn Rand, let alone by some of their contemporary students who are developing these ideas and showing how vibrant a political system and culture can be when human beings are understood as individuals.

The sheer creative power of human beings should make clear that their individuality is undeniable, crucial to every facet of human living, good or bad. Yet, this essential individuality of every person by no means takes away the vital role various social affiliations play for them; human individuals are social beings.

The kind of community worthy of human life is intimately tied to individualism; such a community, even if the most suitable setting for human living, must be chosen by the individuals who occupy it. If this is subverted by forcing individuals into communities, those involuntary communities will not be genuine communities at all.

Individual choice and responsibility are essential to human flourishing.

Indeed, in America, where individualism has flourished more than elsewhere, there are millions of different communities to which individuals belong, often simultaneously, and this is possible because individuals have their right to choose reasonably well protected.

Not only do all individuals join a wide array of communities - family, church, profession, clubs, civic associations, and political parties - but there are vastly different approaches to living that also draw around them large segments of the population who join freely, without any coercion and regimentation. But instead of appreciating the robust nature of individualism, including its support for the healthiest form of communitarianism, its opponents are trying to discredit it in any way they can. Why?

Well, some of their motives may be decent enough - some may indeed fear the impact of narrow economic individualism and thus carp against all individualism. But sometimes their motivations cannot be understood as anything else but a hunger for power over other people's lives. Otherwise, why would the critics ignore perfectly sensible versions of individualism and insist on the caricatures? Over and over again they invoke the caricature even when other, well developed versions are available.

Something like this seems to be the best explanation for wishing to destroy the most significant American discovery, namely, the vital contribution of individuality to human culture. Why would such attacks be launched but to reintroduce subjugation, involuntary servitude, and the demeaning of individuals as individuals in favor of some elite?

No doubt those clamoring for power rationalize their actions with the thought of certain worthy goals: They want a cooperative, harmonious, mutually enhancing community. They often believe that individuals as individuals are dangerous but as members of a community they are wonderful. As the Russian author Tatyana Tolstaya observes in a recent issue of The New Republic:

Taken individually, in short, everyone is not good. Perhaps this is true, but then how did all these scoundrels manage to constitute a good people? The answer is that "the people" is not "constituted of." According to [collectivists] "the people" is a living organism, not a "mere mechanical conglomeration of disparate individuals." This, of course, is the old, inevitable trick of totalitarian thinking: "The people" is posited as unified and whole in its multiplicity. It is a sphere, a swarm, an anthill, a beehive, a body. And a body should strive for perfection; everything in it should be smooth, sleek, and harmonious. Every organ should have its place and its function: The heart and brain are more important than the nails and the hair, and so on. If your eye tempts you, then tear it out and throw it away; cut off sickly members, curb those limbs that will not obey, and fortify your spirit with abstinence and prayer.

That is why they should be in power: They are the head of the organism, of the community; they know what is good; and they ought to be making the decisions as to who remains part of it and who must be cut off.

Members of society do have different roles; the economists speak convincingly of the benefits of the division of labor. The errors of the collectivists are (1) their presumption that they know better than the individuals involved which members of society are less important, and (2) they have the right to eliminate those members. But individuals are ends in themselves, not animals to be sacrificed on the altar of the collectivist state.

At the time of the original publication, Tibor Machan was a philosophy professor. He was smuggled out of Communist Hungary in 1953 and has lived in the United States since 1956.

Reprinted with permission from The Freeman, a publication of the Foundation for Economic Education, Inc., July 1993, vol. 43, No. 7.

ANALYSIS

The foresight of this essay has become more relevant today with, for example, the arrival of a collective takeover of the U.S. health care system. The intrusion, no matter how well intentioned, will likely worsen the overall health care system of the United States, in addition to imposing worthless taxes and penalties on many Americans. The following table contains the major tax and penalty provisions of the socializing of America's health care system. In addition to the $500 billion in tax and penalty increases over the coming ten years, it also worsens America's competitive economic position.

The maps that follow represent winners and losers from Affordable Care Act (ACA or Obamacare). Overall, big winners are businesses within countries that can compete with the United States on certain skill levels and simultaneously provide cheaper labor. Some of the winners include cheap labor countries like China and India and countries with very competitive biotechnology knowledge bases, such as Singapore.

The biggest loser in the health care deal is, of course, the United States. The winners and losers on an international basis are shown graphically in the two national geography maps that follow. The larger the extrusion or the darker the green, the bigger a winner a country is.

The red negative extrusions represent losers from the health care bill. Overall, as stated, countries with highly competitive health care industries on a labor cost and knowledge base benefit at the expense of American businesses.

The loss of freedom readily apparent in the ACA health care bill lowers the tide of all boats, rather than raising it for the downtrodden. If the individualist perspective portrayed in this essay is lost to political force, America will cease to be a choice land. The example of Obamacare is only one example of a wrong step taken by American politicians. In the money management business if you make too many mistakes, you cease to gain business. So it is with countries, if the leaders make too many mistakes, citizens' businesses largely cease to be competitive. Let's hope America's youth learn respect for the truth that is economic individualism.

Tax Increases in ACA ("Obamacare")

	Tax Change	Effective Date	Tax Increase (CBO est.) (Billions)
1	Investment Income Surtax, 3.8% tax increase on households making >$250K ($200KSingle)	1/1/2013	$123.0
2	Medicare Payroll Tax Increase for Self Employed and Other Individuals	1/1/2013	$86.0
3	Individual & Employer Mandate	1/1/2014	$65.0
4	Health Insurers Tax	1/1/2014	$60.1
5	Excise Tax on Comprehensive Health Insurance Plans	1/1/2018	$32.0
6	Biofuel Tax ("Black Liquor")	1/1/2010	$23.6
7	Drug Company Tax	1/1/2010	$22.2
8	Medical Device Manufacturers Tax	1/1/2013	$20.0
9	Tax Increase for Individuals with High Medical Bills	1/1/2013	$15.2
10	Flexible Spending Cap	1/1/2013	$13.2
11	Medicine Cabinet Tax	1/1/2011	$5.0
12	Eliminate Tax Deduction for Employer Provided Drug Coverage, Coordinates with Medicare Part D	1/1/2013	$4.5
13	Tax from "Economic Substance Doctrine"	1/1/2010	$4.5
14	Tax on Indoor Tanning Services	1/1/2010	$2.7
15	HSA Withdrawl Tax Increase	1/1/2011	$1.4
16	Limit on Executive Compensation for Health Insurance Executives	1/1/2013	$0.6
17	Blue Cross/Blue Shield Tax Increase	1/1/2010	$0.4
18	Excise Tax on Charitable Hospitals	1/1/2010	<$0.1
19	Employer Reporting of Insurance on W-2	1/1/2012	<$0.1

Sources:CBO

According to the following charts, current 2012 data suggest the apparent ACA expected results indicates China and Asia will benefit the most at the expense of the United States.

Western Hemisphere Winners/Losers from ACA
(green is a winner, red is a loser)

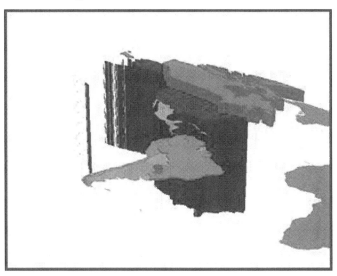

Eastern Hemisphere Winners from ACA
(green is a winner, red is a loser)

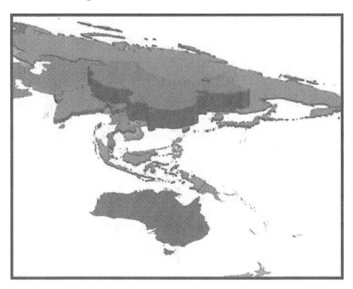

> *Some people regard private enterprise as a predatory tiger to be shot. Others look on it as a cow they can milk. Not enough people see it as a healthy horse, pulling a sturdy wagon.*
>
> ... WINSTON CHURCHILL

PRIVATE ENTERPRISE REGAINED

I am indebted to Betty Knowles Hunt for sending me a column she contributed to the *New Hampshire Morning Union* quoting from Governor Bradford's own history of the Plymouth Bay Colony over which he presided. It is a story that deserves to be far better known, particularly in an age that has acquired a mania for socialism and communism, regards them as peculiarly "progressive" and entirely new, and is sure that they represent "the wave of the future."

Most of us have forgotten that when the Pilgrim Fathers landed on the shores of Massachusetts they established Communist system. Out of their common product and storehouse they set up a system of rationing, though it came to "but a quarter of a pound of bread a day to each person." Even when harvest came, "it arose to but a little." A vicious circle seemed to set in. The people complained that they were too weak from want of food to tend the crops as they should. Deeply religious though they were, they took to stealing from each other. "So as it well appeared," writes Governor

Bradford, "that famine must still insue the next year alIso, if not some way prevented." So the colonists, he continues, "begane to thinke how they might raise as much corne as they could, and obtaine a beter crope than they had done, that they might not still thus languish in miserie. At length [in 1623] after much debate of things, the Gov. (with the advise of the cheefest amongest them) gave way that they should set corne every man for his owne perticuler, and in that regard trust to themselves .... And so assigned to every family a parcell of land.

A Great Success

"This had very good success; for it made all hands very industrious, so as much more corne was planted than other waise would have bene by any means the Gov. or any other could use, and saved him a great deall of trouble, and gave farr better contente.

"The women now wente willingly into the feild, and tooke their litle-ons with them to set corne, which before would aledg weakness, and inabilitie; whom to have compelled would have bene thought great tiranie and oppression.

"The experience that was had in this commone course and condition, tried sundrie years, and that amongst godly and sober men, may well evince the vanitie of that conceite of Platos and other ancients, applauded by some of later times;-that the taking away of propertie, and bringing in communitie into a comone wealth, would make them happy and florishing; as if they were wiser than God. For this comunitie (so farr as it was) was found to breed much confusion and discontent, and retard much imployment that would have been to their benente and comforte.

"For the yong-men that were most able and fltte for labour and service did repine that they should spend their time and streingth to worke for other mens wives and children, without any recompense. The strong, or man of parts, had no more in devission of vietails and cloaths, than he that was weake and not able to doe a quarter the other could; this was thought injuestice ....

"And for men's wives to be commanded to doe servise for other men, as dressing their meate, washing their cloaths, etc., they deemd it a kind of slaverie, neither could many husbands well brooke it ....

"By this time harvest was come, and instead of famine, now God gave them plentie, and the face of things was changed, to the rejoysing of the harts of many, for which they blessed God. And the effect of their particuler [private] planting was well seene, for all had, one way and other, pretty well to bring the year aboute, and some of the abler sorte and more industrious had to spare, and sell to others, so as any generall wante or famine hath not been amongest them since to this day."

The moral is too obvious to need elaboration.

– Henry Hazlitt

ANALYSIS

Henry Hazlitt's views speak to a concern many older generation Americans have for the future of America – the youth's respect for private enterprise and the cycle of business creation and destruction.

Some observers may view the following three graphs of business births and deaths as a sign that things are alive and well. That's not the case; overall, the median by county figures come out to be about 0.23% of the population created a business and 0.20% of the population saw a business die.

The geography of business births and death are shown on the following pages. It may look populated, but are the estimated 900,000 business births and 820,000 business deaths good enough each year? Probably not; a healthy American system should see more along the lines of at least 2% to 3% of the population creating a business every year, with a success rate of at least 15% (it's about 9% today). If Americans are unhappy with large corporations, start a competing business that siphons away business. It's hard, but it's worth it.

In the end, remember this: government intrusion and meddling is not the answer. Don't turn to the government. The question for individuals wanting the best for the future of America then becomes – how can leaders with foresight encourage individuals turn to themselves and their own intellectual, physical, and social capital to improve their lives rather than turning to government support? It's got to happen.

The worst trend in America today is individuals turning to government help, which then in turn gives government bureaucrats some control and feeling that they are doing something worthwhile.

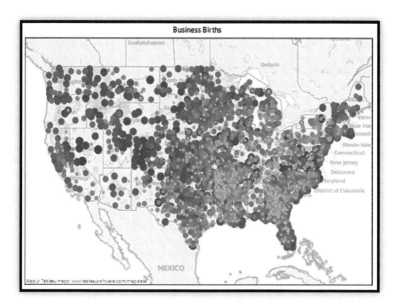

Source: Thomas Young, SBA; each dot means some percent of the county created a business, with the darker or larger the dot, the greater the number of businesses created per capita.

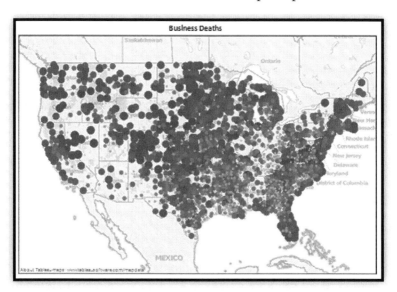

Source: Thomas Young, SBA; each dot means some percent of the county saw a business die, with the darker or larger the dot, the greater then number of business deaths per capita.

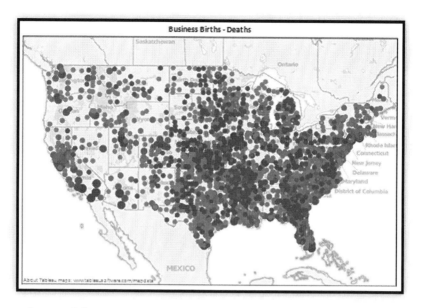

Source: Thomas Young, SBA; each dot means some percent of
the county created a business or saw a business die; red is
where deaths outnumber births, blue is the opposite.

> *"A wise and frugal government which shall restrain men from injuring one another, which shall leave them otherwise free to regulate their own pursuits of industry and improvement, and shall not take from the mouth of labor the bread it has earned. This is the sum of good government."*
>
> ... THOMAS JEFFERSON (1801)

PILGRIMS BEAT COMMUNISM WITH FREE MARKET

Recalling the story of the Pilgrims is a Thanksgiving tradition, but do you know the real story behind their triumph over hunger and poverty at Plymouth Colony nearly four centuries ago? Their salvation stemmed not so much from the charitable gestures of local Indians, but from their courageous decision to embrace the free-market principle of private property ownership a century and a half before Adam Smith wrote The Wealth of Nations.

Writing in his diary of the dire economic straits and self-destructive behavior that consumed his fellow Puritans shortly after their arrival, Governor William Bradford painted a picture of destitute settlers selling their clothes and bed coverings for food while others "became servants to the Indians," cutting wood and fetching water in exchange for "a capful of corn." The most desperate among them starved, with Bradford recounting how one settler, in gathering shellfish along the shore, "was so weak ... he stuck fast in the mud and was found dead in the place."

The colony's leaders identified the source of their problem as a particularly vile form of what Bradford called "communism." Property in Plymouth Colony, he observed, was communally owned and cultivated. This system ("taking away of property and bringing [it] into a commonwealth") bred "confusion and discontent" and "retarded much employment that would have been to [the settlers'] benefit and comfort."

Brink of Extermination

The most able and fit young men in Plymouth thought it an "injustice" that they were paid the same as those "not able to do a quarter the other could." Women, meanwhile, viewed the communal chores they were required to perform for others as a form of "slavery."

On the brink of extermination, the Colony's leaders changed course and allotted a parcel of land to each settler, hoping the private ownership of farmland would encourage self-sufficiency and lead to the cultivation of more corn and other foodstuffs.

As Adam Smith would have predicted, this new system worked famously. "This had very good success," Bradford reported, "for it made all hands very industrious." In fact, "much more corn was planted than otherwise would have been" and productivity increased. "Women," for example, "went willingly into the field, and took their little ones with them to set corn."

The famine that nearly wiped out the Pilgrims in 1623 gave way to a period of agricultural abundance that enabled the Massachusetts settlers to set down permanent roots in the New World, prosper, and play an indispensable role in the ultimate success of the American experiment.

A profoundly religious man, Bradford saw the hand of God in the Pilgrims' economic recovery. Their success, he observed, "may well evince the vanity of that conceit...that the taking away of property... would make [men] happy and flourishing; as if they were wiser than God." Bradford surmised, "God in his wisdom saw another course fitter for them."

Amen to that.

Thanksgiving Story: 2005

Plymouth's Pilgrims may have survived that near-fatal brush with socialism but, sadly, many political leaders remain transfixed by a blind faith in the ability of government to shape and set the course of human behavior.

Case in point: the tenacious liberal belief that no connection exists between the tax burdens we place on capital formation and the economic behavior of those who must shoulder that burden.

The liberal creed holds that investors will take economic risks and create jobs no matter how punitive the tax regime. To liberals, lowering that burden through reductions in the rate of taxation simply bestows an unwarranted windfall on the "rich" and deprives the government of much-needed tax revenue.

Of course, incentives matter every bit as much today as they did four centuries ago. The latest proof comes from figures released by the Treasury Department for the fiscal year that ended on Sept. 30. They vindicate the predictions of conservative economists that the 2003 law, which included a number of pro-growth provisions such as cutting the top tax rate on capital gains and dividends to 15 percent, would be a raging success.

Compared to the previous year:
- Total federal revenues grew by an astonishing 14.6%.
- Corporate receipts exploded, increasing by 47%.
- Payroll tax receipts, an indicator of employment growth, increased by a respectable 8%.

We have much to be thankful for this Thanksgiving season.

Michael Franc *November 22, 2005*

ANALYSIS

With the marginal tax rate set to increase by as much as 13%, the long-term capital gains rate in line to increase by as much as 260%, and the qualified dividend tax rate on track to increase by 33%, without even considering the Obamacare tax increases, Mr. Franc's 2005 remarks are as applicable in today's environment as in the Bush tax cut years. How many jobs will be lost to finance losing government investments?

After doing some econometrics, the likely effect is around 75 million jobs over the employment period covered by the Millennial Generation (up to 2065). The initial effects are hard to extract from the normal job growth numbers, as is shown by the small initial differences by the orange(light) and green(dark) dots in following graph, but the effect will be there, knocking off an anticipated half a percentage point in overall economic growth each year. The jobs really won't be there.

It's not hypothetical guessing. Let's hope the younger generation is able to overcome government spending and tax mistakes made by their parents' generation, or, more desirable, that the older generation currently running the government figures out the errors apparent in tax increases. It's the kids that are hurt the most, although all will be affected by the losing effect. The 75 million forgone jobs are not forgone yet.

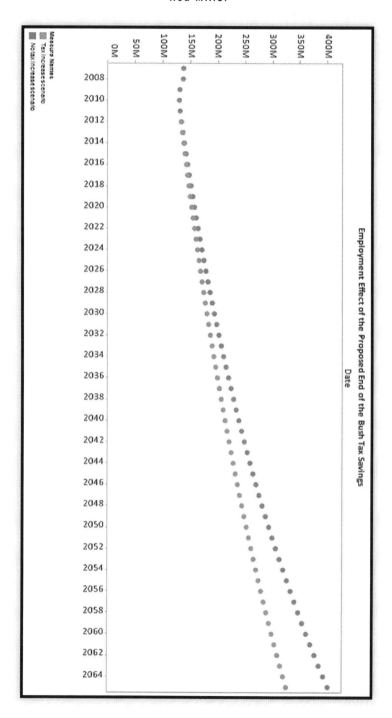

Employment Effect of the Proposed End of the Bush Tax Savings

> *"America's abundance was created not by public sacrifices to the common good, but by the productive genius of free men who pursued their own personal interests and the making of their own private fortunes. They did not starve the people to pay for America's industrialization. They gave the people better jobs, higher wages, and cheaper goods with every new machine they invented, with every scientific discovery or technological advance – and thus the whole country was moving forward and profiting, not suffering, every step of the way."*
>
> … AYN RAND, Capitalism: The Unknown Deal

SHOW ME ANY OTHER COUNTRY

AMERICANS, in general, regard socialism as something alien and unrelated to America, and would never consider joining the Socialist party. Yet, they clamor loudly for every piece of socialistic legislation which is offered-so long as it is sugar-coated with an American label or wrapped in the American flag.

It must be very disheartening for sincere socialists to note the continuing impotence of their party, while, at the same time, pseudo-socialism in free-enterprise wrappings has been able to command such a tremendous following from the rank and file. This is a sad commentary on the political and economic ignorance of the American people. They dismiss socialism with a wave of the hand, and then line up in droves behind social security, socialized industry, medicine, housing and education. They denounce socialism, and yet innocently and ignorantly spout its doctrines day in and day out. Nothing more constructive could happen to the American public than to have it understand socialism clearly is able to identify its doctrines beneath all their various disguises, and then either to endorse or repudiate it's principles-openly and honestly. I have done my own personal job of study, analysis and evaluation of socialism; I take my stand in its opposition, and would like to present some of my reasons for so doing.

There is no question but that socialistic proposals seem logical, just and humanitarian. They sound like the idealistic answer to a muddled world's prayer. In one breath, they denounce the slavery of totalitarianism and the "crazy quilt of capitalism," and offer a Utopian "middle way" which eliminates the liabilities and retains the assets of both collectivism and individualism. They mix the oil of one with the water of the other and present their mixed formula of perfection. It is all very intoxicating and consoling-until one realizes that oil and water will not mix! At that point, it becomes necessary to say to you, Mr. Socialist: "Show me!"

Utopia-On Paper

You say: "We socialists offer logical reasons why we shall have more freedom, and certainly a surer victory over poverty on the basis of public ownership of things necessary to the common life and their democratic control under democratically controlled planning." This is a lovely blue print but show me a concrete example of where this has taken place.

Show me a spot on God's green earth where socialism has increased individual freedom and eliminated poverty. Show me where it has not meant "rigorous and arbitrary regulation," and where it has increased "private initiative and consumer's choice." Show me where it has proved "the road of escape to true freedom as well as to peace and plenty." Show me this Utopia-not on paper, but in reality!

You admit, in your writings, that socialism in Germany, Italy and Russia resulted in Nazism, fascism and communism, but you say these were perversions of true socialism -and you abhor them. That's fine, I do too. But show me where socialism has avoided these pitfalls and led to freedom and prosperity for everyone, as your blueprint says it will.

26

The Cure That Kills

You point out and underscore many of the errors of American capitalism, and I heartily concur in them all, but your solution and mine are at opposite ends of the pole. I am more afraid of your cure than I am of our present ailments! You point to the evil of private monopoly, and then you propose to cure this evil by a bigger and more powerful state monopoly. I find this very inconsistent. If monopolies are destructive of freedom-and I believe with you that they are-then the answer ought to be to curtail or prevent monopolies, not to substitute one for the other.

The only cure for monopolies is freer and wider-spread competition in an economic system which insists that this door of private competition stay open. When you write in one of your pamphlets, "There wasn't much freedom when the 200 largest corporations controlled more than 50 per cent of the business wealth of America," I have to smile at your concern, despite the fact that I would prefer to see fewer "big" businesses and more "middle-sized" businesses. Two hundred businesses with only 50 per cent of our business wealth is still a far cry from monopoly, and not half so glaring a danger as a completely concentrated monopoly such as John L. Lewis enjoys in the coal mines. You say nothing at all about this, and ignore the most stifling monopoly in the world-socialized Russia where everything is owned by the state, and everyone is compelled to belong to one huge closed shop, and to work wherever and for whatever the state decrees.

You admire the British experiment in socialism, but you do not say how socialism is to solve Britain's problems. The key to her post-war struggle still is production, and yet you fail to show socialism's incentive to more production. The weary miners want shorter hours and higher pay. The trade unions of England have geared their output to accommodate their weakest member. How can debt-burdened Britain pay more money for less work-when what she needs is more work for less money? And how can she keep her Labor government in power, except by force or by acceding to the unanswerable demands of the workers who are the bulwark of her support? Poor Britain is damned if she does and damned if she doesn't. So is France. So is Italy. So is Russia-and all of Europe. We may have our troubles here in America, but the socialized world is 100 per cent worse off than we are. It is also note worthy that in the two least-socialized European nations Holland and Belgium-recovery has been most rapid!

What makes you believe that men who are supposed to "manage" in the public interest will be any less subject to the love of power or the human evils of greed and corruption than those who "manage" privately? They are the same people, and they possess the same shortcomings. *Also,* the incentive to good judgment is stronger with private managers who must assume the financial loss for their mistakes, while the government managers can call upon the federal treasury to subsidize their incompetence.

We have the freest, most democratically-controlled government on earth, and yet in the past score of years we have had very little to say about the edicts which have poured forth from government agencies and their appointed directors. Power is intoxicating to all. It feeds upon itself. We the people gain nothing by substituting new people for old in Washington. Our only hope is to take away the power that has been concentrated there, so that no one can use it benevolently or otherwise. Once we allow ourselves to become the subjects of benevolent power, we shall soon find ourselves the slaves of a very un-benevolent power.

Natural Bedfellows

You explain the coalitions of socialists with communists in Europe as "a grim necessity at a critical moment," but this is not the whole answer. You neglect to point out what a broad base of common ground exists between the two parties. Both believe in public ownership instead of private ownership, and both are buddies in their hatred of capitalism, free enterprise, and the profit motive. You differ only in degree and in means, but socialism is closer to communism than it is to capitalism. And when that "critical moment" comes, you will sacrifice your belief in "freedom" before you will relinquish your collectivized program for "security."

Here lies the greatest danger of socialism. Actually, it is the economic philosophy of communism. Those of us who repudiate it do so for two very definite reasons:

First, we believe that economic and political philosophies go hand in hand and are inseparable. We believe it is no accident that "free enterprise" developed along with a free republic, and that it is equally no accident that where a collectivized economy was installed, individual freedom was sacrificed. In the same way, those countries which have tried a hybrid system, half-collectivized and half-free, have in the same proportion increased regimentation, decreased individual initiative and choice, and are in constant danger of swinging further to the left.

Second, despite your emphasis on increased production and plenty via socialism, we can find no examples of such results in proof. Show me a socialized or even a half socialized country which has remotely approached our free-enterprise record of production and plenty. Show me a socialized or half-socialized country which has produced a higher standard of living for workers than capitalistic America. Show me where socialism has produced cheaper cars, telephones, radios, movies, gadgets or comforts, and where they have been wider distributed among the average people, than here in America. Show me any other country where people own as many homes or can match our 75 million life insurance policyholders, or our 50 million bank accounts, or our 80 million bondholders. If you know a better, happier, more envied workers' republic than we have right here in America, where is it?

Don't tell me that this difference is merely because America has large natural resources! India, China and Russia also have great natural resources. Somebody once said: "Only Americans find oil." Why? Don't tell me that our miraculous output of inventions and creations is due to our "natural inventiveness." We are nothing more than a conglomeration of all other peoples. Our Steinmetzes, Pupins, Einsteins and others came to our shores as penniless refugees, and brought their genius with them. Why have we had to erect barriers against those who would come in droves to this land of freedom and opportunity? Why have the socialist countries had to erect barriers to keep their own people at home? Name me some of the major inventions produced under socialism in order to prove that individual incentive still exists there. I do not know of them.

Socialists and communists make the same fatal mistake. They place security ahead of freedom. America is the prime example of a nation which founded itself on the basic principle of individual freedom. It's Constitution bristles with limitations upon the government-and the result has been a greater measure of security for Americans than for all other nations. America offered unlimited rewards for initiative, enterprise and wisdom-and she guaranteed no subsidy for laziness, incompetence or failure. Thus she used the carrot and stick method of encouraging individuals to create, produce and succeed. This free way of life is a rugged, painful business at times, but it has paid the biggest dividends on earth and it has been worth every weary mile of it.

Freedom appeals to man's strength; socialism and communism appeal to man's weakness. Freedom teaches a man to stand independently on his own feet; the others teach him to lose himself in the protective herd. Freedom places its emphasis on man himself; the others lose man in their emphasis on mankind.

Conform or *Be Liquidated*

One of the pleasant-sounding doctrines of socialism and communism is "economic and social planning instead of individual anarchy." But you neglect to mention that for a "plan" to succeed, we must all be fitted into it-whether we like it or not. You would like us to accept the "plan" voluntarily, but if we do not, you fail to explain that we must then be compelled to do so. This is where communists defeat socialists. They have no compunctions about using force to further their ends. "Conform or be liquidated" is their motto. The end justifies the means. Socialists are more squeamish, and that is why the communists will always supplant them when the "emergency" comes along.

In free America, we have recently had an inkling of what this could mean. Under OPA planning of our whole industrial and economic life, when the cattle raisers balked at selling their produce without a normal profit, our President stated in a nation-wide address that he had actually considered government seizure of all the cattle. Shades of Russia! It does not require much imagination to picture the result of such a plan. Cattle raisers would have rebelled. Force would have been used. Fines, imprisonment and death would have followed. Is this so different from Russia's collectivization of her farms, her ruthless "elimination" of rebels, and the subsequent starvation of five million of her farm families? But the communists will argue that the plan was for the benefit of all, and that individuals do not count when society is expected to gain. Nonsense! How can you possibly increase the security of society by destroying the security of its individuals?

Advocates of planning as a stabilizer always forget that planners also must be human, and subject to all the short comings and mistakes of other human beings. Even the most rabid endorsers of OFA admit that the individual injustices were numerous and unavoidable. Yet these individuals were expected to submit and be sacrificed in the interest of the over-all plan.

Government-subsidized potatoes are rotting in the fields by the ton. The planning advocates say: "But this is because we did not control the production." And so it goes. After you control production, then you must control distribution, and back we go to rationing, price fixing, wage fixing and the whole involved, impossible mess. I do not blame the planners. They could be the wisest and best intentioned persons in the world. I blame the whole idea, because it is impossible, impractical, and incapable of justice, and because the taxpayers foot the bill for every inevitable mistake.

There is not a single socialist or communist doctrine that does not sound good, but which is not equally fatal. "Production for use and not for profit" You do not say *who* is to decide what is for use. It is easy to look upon the auto today and call it "useful," but who thought so in its awkward infancy? Would the airplane have been considered "useful"? Or radio? Or splitting the atom? Who among men is so wise that he can know these things in advance, and therefore be trusted with the power to permit or forbid them?

And who profited most from the creation and mass production of the auto together with all its subsequent allied industries? Did Henry Ford? Or did the whole American people, whose standard of living was raised thereby? Did Henry Ford's accumulation of wealth come out of anyone else's pocket? Or did he create a new source of wealth for millions of less gifted people?

Liberty Means Responsibility

My argument against socialism is that America already has the best economic and political system yet devised, and that this is proven by her glorious record-and not in a paper blueprint. America did not become the bread basket, the factory, the bank, and the hope of the world by following the wrong systems or believing in the wrong principles. Her solution is to reacquaint herself with her own best way of life, and to live up to its tenets more faithfully-not to throw it away before she has completely understood or practiced it.

American capitalism has never failed; only some of our human capitalists have failed. Whenever a free-enterpriser achieves his own goal, and then attempts to shut the door of opportunity behind him, or to choke off the free play of competition around him, then he has cheated his own system. Whenever believers in freedom discriminate against minorities, or show favoritism to meritless friends, then they are sabotaging their own constitutional principles and weakening the foundations upon which America was built.

Whenever individuals or groups in America use the political power to gain advantage at the expense of others, then such persons or groups are undermining the structure of our republic, and the results will be evil and unjust. Whenever an American acquires wealth or power-and then fails to be a good and honest steward of these benefits-then he not only denies the principles of America, he denies the principles of Christianity.

The answer, and the only answer, is for all of us to educate ourselves to the responsibilities as well as to the benefits of freedom. Perhaps as a people, we are not morally strong enough to be free. If that is the case, then we shall certainly lose our freedom, and it will not matter much what "ism" supplants Americanism. But this will not prove that our free way of life was not the best way. It will only prove that we were not worthy of it.

–Betty Knowles Hunt

> *"The duty of government is to leave commerce to its own capital and credit as well as all other branches of business, protecting all in their legal pursuits, granting exclusive privileges to none."*
>
> … ANDREW JACKSON

LEGALIZED IMMORALITY

It must be remembered that 95 per cent of the peace, order, and welfare existing in human society is always produced by the conscientious practice of man-to-man justice and person-to-person charity. When any part of this important domain of personal virtue is transferred to government, that part is automatically released from the restraints of morality and put into the area of conscience less coercion. The field of personal responsibility is thus reduced at the same time and to the same extent that the boundaries of irresponsibility are enlarged.

Government cannot manage these fields of human welfare with the justice, economy, and effectiveness that are possible when these same fields are the direct responsibility of morally sensitive human beings. This loss of justice, economy, and effectiveness is increased in the pro- portion that such governmental management is centralized....

Government cannot make men good; neither can it make them prosperous and happy. The evils in society are directly traceable to the vices of individual human beings. At its best government may simply attack the secondary manifestations of these vices. Their primary manifestations are found in the pride, covetousness, lust, envy, sloth, and plain incompetency of individual people. When government goes far beyond this simple duty and deploys its forces along a broad, complicated front, under a unified command, it invariably propagates the very evils that it is designed to reduce.

In the sweet name of "human welfare" such a government begins to do things that would be gravely offensive if done by individual citizens. The government is urged to follow this course by people who consciously or subconsciously seek an impersonal outlet for the "primaries" of human weakness. An outlet in other words, which will enable them to escape the moral responsibility that would be involved in their personal commission of these sins. As a convenience to this popular attitude we are assured that "government should do for the people what the people are unable to do for themselves." This is an extremely dangerous definition of the purpose of government. It is radically different from the purpose stated in the Declaration of Independence; nevertheless it is now widely accepted as correct.

Here is one example of centralized governmental operation: Paul wants some of Peter's property. For moral as well as legal reasons, Paul is unable personally to accomplish this desire. Paul therefore persuades the government to tax Peter in order to provide funds with which the government pays Paul a "subsidy." Paul now has what he wanted. His conscience is clear and he has proceeded "according to law." Who could ask for more? Why, Paul, of course, and at the very next opportunity. There is nothing to stop him now *except the eventual exhaustion of Peter's resources.*

The fact that there are millions of Paul's and Peters involved in such transactions does not change their essential and common characteristic. The Paul's have simply engaged the government "to do for them (the people) that which they are unable to do for themselves." Had the Paul's done this individually and directly without the help of the government, each of them would have been subject to fine and imprisonment. Furthermore, 95 per cent of the Paul's would have refused to do this job because the moral conscience of each Paul would have hurt him if he did. However, where government does it for them, there is no prosecution and no pain in anybody's conscience. This encourages the unfortunate impression that by using the ballot instead of a blackjack we may take whatever we please to take from our neighbor's store of and immunities.

– Clarence Manion

> *"Revealingly, the central function of the Constitution as law—the supreme law—was to impose limitations not on the behavior of ordinary citizens but on the federal government. The government, and those who ran it, were not placed outside the law, but expressly targeted by it. Indeed, the Bill of Rights is little more than a description of the lines that the most powerful political officials are barred from crossing, even if they have the power to do so and even when the majority of citizens might wish them to do so."*
>
> ... GLENN GREENWALD, WITH LIBERTY AND JUSTICE FOR SOME:
> HOW THE LAW IS USED TO DESTROY EQUALITY
> AND PROTECT THE POWERFUL

THE BILL OF RIGHTS

"On February 6, 1788, Massachusetts, by a narrow margin of 19 votes in a convention with a member ship of 335, endorsed the new Constitution, but recommended that a bill of rights be added to protect the States from Federal encroachment on individual liberties.... New York ratified, with a recommendation that a bill of rights be appended...." And so on...

WHAT was the reason-the real reason-that caused those early American patriots to distrust a federal government which they were about to bring into existence? Why did the individual citizens within the various sovereign states demand a bill of rights before ratifying the Constitution? Why did statesmen of the caliber of Washington, Jefferson, Adams, and Franklin wish to severely restrict the authority of the central government and to strictly limit the power of its leaders?

There was a reason, a vital reason-a reason that many present-day Americans have forgotten. A reason, that unless we re-learn it will surely mean the loss of personal freedom and individual liberty for all mankind.

Here is the reason: The power of government is *always* a dangerous weapon in *any* hands. The founders of our government were students of history as well as statesmen. They knew that, without exception, every government in recorded history had at one time or another turned its power-its police force-against its own citizens, confiscated their property, imprisoned them, enslaved them, and made a mockery of personal dignity. That was true of every *type* of government known to mankind. That was true regardless of how the government leaders came to power. It was true-then as now that government leaders *elected by the people* frequently turn out to be the worst enemies of the people who elect them. Hitler was a recent example. He was not the first; he is not likely to be the last.

A New Idea

It was for this reason that the founders of the American republic introduced into that government a completely new idea.

What was this new idea? Was it the regular election of government leaders by the people? As wise a decision as that was, it was not new. The Greeks, among others, had used it.

Was it the wide dispersal of the powers of government among federal, state, and local units? An excellent system, but not new. It had already proved of practical value in France and other countries.

Was the American method of governmental "checks and balances" a new idea? It was a well-conceived plan, but it was not completely original with us. The British system of King, House of Lords, and House of Commons once embodied the same principle.

Here is the new idea: For the first time in known history, a written constitution specified that certain institutions and human relations were to be *outside* the authority of government. The government was specifically forbidden to infringe them or to violate them.

Why Government?

This was a revolutionary concept of government! The idea of inalienable rights and individual freedom had never before been incorporated into a national constitution. Never before in history had the people said to the government: "Thou shalt not." Always the government had been able to say to the people: "You may, or you must." Heretofore, government had *granted* certain freedoms and privileges to the people. But the Bill of Rights said, in effect: "We the people are endowed by our Creator with natural rights and freedoms. The *only* reason for our having a government is to protect and defend these rights and freedoms that we already have as individuals. It is sheer folly to believe that government can give us something that already belongs to us."

These free people then listed in their Constitution those specific functions that they wanted government to handle. Then they forbade the government officials to do anything not commanded of them in the Constitution.

But even so, the people were afraid that the elected leaders of the new government might misunderstand the ideals of human dignity, of individual freedom, of the proper functions of government. So, as specific examples of what they meant, the American people added the Bill of Rights to the Constitution. It might better be called a *Bill of Prohibitions* against government. It is filled with such phrases as: "Congress shall make no law ... the right of the people . . . shall not be infringed . . .," "The right of the people ... shall not be violated ...."

These personal and individual rights include freedom of worship, free speech and a free press, the right to assemble together, the sanctity of person and home, trial by jury, the right to life, liberty, and the private ownership of property.

Finally, to make absolutely sure that no government official could possibly misinterpret his position as servant rather than master, the people added two more blanket restrictions against the federal government. The Bill of Rights specifies that: "The enumeration ... of certain rights shall not be construed to deny ... others retained by the people." And: "The powers not delegated to the United States by the Constitution ... are reserved to the States ... or to the people."

Individual Freedom

It was this philosophy of individual freedom and individual responsibility-reflected in the Bill of Rights-that attracted to this country millions of persons from the government oppressed peoples of Europe. They came here from every country in the world. They represented every color, every race, and every creed. They were in search of *personal freedom,* not government-guaranteed "security." And as a direct result of the individual freedom specified by the Constitution and the Bill of Rights, they earned the greatest degree of security ever enjoyed by any people anywhere.

Those new Americans swelled the tide of immigrants by writing the praise of freedom in their letters to relatives and friends who still lived in the countries with *strong* governments, with *one-man* rule, with *government ownership* of the means of production, with *government guaranteed* "security," with *government* housing, and *state-controlled* education.

Equal Rights

Their letters read, in effect: "Here the government guarantees you nothing except life, liberty, and the right to own whatever you have honestly acquired. Here you have the personal responsibility that goes with individual freedom. There is no law or custom that prevents you from rising as high as you are able. You can associate with anyone who wishes to associate with you. Here in America you can do as you please as long as you do not violate the rights of other persons to do as they please. These rights are recorded in the American Constitution and the Bill of Rights. The same documents specify that three-fourths of the states must be in agreement before these rights can be taken away. And, of course, it is foolish to imagine that the people will ever voluntarily give up their freedom."

Such letters would not be completely true today, because that freedom is gradually being lost. But the "progressive" laws and "popular" court decisions of recent years are not primarily responsible for it. Freedom is seldom lost by a direct vote on the subject. In our case, it just seems to be *seeping* away. The Bill of Rights still exists on paper, but the *spirit* that caused it to be written is disappearing. When that spirit is completely gone, the written words will mean nothing. Thus it behooves us to inquire why that spirit is now weak, and how it can be revived.

Who Is To Blame?

No one person is responsible for sapping that spirit of individualism. No one political party is to blame. The people are as responsible as the elected and appointed leaders. It is we the people who seem to have forgotten that freedom and responsibility are inseparable. It is we the people who are discarding the concept of government that brought forth the Declaration of Independence, the Constitution, and the Bill of Rights.

In short, few of us seem to want to keep government out of our personal affairs and responsibilities Many of us seem to favor various types of government-guaranteed and compulsory "security." We *say* that we want personal freedom, but we *demand* government housing, government price controls, government-guaranteed jobs and wages.

We *boast* that we are responsible persons, but we *vote* for candidates who promise us special privileges, government pensions, government subsidies, and government electricity.

Such schemes are directly contrary to the spirit of the Bill of Rights. Our heritage is being lost more through weakness than through deliberate design. The Bill of Rights still shines in its entire splendor, but many of us are looking in another direction. Many of us are drifting back to that old concept of government that our forefathers feared and rejected. Many of us are now looking to government for security. Many of us are no longer willing to accept individual responsibility for our own welfare. Yet personal freedom cannot exist without individual responsibility.

Your Choice

Thus the American people are on the verge of a final decision. We must choose between the destruction caused by government paternalism, and the security insured by individual freedom with individual responsibility as ex pressed in the Bill of Rights. There is no other choice.

As it must, the choice rests with each of us as individual Americans. No one can tell us what to think or do. No one should. To do so would be a violation of both the spirit and the words of the Bill of Rights. As responsible persons, each of us has the privilege and the obligation to pursue what each considers to be the right course of action. But this above all-before we act, let us understand the *meaning* of our actions, the *direction* in which we are going. – Dean Russell

"A Bill of Rights is what the people are entitled to against every government, and what no just government should refuse, or rest on inference."

... THOMAS JEFFERSON

THE BILL OF RIGHTS
(Amendments 1-10 of the Constitution)

• I •
Congress shall make no law respecting an establishment of religion, or prohibiting the free exercise thereof; or abridging the freedom of speech, or of the press; or the right of the people peaceably to assemble, and to petition the government for a redress of grievances.

• II •
A well-regulated militia being necessary to the security of a Free State, the right of the people to keep and bear arms shall not be infringed.

• III •
No soldier shall, in time of peace, be quartered in any house, without the consent of the owner, nor in time of war but in a manner to be prescribed by law.

• IV •
The right of the people to be secure in their persons, houses, papers, and effects, against unreasonable searches and seizures, shall not be violated, and no warrants shall issue but upon probable cause, supported by oath or affirmation, and particularly describing the place to be searched, and the persons or things to be seized .

• V •
No person shall be held to answer for a capital, or otherwise infamous crime, unless on a presentment or indictment of a grand jury, except in cases arising in the land or naval forces, or in the militia, when in actual service in time of war or public danger; nor shall any person be subject for the same offense to be twice put in jeopardy of life or limb; nor shall be compelled in any criminal case to be a witness against himself, nor be deprived of life, liberty, or property, without due process of law; nor shall private property be taken for public use without just compensation.

• VI •

In all criminal prosecutions, the accused shall enjoy the right to a speedy and public trial, by an impartial jury of the state and district wherein the crime shall have been committed, which district shall have been previously ascertained by law, and to be informed of the nature and cause of the accusation; to be confronted with the witnesses against him; to have compulsory process for obtaining witnesses in his favor, and to have the assistance of counsel for his defense.

• VII •

In suits at common law, where the value in controversy shall exceed twenty dollars, the right of trial by jury shall be preserved, and no fact tried by a jury shall be otherwise re-examined in any court of the United States, than according to the rules of the common law.

• VIII •

Excessive bail shall not be required, nor excessive fines imposed, nor cruel and unusual punishments inflicted.

• IX •

The enumeration in the Constitution, of certain rights, shall not be construed to deny or disparage others retained by the people.

• X •

The powers not delegated to the United States by the Constitution, nor prohibited by it to the States, are re served to the States respectively, or to the people.

> "What is the essence of America? Finding and maintaining that perfect, delicate balance between freedom "to" and freedom "from."
>
> ... MARILYN VOS SAVANT, IN PARADE

THAT SOMETHING

AMERICA has been different from any other nation on earth. Here is why. The men who cut the pattern for Americans a century and three-quarters ago, held a deep conviction that men-all men-are born with qualities that give them a unique status. The simple fact of man's being born a human being, they felt, marks him as the most important thing God ever created-and entitles him to a certain dignity and to self-respect. They believed that in this sense men are born equal and are endowed with certain God-given, not man-given, rights-each being free to live, to be free, to build his life without the handicap of any interference that can be avoided.

These profound thinkers designed our government on the basis of this conviction, as a new kind of government that would be operated by the people themselves. Jefferson said that this was to be a great experiment which would determine for all time whether or not "men may be trusted to govern themselves without a master." He predicted future happiness for Americans "if we can prevent the government from wasting the labors of the people under the pretense of taking care of them."

In the lively decades following 1776, Americans became a great and virile people-self-reliant and free. Most historians of an earlier day believed that we had demonstrated for the entire world to see the truth of Jefferson's theory that men are able to govern themselves. Many are not now so sure. Something seems to have happened to America-and to Americans.

Especially during the depression and World War II we gave up much of our freedom-"temporarily." Since then we have discovered that freedoms relinquished "temporarily" are hard to get back. Emergency "regulations" have led to "planning" and now the government-which according to our rules is supposed to be the servant of the people -is pretty much taking over the running of our lives. This "planning" appears to be changing not only the character of our government but the character of our people. Millions now seem willing to give up their independence for the promise that the government will take care of them.

The great cause for alarm is not that the "planners" want to plan our lives but that we are allowing them to do *so*. And the most tragic aspect of it all is that so many of us, who should be more far-seeing, are helping them, by scurrying to Washington every time our own "security" in the form of special favors is endangered, every time we ourselves want some "planning" -subsidy-from the government.

This country was not built by men who relied on somebody else to take care of them. It was built by men who relied on themselves, who dared to shape their own lives, who had enough courage to blaze new trails-enough confidence in themselves to take the necessary risks. This self-reliance is our American legacy. It is the secret of "that something" which stamped Americans as Americans. Some call it individual initiative; others backbone. But whatever it is called, it is a precious ingredient in our national character-one which we must not lose.

The time has come for us to re-establish the rights for which we stand-to reassert our inalienable rights to human dignity, self-respect, self-reliance-to be again the kind of people who once made America great.

Such a crusade for renewed independence will require a succession of inspired leaders-leaders in spirit and in knowledge of the problem, not just men with political power who are opposed to communism, or to diluted communism, but men who are militantly for the distinctive way of life that was America. We are likely to find such leaders only among those persons who teach self-reliance and who practice it with the strict devotion of belief and understanding.

– J. Ollie Edmunds

ANALYSIS

How are the truths Ollie Edmunds writes of applicable today?

All one has to do is look at the absolute growth in government employment and government programs to see the tentacles of federal, state, and local governments becoming an ever greater part of individuals' lives.

The real issue is: how to get rid of the meddlers and bureaucrats and restore greater dignity in individual responsibility? It won't happen without targeted effort; after all, who is going to convince a student that he would have greater respect for his education if he paid for it himself? Who wants to tell a student that it would be a good idea to weight the costs and benefits of an education in the context of an investment decision? Certainly not the sellers of educational services.

How does one convince fearful individuals that financial regulators largely show up in the form of higher taxes and higher banking costs? What about, for instance, food industry regulators? How does one convince fence sitters that it's by and large better to have greater faith in business (i.e. less fear) than in COLA collecting government employees? It's difficult, but it's a job worth pursuing – freedom depends on it.

The subject is government control – is there evidence that expanding the check book of the federal government is correlated with increased employment? The answer is no, and anyone who says otherwise is probably a government employee or has some sort of benefit connected with government spending.

The following two charts show the lack of evidence graphically. The first chart is from 1967 to 2012. Overall, the slope, which represents the relationship between federal spending and employment, is statistically insignificant, with a slope that's actually negative, indicating that an increase in government spending is correlated with decreased employment of 66 public and private sector jobs for every $1 billion increase in federal spending.

The second chart shows the same thing over the past decade. The same results apply, with the slope getting more negative (380 fewer private and public sector jobs for every $1 billion increase in federal spending).

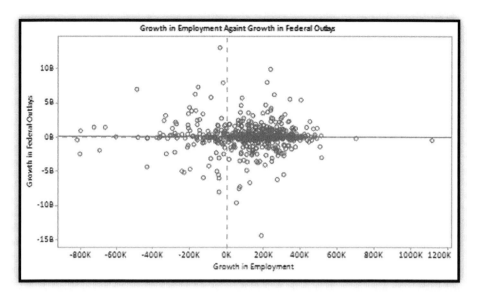

This chart shows the correlation of growth in federal spending against employment growth from 1967 to 2012. The center line that looks almost like a horizontal axis is simply an OLS regression line (the R-squared is less than .01). Overall, evidence on federal spending improving the lives of Americans is non-existent when viewed from a broad picture over a long time horizon.

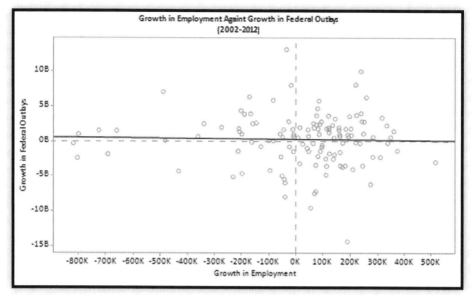

This chart shows the correlation of growth in federal spending against employment growth from 1967 to 2012. The center black line that looks almost like a horizontal axis is simply an OLS regression line (the R-squared is less than .01). Overall, evidence on federal spending improving the lives of Americans is non-existent when viewed from a broad picture over a long time horizon.

Bottom line: updated evidence confirms J. Ollie Edmunds' suggestions from over sixty years earlier.

> *"Anyone who trades liberty for security deserves neither liberty nor security."*
>
> ... BENJAMIN FRANKLIN

THE FIRST LEFTIST

THE first Leftist would not be popular in America today. That is true because the original Leftists wanted to *abolish* government controls over industry, trade, and the professions. They wanted wages, prices, and profits to be determined by competition in a free market, and not by government decree.

They were pledged to free their economy from government planning, and to remove the government-guaranteed special privileges of guilds, unions, and associations whose members were banded together to use the law to set the price of their labor or capital or product above what it would be in a free market. The first Leftists were a group of newly elected representatives to the National Constituent Assembly at the beginning of the French Revolution in 1789. They were labeled "Leftists" merely because they happened to sit on the left side in the French Assembly. The legislators who sat on the right side were referred to as the Party of the Right, or Rightists. The Rightists or "reactionaries" stood for a highly centralized national government, special laws and privileges for unions and various other groups and classes, government economic monopolies in various necessities of life, and a continuation of government controls over prices, production, and distribution.

Early American Ideals

The ideals of the Party of the Left were based largely on the spirit and principles of our own American Constitution. Those first French Leftists stood for individual freedom of choice and personal responsibility for one's own welfare. Their goal was a peaceful and legal limitation of the powers of the central government, a restoration of local self-government, an independent judiciary, and the abolition of special privileges.

Those Leftists, holding a slim majority in the two years' existence of the National Constituent Assembly, did a remarkable job. They limited the extreme powers of the central government. They removed special privileges that the government had granted to various groups and persons. Their idea of personal liberty with absolute equality before the law for all persons was rapidly becoming a reality. But before the program of those first Leftists was completed, a violent minority *from their own ranks-the* revolutionary Jacobins-grasped the power of government and began their reign of terror and tyranny.

That development seems to have risen from this little understood and dangerously deceptive arrangement: Two groups of persons with entirely different motives may sometimes find themselves allied in what appears to be a common cause. As proof that this danger is not understood even today, we need only examine the results of our own "common cause" alliances with various dictators against various other dictators. So it was among the Leftists in France in 1789. The larger faction wanted to limit the powers of government; the leaders of the other group wanted to overthrow the existing rulers and grasp the power themselves.

Separation of Powers

The majority of the original Party of the Left had been opposed to concentrated power regardless of who exercised it. But the violent revolutionists in their midst, led by Robespierre, Danton, and Marat, were opposed to concentrated power only so long as someone else exercised it. Robespierre, who represented himself as spokesman for the people, first said that the division of the powers of government was a good when it diminished the authority of the king. But when Robespierre himself became the leader, he claimed that the division of the powers of government would be a bad thing now that the power belonged "to the people."

Thus, in the name of the people, the ideas of the original Leftists were rejected. For all practical purposes, local self-government disappeared completely, the independence of the judiciary was destroyed, and the new leaders became supreme. The program of the first Party of the Left was dead.

Most of the original Leftists protested. So they too were soon repudiated in the general terror that was called liberty. But since the name Leftist had become identified with the struggle of the individual against the tyranny of government, the new tyrants continued to use that good name for their own purposes. This was a complete perversion of its former meaning. Thus was born what should properly be called the *new* and *second* Left.

The leaders of this new Left were greatly aided in their program of deceiving the people by using this effective device of changing the meaning of words. The term "tyranny" had been used to describe the powers of the old government. And the term "liberty" had been used to describe the ideas of the original Leftists. Well and good. But when the second Leftists in turn became tyrannical, they continued to call it liberty! In the name of liberty, mob violence was encouraged, Habeas Corpus was abolished, and the guillotine was set up!

Look Behind the Label

Now who is opposed to liberty or progress or any of the various other desirable ideals that government officials claim will result from their "unselfish programs for the people"? Probably no one ...

Thus do the people tend to accept almost any idea-communism, socialism, imperialism, or whatever-if those ideas are advanced under attractive labels such as freedom from want, defense against aggression, welfare, equality, liberty, fellowship, and security. Since most of the world today still suffers from this disease of "word confusion," it is hardly surprising that the French people in the 1790's were also misled by the same device. The rallying cry of this new Left was: All power to the people. And, as always, it sounded good to the people. But the point that the French people missed is the same point that haunts the world today.

It is this: The people cannot themselves individually exercise the power of government; the power must be held by one or a few persons. Those who hold the power *always* claim that they use it for the people, whether the form of government is a kingdom, a dictatorship, a democracy, or whatever. If the people truly desire to retain or to regain their freedom, their attention should first be directed to the principle of *limiting the power of government itself* instead of merely demanding the right to vote on what party or person is to hold the power. For is the victim of government power any the less deprived of his life, liberty, or property merely because the depriving is done in the name of-or even with the consent of-the majority of the people?

It was on this point that Hitler, for instance, misled the Germans, and Stalin deceived the Russians. Both of them hastened to identify themselves as champions of the people. And there appears to be little or no doubt but that the majority of the people approved or acquiesced in the overall programs that were initiated in their names.

As the "leaders" murdered millions of individual persons, their excuse for their deeds was that they were doing them "for the people."

As they enslaved countless millions of human beings, they brushed all criticism aside by exclaiming: "But the people voted for me in the last election."

As they confiscated property and income, they claimed to be doing it "for the general welfare" and by "a mandate from the people."

Hitler and Stalin merely adapted to their time and circumstances the philosophy of the French Jacobins, the new Leftists, who declared that power is always too great in tyrannical hands, but that it can never be too great in the hands of the people-meaning Hitler, Stalin, a Jacobin leader, or any other person who wishes to possess and increase the power of government over the individual citizen.

What Is *Government?*

Here is another illogical reason why the people of France traded the freedom-with-responsibility offered by the policy of the first Leftists for the bloody tyranny offered by the policy of the second Leftists: They believed that an organized police force-government-could be used to force people to be good and virtuous.

It is true that this organized force of government can be used, and should be used, to restrain and punish persons who commit evil acts-murder, theft, defamation, and such-against their fellow men; but this force that is government *cannot* be used to force persons to be good or brave or compassionate or charitable or virtuous in any respect. All virtues must come from within a person; they *cannot* be imposed by force or threats of force. Since that is so, it follows that almost all human relations and institutions should be left completely outside the authority of government, with no government regulation whatever. But this seems to be a difficult idea for most persons to grasp.

The idea of concentrated government power-force against persons-is easy to grasp. And it is easy to imagine that this power can be used to force equality upon unequal persons. Possibly this explains why so many persons believe that the world could be near-perfect if only *they* had the power of government to force other people to do what they think best for them. That concept of government is, however, the direct road to despotism. Any person who holds it is, by definition, a would-be dictator-one who desires to make mankind over in his own image; to force other persons to follow *his* concepts of morality, economics, social relationships, and government. The fact that such would-be dictators may seem to have fine intentions, and wish only to do good for the people, does not justify their arrogant desire to have authority over others.

Thus it was that the terror of the second Leftists reversed the advance of freedom which had begun in France in 1789. And the French Revolution finally became nothing more than a fight among would-be rulers to gain possession of the power of government.

The new Leftists-as is the case with all persons who desire authority over other persons-did not fear the power of government. They adored it. Like Hitler, Stalin, and other despots, their primary reason for inciting the people to reject the old order was to get this power for themselves. And the people did not object at first because they did not understand that the power of government is dangerous in *any* hands. They just thought that it was dangerous in the hands of a king. So they took the power from the king and transferred it to a "leader." They failed to see that it was a brutal restoration of the very thing they had rebelled against! In fact, those second Leftists held far more power than Louis XVI ever had.

Is there a lesson for present-day America to be learned from this French experiment with a highly centralized "people's government"?

The majority of the American people voted approval of this "Robespierre philosophy of government" as expressed by the holder of a high political office in 1936: "... in 34 months we have built up new instruments of public power. In the hands of a people's government this power is wholesome and proper. But in the hands of political puppets of an economic autocracy, such power would provide shackles for the liberties of the people."

When translated into simple English, that statement reads: Power is a good thing, so long as I am the one who has it.

That concept of increasing the power of the national government seems to have even more support today, by the leaders of *both* major political parties, than it had in 1936. All of them claim, of course, that they will use the power "for the good of the people."

Something for Nothing

Have we fully considered where this road may lead? Have we forgotten the teachings of our forefathers and their warning that the only hope for permanent liberty lies in restricting the power of government itself, regardless of who the government officials are or how they may be selected? Have we forgotten their warning to be especially wary of the demagogues who promise us something for nothing?

Our founding fathers, along with the first Leftists who were of the same political faith, were well aware that individual freedom and personal responsibility for one's own welfare are equal and inseparable parts of the same truth. They knew that history amply supports this truism: When personal responsibility is lost-whether it be taken by force or given up voluntarily-individual freedom does not long endure.

– Dean Russell

> *"I think the American Dream says that anything can happen if you work hard enough at it and are persistent, and have some ability. The sky is the limit to what you can build, and what can happen to you and your family."*
>
> ... SANFORD I. WEILL

FOR THE BETTER ECONOMIC LIFE

Women were not freed from their 18th Century servitude by feminist agitation, but by the invention of the sewing machine, the washing machine, the refrigerator, and the dishwasher, together with the revolutionary developments for handling and distributing foodstuffs.

Peasantry on the farm was not banished by reform or edict, but by the iron plow, the reaper, and the tractor.

The 12-hour shift and the six-day week could not have disappeared from the scene through laws or social upheaval. It was modern machinery, developed by research that made it possible for the American workman of 1950 to produce many times as much goods as the workman of 1850.

The automobile, pre-eminently a product of research, has widened and enriched lives in a manner impossible to achieve through legislation. At every hand, it is plain that the improvements leading to advancement have their origin in invention and development. There is no alternative.

Ideas formed in a man's mind, after it has been trained and sharpened by education and experience, are the basis of successful research. Without the creative brain of the scientist, all investment in research is worthless. American scientific laboratories are the best equipped in the world. Yet continued progress will be insured only if the rights of the individual to exercise freely his initiative are reestablished and jealously guarded.

American research prospered by providing rewards for success; the inventive genius of the nation was kept alive by adding to it what Lincoln called "the fuel of incentive." Further, the integrity of American research was kept inviolate; the research worker was spared the necessity of finding "political" conclusions as the goal of his investigations.

In this atmosphere of free inquiry and of freedom of the individual to enjoy the fruits of his labor, science here flourished. Elsewhere in the world, it has suffered serious setbacks.

The German scientist, once a leader, found under Hitler that he was falling behind. Specified results at a specified time could not be guaranteed, no matter how urgent or peremptory the orders. The Russian scientist under communism has learned that his findings must satisfy the official view, regardless of the facts. The British scientist under socialism has seen the rewards of his enterprise virtually confiscated by taxation.

Without freedom, scientific research and the progress in its wake will falter in the United States, as has happened elsewhere. The individual must be assured the freedom of incentive. The university scientist must have freedom of inquiry, of discussion, and of publication.

And sponsors of industrial research, such as American companies, must have the freedom and incentive to win as well as to lose-the freedom to grow and expand, as is necessary to fulfill their responsibilities. The means to carry on future research will be forthcoming only as long as it can pay its way.

When it can no longer do *so,* it will stop, and let the retrogression process begin. In that event, a well-known principle would again be proved: A hoop rolling downhill moves faster than one going up.

– Crawford H. Greenewalt

> *"The greatest country, the richest country, is not that which has the most capitalists, monopolists, immense grabbings, vast fortunes, with its sad, sad soil of extreme, degrading, damning poverty, but the land in which there are the most homesteads, freeholds — where wealth does not show such contrasts high and low, where all men have enough — a modest living— and no man is made possessor beyond the sane and beautiful necessities."*
>
> ... WALT WHITMAN, AMERICAN POET (1819-1892)

INEQUITY OF WEALTH AND INCOMES

The market economy-capitalism-is based on private ownership of the material means of production and private entrepreneurship. The consumers, by their buying or abstention from buying, ultimately determine what should be produced and in what quantity and quality. They render profitable the affairs of those businessmen who best comply with their wishes and unprofitable the affairs of those who do not produce what they are asking for most urgently. Profits convey control of the factors of production into the hands of those who are employing them for the best possible satisfaction of the most urgent needs of the consumers, and losses withdraw them from the control of the inefficient businessmen. In a market economy not sabotaged by the government the owners of property are mandatories of the consumers as it were. On the market a daily repeated plebiscite determines who should own what and how much. It is the consumers who make some people rich and other people penniless.

Inequality of wealth and incomes is an essential feature of the market economy. It is the implement that makes the consumers supreme in giving them the power to force all those engaged in production to comply with their orders. It forces all those engaged in production to the utmost exertion in the service of the consumers. It makes competition work. He who best serves the consumers profits most and accumulates riches.

In a society of the type that Adam Ferguson, Saint-Simon, and Herbert Spencer called militaristic and present-day Americans call feudal, private property of land was the fruit of violent usurpation or of donations on the part of the conquering warlord. Some people owned more, some less, and some nothing because the chieftain had determined it that way. In such a society it was correct to assert that the abundance of the great landowners was the corollary of the indigence of the land less.

But it is different in a market economy. Bigness in business does not impair, but improves the conditions of the rest of the people. The millionaires are acquiring their fortunes in supplying the many with articles that were previously beyond their reach. If laws had prevented them from getting rich, the average American household would have to forgo many of the gadgets and facilities that are today its normal equipment. This country enjoys the highest standard of living ever known in history because for several generations no attempts were made toward "equalization" and "redistribution." Inequality of wealth and incomes is the cause of the masses' well-being, not the cause of anybody's distress. Where there is a "lower degree of inequality," there is necessarily a lower standard of living of the masses.

Demand for "Distribution"

In the opinion of the demagogues inequality in what they call the "distribution" of wealth and incomes is in itself the worst of all evils. Justice would require an equal distribution. It is therefore both fair and expedient to confiscate the surplus of the rich or at least a considerable part of it and to give it to those who own less. This philosophy tacitly presupposes that such a policy will not impair the total quantity produced. But even if this were true, the amount added to the average man's buying power would be much smaller than extravagant popular illusions assume. In fact the luxury of the rich absorbs only a slight fraction of the nation's total consumption. The much greater part of the rich men's incomes is not spent for consumption, but saved and invested. It is precisely this that accounts for the accumulation of their great fortunes. If the funds which the successful businessmen would have ploughed back into productive employment are used by the state for current expenditure or given to people who consume them, the further accumulation of capital is slowed down or entirely stopped. Then there is no longer any question of economic improvement, technological progress, and a trend toward higher average standards of living.

When Marx and Engels in the Communist Manifesto recommended "a heavy progressive or graduated income tax" and "abolition of all right of inheritance" as measures "to wrest, by degrees, all capital from the bourgeoisie," they were consistent from the point of view of the ultimate end they were aiming at, viz., the substitution of socialism for the market economy. They were fully aware of the inevitable consequences of these policies. They openly declared that these measures are "economically untenable" and that they advocated them only because "they necessitate further inroads" upon the capitalist social order and are "unavoidable as a means of entirely revolutionizing the mode of production," i.e., as a means of bringing about socialism.

But it is quite a different thing when these measures which Marx and Engels characterized as "economically untenable" are recommended by people who pretend that they want to preserve the market economy and economic freedom. These self-styled middle-of-the-road politicians are either hypocrites who want to bring about socialism by deceiving the people about their real intentions, or they are ignoramuses who do not know what they are talking about. For progressive taxes upon incomes and upon estates are incompatible with the preservation of the market economy.

The middle-of-the-road man argues this way: "There is no reason why a businessman should slacken in the best conduct of his affairs only because he knows that his profits will not enrich him but will benefit all people. Even if he is not an altruist who does not care for lucre and who unselfishly toils for the common weal, he will have no motive to prefer a less efficient performance of his activities to a more efficient. It is not true that the only incentive that impels the great captains of industry is acquisitiveness. They are no less driven by the ambition to bring their products to perfection."

Supremacy of the Consumers

This argumentation entirely misses the point. What matters is not the behavior of the entrepreneurs but the supremacy of the consumers. We may take it for granted that the businessmen will be eager to serve the consumers to the best of their abilities even if they themselves do not derive any advantage from their zeal and application. They will accomplish what according to their opinion best serves the consumers. But then it will no longer be the consumers that determine what they get. They will have to take what the businessmen believe is best for them. The entrepreneurs, not the consumers, will then be supreme. The consumers will no longer have the power to entrust control of production to those businessmen whose products they like most and to relegate those whose products they appreciate less to a more modest position in the system.

If the present American laws concerning the taxation of the profits of corporations, the incomes of individuals and inheritances had been introduced about sixty years ago, all those new products whose consumption has raised the standard of living of the "common man" would either not be produced at all or only in small quantities for the benefit of a minority. The Ford enterprises would not exist if Henry Ford's profits had been taxed away as soon as they came into being. The business structure of 1895 would have been preserved. The accumulation of new capital would have ceased or at least slowed down considerably. The expansion of production would lag behind the increase of population. There is no need to expatiate about the effects of such a state of affairs.

Profit and loss tell the entrepreneur what the consumers are asking for most urgently. And only the profits the entrepreneur pockets enable him to adjust his activities to the demand of the consumers. If the profits are expropriated, he is prevented from complying with the directives given by the consumers. Then the market economy is deprived of its steering wheel. It becomes a senseless jumble.

People can consume only what has been produced. The great problem of our age is precisely this: Who should determine what is to be produced and consumed, the people or the State, the consumers themselves or a paternal government? If one decides in favor of the consumers, one chooses the market economy. If one decides in favor of the government, one chooses socialism. There is no third solution. The determination of the purpose for which each unit of the various factors of production is to be employed cannot be divided.

Demand for Equalization

The supremacy of the consumers consists in their power to hand over control of the material factors of production and thereby the conduct of production activities to those who serve them in the most efficient way. This implies inequality of wealth and incomes. If one wants to do away with inequality of wealth and incomes, one must abandon capitalism and adopt socialism. (The question whether any socialist system would really give income equality must be left to an analysis of socialism.)

But, say the middle-of-the-road enthusiasts, we do not want to abolish inequality altogether. We want merely to substitute a lower degree of inequality for a higher degree.

These people look upon inequality as upon an evil. They do not assert that a definite degree of inequality which can be exactly determined by a judgment free of any arbitrariness and personal evaluation is good and has to be preserved unconditionally. They, on the contrary, declare inequality in itself as bad and merely contend that a lower degree of it is a lesser evil than a higher degree in the same sense in which a smaller quantity of poison in a man's body is a lesser evil than a larger dose. But if this is so, then there is logically in their doctrine no point at which the endeavors toward equalization would have to stop.

Whether one has already reached a degree of inequality which is to be considered low enough and beyond which it is not necessary to embark upon further measures toward equalization is just a matter of personal judgments of value, quite arbitrary, different with different people and changing in the passing of time. As these champions of equalization appraise confiscation and "redistribution" as a policy harming only a minority, viz., those whom they consider to be "too" rich, and benefiting the rest - the majority - of the people, they cannot oppose any tenable argument to those who are asking for more of this allegedly beneficial policy. As long as any degree of inequality is left, there will always be people whom envy impels to press for a continuation of the equalization policy. Nothing can be advanced against their inference: If inequality of wealth and incomes is an evil, there is no reason to acquiesce in any degree of it, however low; equalization must not stop before it has completely leveled all individuals' wealth and incomes.

The history of the taxation of profits, incomes, and estates in all countries clearly shows that once the principle of equalization is adopted, there is no point at which the further progress of the policy of equalization can be checked. If, at the time the Sixteenth Amendment was adopted, somebody had predicted that some years later the income tax progression would reach the height it has really attained in our day, the advocates of the Amendment would have called him a lunatic.

It is certain that only a small minority in Congress will seriously oppose further sharpening of the progressive element in the tax rate scales if such a sharpening should be suggested by the Administration or by a congressman anxious to enhance his chances for reelection. For, under the sway of the doctrines taught by contemporary pseudo-economists, all but a few reasonable men believe that they are injured by the mere fact that their own income is smaller than that of other people and that it is not a bad policy to confiscate this difference.

There is no use in fooling ourselves. Our present taxation policy is headed toward a complete equalization of wealth and incomes and thereby toward socialism. This trend can be reversed only by the cognition of the role that profit and loss and the resulting inequality of wealth and incomes play in the operation of the market economy. People must learn that the accumulation of wealth by the successful conduct of business is the corollary of the improvement of their own standard of living and vice versa. They must realize that bigness in business is not an evil, but both the cause and effect of the fact that they themselves enjoy all those amenities whose enjoyment is called the "American way of life."

– Ludwig von Mises

Editor's Note: Last January the Economic Policy Institute and the Center on Budget and Policy Priorities released a study decrying the growing income inequality in America and calling on government to rectify this alleged injustice. "The economic prosperity of the 1990's has not been shared equally," wrote the authors. There is no better response than what Ludwig von Mises (1881-1973), the great economist of the Austrian school, wrote in Ideas on Liberty in May 1955

Reprinted with permission from The Freeman, a publication of The Foundation for Economic Education, Inc., April 2000, Vol. 50, No. 4.

> *"Our country is the best country in the world. We are swimming in prosperity and our President is the best president in the world. We have larger apples and better cotton and faster and more beautiful machines. This makes us the greatest country in the world. Unemployment is a myth. Dissatisfaction is a fable. In preparatory school America is beautiful. It is the gem of the ocean and it is too bad. It is bad because people believe it all because they become indifferent. Because they marry and reproduce and vote and they know nothing."*
>
> … JOHN CHEEVER

A STRANGE INDIFFERENCE

An unusual thing happened to me one night several months ago. I had worked late in my home office, and my wife had fallen asleep with the bedroom television on. As I prepared for bed, a late-night talk-show was being broadcast. The talk-show guest was a well-known consumer advocate, who was crowing about his success at having a certain controversial but otherwise harmless product outlawed in many cities and tightly regulated in a few states. I watched for a few minutes with no particular interest, and then it struck me how strange that was - that I had no particular interest.

My "arguments with the television" are somewhat of a family joke. Indeed, it had been unusual for me to get through a newscast without becoming livid over the course of local and national events. Yet there I was, listening to a recital of how one more freedom of choice was being eliminated, and I really didn't care. That startled me.

It wasn't fatigue. I'm a night person, and usually have to force myself to bed. It wasn't preoccupation. I had completed the task I had been working on, and felt satisfied with my accomplishment. Perhaps, I thought, I had been emotionally drained by recent months, and the increasing attacks on our liberties.

I had been angered at having to obtain a Social Security number for my ten-year-old son. I was depressed by calls for tighter regulation of financial markets. I was frightened by the efforts to increase my already oppressive tax load, and calls for the creation of vast new bureaucracies. And, nearly every day, I was shocked by the indifference of my neighbors to the tightening controls on their lives. As I turned off the TV it seemed the topic being discussed was trivial compared to some things yet I couldn't stop wondering at my own apathy.

As I lay in the dark, an odd, out-of-place memory came to mind. I recalled the two years I had lived in Europe. It occurred to me that I could remember almost nothing of the events that had gone on around me at the time. The reason for this was fairly obvious. While I had been in Europe, I had not been of Europe. To me, "the world" had been America, several thousand miles away. I had felt as removed from the culture around me as I would have been were I observing a tribe of aborigines. European affairs had aroused not the slightest emotion in me.

My mind went off on other strange tangents. I thought of my grandfather, who had come to America at the turn of the century, leaving a comparatively prosperous life in Europe to live in a strange land where he couldn't speak the language, and had to work as a common laborer. Despite stories of oppression by the czar's armies, it was never clear to me why he had thrown up his hands and given up on his native country, when thousands of others, including his own brother, chose to remain. When and why had the idea to leave first played across his mind, and what was he feeling when the idea became a decision?

My thoughts turned to John Steinbeck's novel, The Grapes of Wrath, about the desperate flight of the Okies from the dust bowl of the Midwest to seek work in California. Several times in the book Steinbeck wrote that, when the migrant men got mad, their women felt relieved, because they knew that men who still could get mad, and shout, and curse had not reached a breaking point.

I wondered - was my current, momentary apathy a passing mood, or was it a symptom that, in my heart, I was giving up on America? Did I now feel as alienated from my neighbors as I once had from the Germans who had bustled about me on the streets of Frankfurt? I had daydreamed about expanding my business to some emerging country, but had passed the idea off as merely a mid-life adventure fantasy - was I actually repeating a thought process that had brought my grandfather to abandon his roots, ninety years before?

As I drifted off to sleep, I reflected that men will get mad, and shout, and curse - even at television sets - when they see hope being stolen from them. It's when they think that all hope for the future is gone that they fall silent, and no one can be sure what they'll do then.

Rights for Robots

Millions of our people now look to the government much in the same fashion that their fathers of Victorian times looked to God. Political authority has taken the place of heavenly guidance.

Herbert Spencer in that wonderful prophecy, The Man Versus the State, explained in detail what would happen. He foretold with exactitude the present rush of the weaklings for jobs as planners and permitters, telling other people what not to do.

You will have noticed that while we are all under the thumb of authority, authority becomes composed of those who, lacking the courage to stand on their own feet and accept their share of personal responsibility, seek the safety of official positions where they escape the consequences of error and failure. Active, energetic, and progressive persons, instead of leading the rest, are allowed to move only by the grace and favor of that section of the population which from its very nature lacks all the qualities needed to produce the desired results. Authority is the power to say no, which requires little or no ability.

On a broad view, the all-important issue in the world today is individualism versus collectivism.

The Individualist thinks of millions of single human souls, each with a spark of divine genius, and visualizes that genius applied to the solution of his own problems. His conception is infinitely higher than that of the politician or planner who at best regards these millions as material for social or political experiment or, at worst, cannon fodder.

– Andrew E. Barniskis

> *"Socialism needs to pull down wealth; liberalism seeks to raise up poverty. Socialism would destroy private interests, Liberalism would preserve {them} ... by reconciling them with public right. Socialism would kill enterprise; Liberalism would rescue enterprise from the trammels of privilege and preference. Socialism assails the preeminence of the individual; Liberalism seeks ... to build up a minimum standard for the mass. Socialism exalts the rule; Liberalism exalts the man. Socialism attacks capitalism; Liberalism attacks monopoly."*
>
> ... WINSTON CHURCHILL

LIBERALISM STANDS FOR FREEDOM

THE story about the Grand Inquisitor in Dostoevsky's novel, *The Brothers Karamazov,* pictures Christ as appearing in the streets of Seville during the Spanish Inquisition just as a large number of heretics had been burned at the stake. The Grand Inquisitor arrested Christ, visited him in his cell, and said:

Thou wouldst go into the world . . . with some promise of freedom which men ... cannot even understand, which they fear and dread-for nothing has ever been more insupportable for a man and a human society than freedom. But seest Thou these stones in this parched and barren wilderness? Turn them into bread, and mankind will run after Thee like a flock of sheep, grateful and obedient.... But Thou wouldst *not deprive man of freedom and didst reject the offer, thinking, what is that freedom worth, if obedience is bought with bread? Thou didst reply that man lives not by bread alone.**

*Fyodor Sostoevsky, *The Brothers Karamazov* (New York: The Macmillan Company, 1927), p. 266.

The Grand Inquisitor was a good man, devoted to the public welfare. But he believed in an authoritarian concept of life and he regarded Christ as a dangerous agitator. The Grand Inquisitor believed in using authority to regiment man for the good of society. He told Christ that liberalism would not work; that freedom is something that men "fear and dread," but that men will follow, like a flock of sheep, anyone who will give them, or promise them, bread. His views foreshadowed those of today's neo-liberals who want man to surrender his freedom for the politician's promise of security, and to exchange his liberties for subsidies from the all-powerful "Social Welfare" State.

The Soul of Man

Today we are witnessing a great struggle for the soul and mind of man. We are witnessing a struggle between the authoritarian and the liberal concepts of life. In this struggle those who now falsely call themselves liberals are lined up on the totalitarian side. That is not where they intend to stand but it is nevertheless where they do stand. They stand there because they have abandoned the philosophy of traditional liberalism, which placed its main emphasis upon individual freedom.

The philosophy of neo-liberalism wants to create an egalitarian society and to use the coercive power of the state to equalize possessions and incomes even though in the process the individual is deprived of freedom.

There is a sharp distinction between liberalism and the fraudulent substitute that passes for it today. Throughout history two basic philosophies of life have been in deadly conflict. One concept, the liberal concept, is based upon the belief in the importance of the individual soul and personality. It is based upon the theory that the state was made to serve man, not man to serve the state. The other concept, the authoritarian concept, assumes that man, the individual, is of no importance. It assumes that man, collectively, as represented by the state, the church, the labor union or some other collective aggregate, alone is important. One concept exalts man, the other debases him.

The Struggle of Man

To anyone familiar with the historic meaning of liberalism, it is crystal clear that what passes for liberalism today is in fact its direct opposite. The principle of authority, which now masquerades as liberalism and which has enslaved the human spirit during the greater part of recorded history, has been challenged effectively only by that concept of life which historically is known as liberalism. In simpler terms, the history of liberalism is the history of man's struggle for freedom and liberty. Although the roots of liberalism lie deep in history, the philosophy that was later to be known as liberalism began to develop with the long struggle between Parliament and the Crown in England, and with the rise of the Dutch Republic in Holland. The right of free speech was asserted as early as 1644 by John Milton in *Areopagitica,* an essay published in defiance of law, to protest against censorship. But John Locke, the philosopher of the Glorious Revolution of 1688, was the first to expound the principles of liberalism as a comprehensive philosophy of government. A century later, the American Revolution established a new type of government based upon the doctrines of Locke; and Adam Smith formulated the liberal doctrine in economic terms.

Fear of Authority

The Declaration of Independence and the Constitution of the United States stem directly from the writings of John Locke. Our Constitution expresses the fear of governmental authority, which is characteristic of liberalism. It does so in the Bill of Rights which, to protect the rights of man, places constitutional limits upon governmental authority. It does so in our system of governmental checks and balances, which was conceived, not by the draftsmen of our Constitution, but by John Locke. Our Constitution was designed primarily to safeguard liberty. It shows distrust of the President, of Congress and of the courts, and makes each a check upon the other two. Nowhere is the fear of authoritarian government expressed more graphically than in John Stuart Mill's essay *On Liberty:*

The struggle between Liberty and Authority is the most conspicuous feature in the portions of history with which we are earliest familiar ... By liberty, was meant protection against the tyranny of the political rulers. The rulers were conceived ... as in a necessarily antagonistic position to the people whom they ruled.

To prevent the weaker members of the community from being preyed upon by innumerable vultures, it was needful that there should be an animal of prey stronger than the rest, commissioned to keep them down. But as the king of the vultures would be no less bent upon preying on the flock than any of the minor harpies, it was indispensable to be in a perpetual attitude of defense against his beak and claws. The aim, therefore, of patriots was to set limits to the power which the ruler should be suffered to exercise over the community; and this limitation was what they meant by liberty.

"All Men Are Created Equal"

The statement in the Declaration of Independence that "all men are created equal" was not intended to mean that they are equal in intelligence, in physical strength, in character or in any other respect in which individuals differ. On the contrary, that statement means that under a just government, all men are equal under the law. This was then a new and revolutionary doctrine in direct conflict with the principle of authority under which men are not equal under the law. Under the rule of authority a man's status in the social structure determines what laws apply to him. Two examples will illustrate the point: (1) In France, before the French Revolution, the nobility and clergy were not subject to certain taxes imposed upon other classes of society. (2) In England, under the Statute of Artificers enacted in the reign of Queen Elizabeth, a workman was not permitted to leave his parish without the consent of his last employer. The special privileges of French nobles and clergy and the discriminatory restraints upon the freedom of English workmen were based on their status in society.

This concept of status is in direct conflict with the liberal philosophy of equality under the law. This means the application to everyone alike of impersonal rules and principles of law. As Locke expressed it: Freedom of man under government is to have a standing rule to live by, common to everyone of that society and made by the legislative power vested in it.*

*John Locke, *Treatise on Government*, II, 1690

As Aristotle expressed it:

The only stable state is the one in which all men are equal before the law**

**Aristotle, *Politics*, V.

The Liberal Concept

In the last two decades, we have gone a long way from the liberal concepts of individual freedom, limited government. Equality under the law and the rule of law as contrasted with the rule of men. This trend is the result of neo-liberalism which has changed the popular meaning of the term "liberalism" so that to most people today it stands for a philosophy diametrically opposed to traditional liberalism.

Equality under the law has been undermined by giving special privileges to powerful groups. The special privileges now granted members of labor unions in no way differ in principle from the special privileges that the French nobles and clergy once enjoyed. Labor unions are exempt from the anti-trust laws. In many states they cannot be sued although the congregation of a church may be sued. They are immune from injunctions, except to a very limited degree. Before the Taft-Hartley Law, the United States Supreme Court held that they could lawfully engage in racketeering and extortion under the threats of violence.* Thus the principle of equality under the law has given way to the discredited, reactionary, medieval concept of *status* under which a person's position in society determines the laws to which he is subject.

*U.S. v. Local 807 International Brotherhood of Teamsters, 315 U.S. 521 (1942).

The Rule of Law

If equality under the law is one test of liberalism, another is the concept of the rule of law rather than the rule of men. This basic idea rests on the assumption that the power of the state should be exerted according to the law rather than through the arbitrary action of officials. But today in administrative agencies of the government, the arbitrary judgment of officials is substituted for the rule of law. We quote Roscoe Pound, former Dean of the Harvard Law School:

As a result ... of the hostility of administrative agencies to all attempts to impose effective legal checks upon them we have been coming in practice to a condition of what may be called administrative absolutism ... To them [government officials] ... law is whatever is done by administrative agencies. What they do is law because they do it.... Instead of our fundamental doctrine that government is to be carried on according to law we are told that what the government does is law. **

** Roscoe Pound, *Administrative Agencies and the Law.*

Another test of liberalism is the doctrine that freedom can exist only under a government of defined and limited powers. This Lockian principle is written into our Constitution. But our Supreme Court, bowing to popular pressure, has for all practical purposes wiped out the constitutional limitations upon the power of government. The commerce clause has been stretched so far that the Court has upheld the government's claims to jurisdiction over the terms of employment of elevator operators in city office buildings and of those employed in hosts of other purely local activities on the tenuous ground that, since these local activities are related, however remotely, to interstate commerce, the federal government has jurisdiction.

The Decay of Liberalism

The change from the liberal philosophy of a free society to the neo-liberal philosophy of the Social Welfare State did not develop overnight. In both England and the United States early liberals were interested not only in promoting the extension of individual liberty, in broadening the franchise and in obtaining the greatest measure of political equality among men, but they were also strongly imbued with humanitarian ideas. They were shocked by many of the evils that characterized the industrial revolution in England and in the United States, and they sought to reform them. As time went on, many who designated themselves as liberals became more and more interested in reform and less and less interested in freedom. They wished to use the coercive power of the state to limit liberty in order to protect the weak against the strong. But the term "liberal" was identified historically with individual freedom. Neo-liberals resolved this difficulty by gradually debasing the word "freedom" and changing its meaning. This changed meaning began to evolve in our universities and in intellectual circles based largely upon German idealistic philosophy, which taught that man is subordinate to a higher force or purpose and that it is only as he serves this higher purpose and makes his desires conform to it that he becomes really free. If this higher force is conceived of as the state, then man is only free as he serves the state. This is a collectivist and authoritarian conception of freedom. Marxian communism teaches that the legal liberty of western democracies is merely "formal liberty" without substance.

The Communist View

This communist view of liberty is constantly reiterated by our neo-liberal left. We are told again and again by those who claim to speak for liberalism that society must give the average man *"actual* as distinct from merely *legal* liberty"; that political freedom is meaningless without "industrial democracy"; that the old kind of liberty was "license for the few and economic serfdom for the many"; and that, because of inequalities in wealth, the average man has no opportunity and therefore no real freedom. The old-fashioned liberal looked up to the man of moderate means who skimped and saved to put his children through college. The neo-liberal thinks that he has been victimized and that the government should perform this duty for him.

Expedient Bedfellows

It is a curious thing that although most of our neo-liberals are bitterly opposed to totalitarianism, they nevertheless adopt the communist definition of freedom. It is necessary for them to do so to provide a moral justification for the "Social Welfare" State which they advocate. They have adopted the definition of freedom which the Communists share with the Fascists. It is a definition upon which right wing and left wing totalitarians agree. Let us look at the record.

Molotov, in an attack upon Bernard M. Baruch at the United Nations General Assembly, expressed the communist view of freedom. He said:

[Baruch's] concept of freedom is far removed from the real aspirations of common people for freedom. He would like to see all people satisfied with freedom under which only the lucky ones can enjoy the benefits of life.*

Lenin wrote:

"No amount of political freedom will satisfy the hungry masses."**

Oswald Mosley, the British Fascist, wrote:

Real freedom means good wages, short hours, security in employment, good homes, leisure and recreation with family and friends.***

*Address before the United Nations General Assembly, October 30, 1946.

**Draft of Bolshevik Theses, March 17, 1917.

***Fascism, 1936.

Juan D. Peron, in a series of newspaper articles, contrasted the liberal idea of freedom with the totalitarian definition of freedom which he shares with neo-liberals, Communists and his fellow Fascists. He wrote:

The equality of the French Revolution consisted in equal treatment of all persons, whereas present equality consists of an unequal treatment to compensate the differences.

The liberty of the French Revolution was incompatible ... with the professional syndicates [labor unions], whereas in the present, the syndicates or unions constitute the indispensable requirement for individual and collective freedom of the working classes. In the nineteenth century, or at least in its beginnings, it was impossible to understand the interventionism of the state in social matters, whereas in the twentieth century we cannot understand the relationship between capital and labor unless we look at it on the basis of state intervention.... Respect for contractual freedom was an unchangeable point of this policy of freedom; but in our times, it will be very rare to find a contract in which the state does not intervene.... Liberty will bestow fewer rights upon the individual to do as he sees fit, because liberty will increase the obligation to do whatever is best for the community. ****

Peron has written a platform on which the whole left wing could stand. This should surprise no one because neo-liberalism, in common with fascism and communism, is basically authoritarian. Peron has rationalized and put in logical form the general philosophy of those who now call themselves liberals. It will be noted that Peron's concept of freedom, which the left wing has adopted, is that of license for the *organization* at the sacrifice of freedom for the *individual.* To illustrate, the closed shop deprives the individual workman of the liberty of choice to go into the union or to stay out of the union as he pleases. But in neo-liberal eyes the closed shop and the union shop increase the freedom of the workman because they increase the power of the organizations which claim to represent him. The same is true of permitting labor unions to coerce and intimidate both their own members and unorganized workmen. This is a collectivist concept of freedom on which the Russian Communist, Molotov, the British Fascist, Oswald Mosley, the Fascist dictator of Argentina, Juan Peron, and neo-liberals all agree.

****St. Louis Globe-Democrat, June 8, 1948

A Necessary Evil

The Grand Inquisitor was intellectually honest and recognized that freedom and free bread is alternatives. But Communists, Fascists and our neo-liberal left wing argue that government bounties of free bread and freedom are identical.

Traditional liberalism regards government as a necessary evil. It fears government and seeks to impose restraints upon its power. As Woodrow Wilson expressed it, *"The history of liberty is the history of limitations of governmental power, not the increase of it."*****

Today's neo-liberals believe in increasing the authority of the state at the expense of individual liberty. Communists look upon the centralization of all power in the state as a necessary prelude to the police state which is their goal. But, many neo-liberals abhor the police state. They merely want to do good and improve the lot of mankind. But they want the government to have *unlimited* power to do good. They look upon the citizen with suspicion and upon the government with approval. They seek to build a government of unlimited powers to control and regiment the individual for the good of society, to prevent the strong from taking advantage of the weak, to offset inequalities in incomes and wealth, and to play the historic role of Robin Hood who robbed the rich and distributed some of the proceeds to the poor. Neo-liberals unwittingly are playing the communist game. They mean well but they fail to recognize the harsh truth of Lord Acton's dictum: *"All power tends to corrupt, and absolute power corrupts absolutely."* If we follow them we shall end as slaves of an authoritarian state. That is not the goal of neo-liberals but it is nevertheless the destination toward which they are headed.

– Towner Phelan

*****Speech in New York, September 9, 1912.*

> *"The true theory of our Constitution is surely the wisest and best, that the States are independent as to everything within themselves and united as to everything respecting foreign affairs. Let the General Government be reduced to foreign concerns only, and let our affairs be disentangled from those of all other nations, except as to commerce, which the merchants will manage the better, the more they are left free to manage for themselves, and our General Government may be reduced to a very simple organization, and a very inexpensive one; a few plain duties to be performed by a few servants."*
>
> ... THOMAS JEFFERSON

SOME WANDERING THOUGHTS

MAYBE the whole idea is impossible, but what do you think of my wandering thoughts?

We all complain that the federal government is encroaching upon the authority of state and local governments and the rights of individuals. It takes unto itself more and more of the functions historically exercised by states and localities. Under the old way, "home government" was a blessing for the nation as a whole.

My thoughts went far off the beaten paths. Why should we not forbid the federal government to collect taxes? Let state and local governments collect all taxes, if needed. Then reverse the present trend by giving state grants to the federal government to cover the expenses involved for its then *limited services.* Why federal "grants" to states and localities when the residents of the various states and localities furnish this money in the first place, and have to pay for the administration and handling of these funds which, if they come back at all, look awfully sick after deductions for "services rendered" by the federal government?

Then the federal government would have to submit its budgets to state legislatures where they could be scrutinized before acceptance. The people would thus have a broader picture of the cost of government. The centralization of power and even the "ism" of the "welfare state" would be well on the way to elimination. Taxes, I am sure, could be cut to a fraction under such a change, putting the "bureaucrats" in Washington under the "dole" from the states. That would be the kind of "social security" we could stand. The power of the individual state and local governments, and through them the power of the individual voters, could be re-established.

In 1916, Lenin advised Swiss workers that direct federal taxation would be an instrument through which Switzerland could be socialized. The same for the United States.

— *John Unkel*

> *"Perhaps one of the most important accomplishments of my administration has been minding my own business"*
>
> ... CALVIN COOLIDGE

ON MINDING ONE'S OWN BUSINESS

THE passion for dealing with social questions is one of the marks of our time. Every man gets some experience of, and makes some observations on social affairs. Except matters of health, probably none have such general interest as matters of society. Except matters of health, none are so much afflicted by dogmatism and crude speculation as those which appertain to society. The amateurs in social science always ask: What shall we do? What shall we do with Neighbor A? What shall we do for Neighbor B? What shall we make Neighbor A do for Neighbor B? It is a fine thing to be planning and discussing broad and general theories of wide application. The amateurs always plan to use the individual for some constructive and inferential social purpose, or to use the society for some constructive and inferential individual purpose. For A to sit down and think, what shall

I do? is commonplace; but to think what B ought to do is interesting, romantic, moral, self-flattering, and public-spirited all at once. It satisfies a great number of human weaknesses at once. To go on and plan what a whole class of people ought to do is to feel one's self a power on earth, to win a public position, to clothe one's self in dignity. Hence we have an unlimited supply of reformers, philanthropists, humanitarians, and would-be managers-in-general of society.

The First Duty

Every man and woman in society has one big duty. That is, to take care of his or her own self. This is a social duty. For, fortunately, the matter stands so that the duty of making the best of one's self individually is not a separate thing from the duty of filling one's place in society, but the two are one, and the latter is accomplished when the former is done. The common notion, however, seems to be that one has a duty to society, as a special and separate thing, and that this duty consists in considering and deciding what other people ought to do. Now, the man who can do anything for or about anybody else than himself is fit to be head of a family; and when he becomes head of a family he has duties to his wife and his children, in addition to the former big duty.

Then, again, any man who can take care of himself and his family is in a very exceptional position if he does not find in his immediate surroundings people who need his care and have some sort of a personal claim upon him. If, now, he is able to fulfill all this, and to take care of anybody outside his family and his dependents, he must have a surplus of energy, wisdom, and moral virtue beyond what he needs for his own business. No man has this; for a family is a charge which is capable of infinite development, and no man could suffice to the full measure of duty for which a family may draw upon him. Neither can a man give to society so advantageous an employment of his services, whatever they are, in any other way as by spending them on his family. Upon this, however, I will not insist. I recur to the observation that a man who proposes to take' care of other people must have himself and his family taken care of, after some sort of a fashion, and must have an as yet unexhausted store of energy.

A Twofold Danger

The danger of minding other people's business is twofold. First, there is the danger that a man may leave his own business unattended to; and, second, there is the danger of an impertinent interference with another's affairs. The "friends of humanity" almost always run into both dangers. I am one of humanity, and I do not want any volunteer friends. I regard friendship as mutual, and I want to have my say about it. I suppose that other components of humanity feel in the same way about it. If so, they must regard anyone who assumes the *role* of a friend of humanity as impertinent. The reference of the friend of humanity back to his own business is obviously the next step.

Yet we are constantly annoyed, and the legislatures are kept constantly busy, by the people who have made up their minds that it is wise and conducive to happiness to live in a certain way, and who want to compel everybody else to live in their way. Some people have decided to spend Sunday in a certain way, and they want laws passed to make other people spend Sunday in the same way. Some people have resolved to be teetotalers, and they want a law passed to make everybody else a teetotaler. Some people have resolved to eschew luxury, and they want taxes laid to make others eschew luxury. The taxing power is especially something after which the reformer's finger always itches. Sometimes there is an element of self-interest in the proposed reformation, as when a publisher wanted a duty imposed on books, to keep Americans from reading books which would unsettle their Americanism; and when artists wanted a tax laid on pictures, to save Americans from buying bad paintings.

I make no reference here to the giving and taking of counsel and aid between man and man: of that I shall say something in the last chapter. The very sacredness of the relation in which two men stand to one another when one of them rescues the other from vice separates that relation from any connection with the work of the social busybody, the professional philanthropist, and the empirical legislator.

Social Quacks

The amateur social doctors are like the amateur physicians -they always begin with the question of *remedies,* and they go at this without any diagnosis or any knowledge of the anatomy or physiology society. They never have any doubt of the efficacy of their remedies. They never take account of any ulterior effects which may be apprehended from the remedy itself. It generally troubles them not a whit that their remedy implies a complete reconstruction of society, or even a reconstitution of human nature. Against all such social quackery the obvious in junction to the quacks is, to mind their own business.

The social doctors enjoy the satisfaction of feeling themselves to be more moral or more enlightened than their fellow-men. They are able to see what other men ought to do when the other men do not see it. An examination of the work of the social doctors, however, shows that they are only more ignorant and more presumptuous than other people. We have a great many social difficulties and hardships to contend with. Poverty, pain, disease, and misfortune surround our existence. We fight against them all the time. The individual is a centre of hopes, affections, desires, and sufferings. When he dies, life changes its form, but does not cease. That means that the person-the centre of all the hopes, affections, etc.-after struggling as long as he can, is sure to succumb at last. We would, therefore, as far as the hardships of the human lot are concerned, go on struggling to the best of our ability against them but for the social doctors, and we would endure what we could not cure. But we have inherited a vast number of social ills which never came from Nature. They are the complicated products of all the tinkering, muddling, and blundering of social doctors in the past. These products of social quackery are now buttressed by habit, fashion, prejudice, platitudinarian thinking, and new quackery in political economy and social science.

The greatest reforms which could now be accomplished would consist in undoing the work of statesmen in the past, and the greatest difficulty in the way of reform is to find out how to undo their work without injury to what is natural and sound. All this mischief has been done by men who sat down to consider the problem (as I heard an apprentice of theirs once express it), what kind of a society do we want to make? When they had settled this question *a priori* to their satisfaction, they set to work to make their ideal society, and today we suffer the consequences. Human society tries hard to adapt itself to any conditions in which it finds itself, and we have been warped and distorted until we have got used to it, as the foot adapts itself to an ill-made boot. Next, we have come to think that that is the right way for things to be; and it is true that a change to a sound and normal condition would for a time hurt us, as a man whose foot has been distorted would suffer if he tried to wear a well-shaped boot. Finally, we have produced a lot of economists and social philosophers who have invented sophisms for fitting our thinking to the distorted facts.

Society, therefore, does not need any care or supervision. If we can acquire a science of society, based on observation of phenomena and study of forces, we may hope to gain some ground slowly toward the elimination of old errors and the re-establishment of a sound and natural social order. Whatever we gain that way will be by growth, never in the world by any reconstruction of society on the plan of some enthusiastic social architect. The latter is only repeating the old error over again, and postponing all our chances of real improvement.

Society needs first of all to be freed from these meddlers-that is, to be let alone. Here we are, then, once more back at the old doctrine *Laissez faire.* Let us translate it into blunt English, and it will read, Mind your own business. It is nothing but the doctrine of liberty. Let every man be happy in his own way. If his sphere of action and interest impinges on that of any other man, there will have to be compromise and adjustment. Wait for the occasion. Do not attempt to generalize those interferences or to plan for them *a priori.* We have a body of laws and institutions which have grown up as occasion has occurred for adjusting rights. Let the same process go on. Practice the utmost reserve possible in your interferences even of this kind, and by no means seize occasion for interfering with natural adjustments. Try first long and patiently whether the natural adjustment will not come about through the play of interests and the voluntary concessions of the parties.

The Root of Dictatorship

I have said that we have an empirical political economy and social science to fit the distortions of our society. The test of empiricism in this matter is the attitude which one takes up toward *laissez faire.* It no doubt wounds the vanity of a philosopher who is just ready with a new solution of the universe to be told to mind his own business. So he goes on to tell us that if we think that we shall, by being let alone, attain to perfect happiness on earth, we are mistaken. The halfway men, the professorial socialists, join him.

They solemnly shake their heads, and tell us that he is right-that letting us alone will never secure us perfect happiness. Under all this lies the familiar logical fallacy, never expressed, but really the point of the whole, that we *shall* get perfect happiness if we put ourselves in the hands of the world-reformer. We never supposed that *laissez faire* would give us perfect happiness. We have left perfect happiness entirely out of our account. If the social doctors will mind their own business, we shall have no troubles but what belong to Nature. Those we will endure or combat as we can. What we desire is that the friends of humanity should cease to add to them. Our disposition toward the ills which our fellow-man inflicts on us through malice or meddling is quite different from our disposition toward the ills which are inherent in the conditions of human life.

To mind one's own business is a purely negative and unproductive injunction, but, taking social matters as they are just now, it is a sociological principle of the first importance. There might be developed a grand philosophy on the basis of minding one's own business. – William Graham Sumner

> "*Trusting people to be creative and constructive when given more freedom does not imply an overly optimistic belief in the perfectibility of human nature. It is, rather, belief that the inevitable errors and sins of the human condition are far better overcome by individuals working together in an environment of trust and freedom and mutual respect than by individuals working under a multitude of rules, regulations, and restraints imposed upon them by another group of imperfect individuals.*"
>
> ... PETER SENGE

PEACE OR POLITICS

PEACE is the business of Society. Society is a cooperative effort, springing spontaneously from man's urge to improve on his circumstances. It is voluntary, completely free of force. It comes because man has learned that the task of life is easier of accomplishment through the exchange of goods, services, and ideas. The greater the volume and the fluidity of such exchanges the richer and fuller the life of every member of Society. That is the law of association; it is also the law of peace.

It is in the market place that man's peaceful ways are expressed. Here the individual voluntarily gives up possession of what he has in abundance, to gain possession of what he lacks. It is in the market place that Society flourishes, because it is in the market place that the individual flourishes. Not only does he find here the satisfactions for which he craves, but he also learns of the desires of his fellow-man so that he might the better serve him. More than that, he learns of and swaps ideas, hopes, and dreams, and comes away with values of greater worth to him than even those congealed in material things.

The law of association -the supreme law of Society is self-operating; it needs no enforcement agency. Its motor force is in the nature of man. His insatiable appetite for material, cultural, and spiritual desires drives him to join up. The compulsion is so strong that he makes an automobile out of an oxcart, a telephone system out of a drum, so as to overcome the handicaps of time and space; contact is of the essence in the market-place technique. Society grows because the seed of it is in the human being; it is made of man, but not by men.

The only condition necessary for the growth of Society into One Worldism is the absence of force in the market place; which is another way of saying that politics is a hindrance to, and not an aid of, peace. Any intervention in the sphere of voluntary exchanges stunts the growth of Society and tends to its disorganization. It is significant that in war, which is the ultimate of politics, every strategic move is aimed at the disorganization of the enemy's means of production and exchange -the disruption of his market place. Likewise, when the State intervenes in the business of Society, which is production and exchange, a condition of war exists, even though open conflict is prevented by the superior physical force the State is able to employ. Politics in the market place is like a bull in the china shop.

The essential characteristic of the State is force; it originates in force and exists by it. The rationale of the State is that conflict is inherent in the nature of man and he must be coerced into behaving, for his own good. That is a debatable doctrine, but even if we accept it the fact remains that the coercion must be exercised by men who are, by definition, as "bad" as those upon whom the coercion is exercised. The State is men. And the doctrine of the super-personal State cannot cover up that disturbing fact.

Getting down to the facts of experience, political power has never been used for the "general good," as advertised, but has always been used to further the interests of those in power or those who can support them in this purpose. To do so it must intervene in the market place. The advantages that political power confers upon its priesthood and their cohorts consist of what it skims from the abundance created by Society. Since it cannot make a single good, it lives and thrives by what it takes. What it takes deprives producers of the fruits of their labors, impoverishes them, and this causes a feeling of hurt. Intervention in the market place can do nothing else, then, than to create friction. Friction is incipient war.

– Frank Chodorov

> *"Individual rights are not subject to a public vote; a majority has no right to vote away the rights of a minority; the political function of rights is precisely to protect minorities from oppression by majorities (and the smallest minority on earth is the individual)."*
>
> … AYN RAND

THE INDIVIDUAL IN SOCIETY

THE words freedom and liberty signified for the most eminent representatives of mankind one of the most precious and desirable goods. Today it is fashionable to sneer at them. They are, trumpets the modern sage, "slippery" notions and "bourgeois" prejudices.

Freedom and liberty are not to be found in nature. In nature there is no phenomenon to which these terms could be meaningfully applied. Whatever man does, he can never free himself from the restraints which nature imposes upon him. If he wants to succeed in acting, he must submit unconditionally to the laws of nature.

Freedom and liberty always refer to inter human relations. A man is free as far as he can live and get on without being at the mercy of arbitrary decisions on the part of other people. In the frame of society everybody depends upon his fellow citizens. Social man cannot become independent without forsaking all the advantages of social cooperation.

The fundamental social phenomenon is the division of labor and its counterpart-human cooperation. Experience teaches man that cooperative action is more efficient and productive than isolated action of self-sufficient individuals. The natural conditions determining man's life and effort are such that the division of labor increases output per unit of labor expended. These natural facts are: (1) the innate inequality of men with regard to their ability to perform various kinds of labor, and (2) The unequal distribution of the nature-given, non human opportunities of production on the surface of the earth. One may as well consider these two facts as one and the same fact, namely, the manifoldness of nature which makes the universe a complex of infinite varieties.

Innate Inequality

The division of labor is the outcome of man's conscious reaction to the multiplicity of natural conditions. On the other hand, it is itself a factor bringing about differentiation. It assigns to the various geographic areas specific functions in the complex of the processes of production. It makes some areas urban, others rural; it locates the various branches of manufacturing, mining, and agriculture in different places. Still more important, however, is the fact that it intensifies the innate inequality of men. Exercise and practice of specific tasks adjust individuals better to the requirements of their performance; men develop some of their inborn faculties and stunt the development of others. Vocational types emerge, people become specialists.

The division of labor splits the various processes of production into minute tasks, many of which can be performed by mechanical devices. It is this fact that made the use of machinery possible and brought about the amazing improvements in technical methods of production. Mechanization is the fruit of the division of labor, its most beneficial achievement, not its motive and fountain spring. Power-driven specialized machinery could be employed only in a social environment under the division of labor. Every step forward on the road toward the use of more specialized, more refined, and more productive machines requires a further specialization of tasks.

Within Society

Seen from the point of view of the individual, society is the great means for the attainment of all his ends. The preservation of society is an essential condition of any plans an individual may want to realize by any action whatever. Even the refractory delinquent who fails to adjust his conduct to the requirements of life within the societal system of cooperation does not want to miss any of the advantages derived from the division of labor. He does not consciously aim at the destruction of society. He wants to lay his hands on a greater portion of the jointly produced wealth than the social order assigns to him. He would feel miserable if antisocial behavior were to become universal and its inevitable outcome, the return to primitive indigence, resulted.

Liberty and freedom are the conditions of man within a contractual society. Social cooperation under a system of private ownership of the means of production means that within the range of the market the individual is not bound to obey and to serve an overlord. As far as he gives and serves other people, he does so of his own accord in order to be rewarded and served by the receivers. He exchanges goods and services; he does not do compulsory labor and does not pay tribute. He is certainly not independent. He depends on the other members of society. But this dependence is mutual. The buyer depends on the seller and the seller on the buyer.

Self-Interest

The main concern of many writers of the nineteenth and twentieth centuries was to misrepresent and to distort this obvious state of affairs. The workers, they said, are at the mercy of their employers. Now, it is true that the employer has the right to fire the employee. But if he makes use of this right in order to indulge in his whims, he hurts his own interests. It is to his own disadvantage if he discharges a better man in order to hire a less efficient one. The market does not directly prevent anybody from arbitrarily inflicting harm on his fellow citizens; it only puts a penalty upon such conduct. The shopkeeper is free to be rude to his customers provided he is ready to bear the consequences. The consumers are free to boycott a purveyor provided they are ready to pay the costs. What impels every man to the utmost exertion in the service of his fellow men and curbs innate tendencies toward arbitrariness and malice is, in the market, not compulsion and coercion on the part of gendarmes, hangmen, and penal courts; it is self-interest. The member of a contractual society is free because he serves others only in serving himself. What restrains him is only the inevitable natural phenomenon of scarcity. For the rest he is free in the range of the market.

In the market economy the individual is free to act within the orbit of private property and the market. His choices are final. For his fellow men his actions are data which they must take into account in their own acting. The coordination of the autonomous actions of all individuals is accomplished by the operation of the market. Society does not tell a man what to do and what not to do. There is no need to enforce cooperation by special orders or prohibitions. Non-cooperation penalizes itself. Adjustment to the requirements of society's productive effort and the pursuit of the individual's own concerns are not in conflict. Consequently no agency is required to settle such conflicts. The system can work and accomplish its tasks without the interference of an authority issuing special orders and prohibitions and punishing those who do not comply.

Compulsion and Coercion

Beyond the sphere of private property and the market lies the sphere of compulsion and coercion; here are the dams which organized society has built for the protection of private property and the market against violence, malice, and fraud. This is the realm of constraint as distinguished from the realm of freedom. Here are rules discriminating between what is legal and what is illegal, what is permitted and what is prohibited. And here is a grim machine of arms, prisons, and gallows and the men operating it, ready to crush those who dare to disobey.

It is important to remember that government interference always means either violent action or the threat of such action. Government is in the last resort the employment of armed men, of policemen, gendarmes, soldiers, prison guards, and hangmen. The essential feature of government is the enforcement of its decrees by beating, killing, and imprisoning. Those who are asking for more government interference are asking ultimately for more compulsion and less freedom.

Liberty and freedom are terms employed for the description of the social conditions of the individual members of a market society in which the power of the indispensable hegemonic bond, the state, is curbed lest the operation of the market be endangered. In a totalitarian system there is nothing to which the attribute "free" could be attached but the unlimited arbitrariness of the dictator.

There would be no need to dwell upon this obvious fact if the champions of the abolition of liberty had not purposely brought about a semantic confusion. They realized that it was hopeless for them to fight openly and sincerely for restraint and servitude. The notions liberty and freedom had such prestige that no propaganda could shake their popularity. Since time immemorial in the realm of Western civilization, liberty has been considered as the most precious good. What gave to the West its eminence was precisely its concern about liberty, a social ideal foreign to the oriental peoples. The social philosophy of the Occident is essentially a philosophy of freedom. The main content of the history of Europe and the communities founded by European emigrants and their descendants in other parts of the world was the struggle for liberty. "Rugged" individualism is the signature of our civilization. No open attack upon the freedom of the individual had any prospect of success.

New Definitions

Thus the advocates of totalitarianism chose other tactics. They reversed the meaning of words. They call true or genuine liberty the condition of the individuals under a system in which they have no right other than to obey orders. They call themselves true *liberals* because they strive after such a social order. They call democracy the Russian methods of dictatorial government. They call the labor union methods of violence and coercion "industrial democracy." They call freedom of the press a state of affairs in which only the government is free to publish books and newspapers. They define liberty as the opportunity to do the "right" things, and, of course, they arrogate to themselves the determination of what is right and what is not. In their eyes government omnipotence means full liberty. To free the police power from all restraints is the true meaning of their struggle for freedom.

The market economy, say these self-styled liberals, grants liberty only to a parasitic class of exploiters, the bourgeoisie; that these scoundrels enjoy the freedom to enslave the masses; that the wage earner is not free; that he must toil for the sole benefit of his masters, the employers; that the capitalists appropriate to themselves what according to the inalienable rights of man should belong to the worker; that under socialism the worker will enjoy freedom and human dignity because he will no longer have to slave for a capitalist; that socialism means the emancipation of the common man, means freedom for all; that it means, moreover, riches for all.

These doctrines have been able to triumph because they did not encounter effective rational criticism. It is useless to stand upon an alleged "natural" right of individuals to own property if other people assert that the foremost "natural" right is that of income equality. Such disputes can never be settled. It is beside the point to criticize non essential, attendant features of the socialist program. One does not refute socialism by attacking the socialists' stand on religion, marriage, birth control, and art.

A *New Subterfuge*

In spite of these serious shortcomings of the defenders of economic freedom it was impossible to fool all the people all the time about the essential features of socialism. The most fanatical planners were forced to admit that their projects involve the abolition of many freedoms people enjoy under capitalism and "plutodemocracy." Pressed hard, they resorted to a new subterfuge. The freedom to be abolished, they emphasize, is merely the spurious "economic" freedom of the capitalists that harms the common man; that outside the "economic sphere" freedom will not only be fully preserved, but considerably expanded. "Planning for Freedom" has lately become the most popular slogan of the champions of totalitarian government and the Russification of all nations.

The fallacy of this argument stems from the spurious distinction between two realms of human life and action, the "economic" sphere and the "non-economic" sphere. Strictly speaking, people do not long for tangible goods as such, but for the services which these goods are fitted to render them. They want to attain the increment in well being which these services are able to convey. It IS a fact that people, in dealing on the market, are motivated not only by the desire to get food, shelter, and sexual enjoyment, but also by manifold "ideal" urges. Acting man is always concerned both with "material" and "ideal" things. He chooses between various alternatives, no matter whether they are to be classified as material or ideal. In the actual scales of value, material and ideal things are jumbled together.

Preserving the Market

Freedom, as people enjoyed it in the democratic countries of Western civilization in the years of the old liberalism's triumph, was not a product of constitutions, bills of rights, laws, and statutes. Those documents aimed only at safe guarding liberty and freedom, firmly established by the operation of the market economy, against encroachments on the part of officeholders. No government and no civil law can guarantee and bring about freedom otherwise than by supporting and defending the fundamental institutions of the market economy. Government means always coercion and compulsion and is by necessity the opposite of liberty. Government is a guarantor of liberty and is compatible with liberty only if its range is adequately restricted to the preservation of economic freedom. Where there is no market economy, the best-intentioned provisions of constitutions and laws remain a dead letter.

Competition

The freedom of man under capitalism is an effect of competition. The worker does not depend on the good graces of an employer. If his employer discharges him, he finds another employer. The consumer is not at the mercy of the shopkeeper. He is free to patronize another shop if he likes. Nobody must kiss other people's hands or fear their disfavor. Interpersonal relations are businesslike. The exchange of goods and services is mutual; it is not a favor to sell or to buy, it is a transaction dictated by selfishness on either side.

It is true that in his capacity as a producer every man depends either directly, as does the entrepreneur, or in directly, as does the hired worker, on the demands of the consumers. However, this dependence upon the supremacy of the consumers is not unlimited. If a man has a weighty reason for defying the sovereignty of the consumers, he can try it. There is in the range of the market a very substantial and effective right to resist oppression. Nobody is forced to go into the liquor industry or into a gun factory if his conscience objects. He may have to pay a price for his conviction; there are in this world no ends the attainment of which is gratuitous. But it is left to a man's own decision to choose between a material advantage and the call of what he believes to be his duty. In the market economy the individual alone is the supreme arbiter in matters of his satisfaction.

Consumers Choose

Capitalist society has no means of compelling a man to change his occupation or his place of work other than to reward those complying with the wants of the consumers by higher pay. It is precisely this kind of pressure which many people consider as unbearable and hope to see abolished under socialism. They are too dull to realize that the only alternative is to convey to the authorities full power to determine in what branch and at what place a man should work.

In his capacity as a consumer man is no less free. He alone decides what is more and what is less important for him. He chooses how to spend his money according to his own will.

The substitution of economic planning for the market economy removes all freedom and leaves to the individual merely the right to obey. The authority directing all economic matters controls all aspects of a man's life and activities. It is the only employer. All labor becomes compulsory labor because the employee must accept what the chief deigns to offer him. The economic tsar determines what and how much of each the consumer may consume. There is no sector of human life in which a decision is left to the individual's value judgments. The authority assigns a definite task to him, trains him for this job, and employs him at the place and in the manner it deems expedient.

The "Planned" Life Is Not Free

As soon as the economic freedom which the market economy grants to its members is removed, all political liberties and bills of rights become humbug. Habeas Corpus and trial by jury are a sham if, under the pretext of economic expediency, the authority has full power to relegate every citizen it dislikes to the arctic or to a desert and to assign him "bard labor" for life. Freedom of the press is a mere blind if the authority controls all printing offices and paper plants. And so are all the other rights of men.

A man has freedom as far as he shapes his life according to his own plans. A man whose fate is determined by the plans of a superior authority, in which the exclusive power to plan is vested, is not free in the sense in which the term "free" was used and understood by all people until the semantic revolution of our day brought about a confusion of tongues.

– Ludwig von Mises

> *"Every gun that is made, every warship launched, every rocket fired signifies in the final sense, a theft from those who hunger and are not fed, those who are cold and are not clothed. This world in arms is not spending money alone. It is spending the sweat of its laborers, the genius of its scientists and the hopes of its children. This is not a way of life at all in any true sense. Under the clouds of war, it is humanity hanging on a cross of iron."*
>
> … DWIGHT D. EISENHOWER

THE MOST DREADED ENEMY OF LIBERTY

OF all the enemies to public liberty war is, perhaps, the most to be dreaded, because it comprises and develops the germ of every other. War is the parent of armies; from these proceed debts and taxes; and armies, and debts, and taxes are the known instruments for bringing the many under the domination of the few. In war, too, the discretionary power of the Executive is extended; its influence in dealing out offices, honors, and emoluments is multiplied; and all the means of seducing the minds, are added to those of subduing the force, of the people.... [There is also an] inequality of fortunes, and the opportunities of fraud, growing out of a state of war, and ... degeneracy of manners and of morals ... No nation could preserve its freedom in the midst of continual warfare ... [It should be well understood] that the powers proposed to be surrendered {by the Third Congress} to the Executive were those which the Constitution has most jealously appropriated to the Legislature.... The Constitution expressly and exclusively vests in the Legislature the power of declaring a state of war ... the power of raising armies ... the power of creating offices .... A delegation of such powers [to the President] would have struck, not only at the fabric of our Constitution, but at the foundation of all well organized and well checked governments.

The separation of the power of declaring war from that of conducting it is wisely contrived to exclude the danger of its being declared for the sake of its being conducted.

The separation of the power of raising armies from the power of commanding them is intended to prevent the raising of armies for the sake of commanding them.

The separation of the power of creating offices from that of filling them is an essential guard against the temptation to create offices for the sake of gratifying favourites or multiplying dependents.

– James Madison

> *"In too many cases, if our Government had set out determined to destroy the family, it couldn't have done greater damage than some of what we see today. Too often these programs, well-intentioned, welfare programs for example, which were meant to provide for temporary support, have undermined responsibility. They've robbed people of control of their lives, destroyed their dignity, in some cases – and we've tried hard to change this – encouraged people, man and wife, to live apart because they might just get a little bit more to put in their pockets."*
>
> ... PRESIDENT GEORGE H. W. BUSH

THE GUARANTEED LIFE

"A GOVERNMENT is a group of men organized to sell protection to the inhabitants of a limited area at monopolistic prices." So said Peter Stuyvesant in *Knickerbocker Holiday,* and so I believe now. In other words there's no such thing as a "good" government; one and all they partake of the nature of rackets. But government is better than anarchy, and was invented as an insurance against anarchy. And some kinds of government are far better than others. Specifically, our American experiment has worked so well that we can point to it as one of the most successful in the history of the world, if not the most successful.

In *Knickerbocker Holiday* I tried to remind the audience of the attitude toward government which was prevalent in this country at the time of the revolution of 1776 and throughout the early years of the republic. At that time it was generally believed, as I believe now, that the gravest and most constant danger to a man's life, liberty and happiness is the government under which he lives.

It was believed then that a civilization is a balance of selfish interests, and that a government is necessary as an arbiter among these interests, but that the government must never be trusted, must be constantly watched, and must be drastically limited in its scope, because it, too, is a selfish interest and will automatically become a monopoly in crime and devour the civilization over which it presides unless there are definite and positive checks on its activities. The Constitution is a monument to our fore fathers' distrust of the state, and the division of powers among the legislative, judicial and executive branches succeeded so well for more than a century in keeping the sovereign authority in its place that our government has become widely regarded as a naturally wise and benevolent institution, capable of assuming the whole burden of social and economic justice. But there was nothing natural or accidental about it. Our government has done so well because of the wary thinking that went into its making.

A Selfish Interest

The thinking behind our Constitution was dominated by such men as Franklin and Jefferson, men with a high regard for the rights of the individual, combined with a cold and realistic attitude toward the blessings of central authority. Knowing that government is a selfish interest, they treated it as such, and asked of it no more than a selfish interest can give. But the coddled young reformer of our day, looking out on his world, finding merit often unrewarded and chicanery triumphant throws prudence to the winds and grasps blindly at any weapon which seems to him likely to destroy the purse-proud haves and scatter their belongings among the deserving have-nots. Now he is right in believing that the accumulation of too much wealth and power in a few hands is a danger to his civilization and his liberty. But when the weapon he finds is economic planning, and when the law he enacts sets up bureaus to run the nation's business, he is fighting a lesser evil by accepting a greater and more deadly one, and he should be aware of that fact.

Monopolistic Prices

A government is always "organized to sell protection to the inhabitants of a limited area at monopolistic prices." The members of a government are not only in business, but in a business which is in continual danger of lapsing into pure gangsterism, pure terrorism and plundering, buttered over at the top by a hypocritical pretense at patriotic unselfishness. The continent of Europe has seen too many such governments lately, and our own government is rapidly assuming economic and social responsibilities which take us in the same direction. Whatever the motives behind a government-dominated economy, it can have but one result, a loss of individual liberty in thought, speech and action. A guaranteed life is not free. Social security is a step toward the abrogation of the individual and his absorption into that robot which he has invented to serve him-the paternal state.

When I have said this to some of the youthful proponents of guaranteed existence, I have been met with the argument that men must live, and that when the economic machinery breaks down men must be cared for lest they starve or revolt. This is quite true and nobody is opposed to helping his fellow man. But the greatest enemies of democracy, the most violent reactionaries, are those who have lost faith in the capacity of a free people to manage their own affairs and wish to set up the government as a political and social guardian, running their business and making their decisions for them. This is statism, or Stalinism, no matter who advocates it and its plain treason to freedom.

Ward of the State

And life is infinitely less important than freedom. A free man has a value to himself and perhaps to his time; a ward of the state is useless to himself-useful only as so many foot-pounds of energy serving those who manage to set themselves above him. A people who have lost its freedom might better be dead, for it has no importance in the scheme of things except as an evil power behind a dictator. In our hearts we all despise the man who wishes the state to take care of him, who would not rather live meagerly as he pleases than suffer a fat and regimented existence. Those who are not willing to sacrifice their lives for their liberty have never been worth saving. Throughout remembered time every self-respecting man has been willing to defend his liberty with his life. If our country goes totalitarian out of a soft-headed humanitarian impulse to make life easy for the many, we shall get what we vote for and what we deserve, for the choice is still before us, but we shall have betrayed the race of men, and among them the very have-nots whom we subsidize. Our Western continent still has the opportunity to resist the government-led rush of barbarism which is taking Europe back toward Attila, but we can only do it by running our government, and by refusing to let it run us.

Dishonest Business

If the millions of workingmen in this country who are patiently paying their social security dues could glimpse the bureaucratic absolutism which that act presages for themselves and their children they would repudiate the whole monstrous and dishonest business overnight. When a government takes over a people's economic life it becomes absolute, and when it has become absolute it destroys the arts, the minds, the liberties and the meaning of the people it governs. It is not an accident that Germany, the first paternalistic state of modern Europe, was seized by an uncontrollable dictator who brought on the second world war; not an accident that Russia, adopting a centrally administered economy for humanitarian reasons, has arrived at a tyranny bloodier and more absolute than that of the Czars. And if England does not turn back soon she will go this same way. Men who are fed by their government will soon be driven down to the status of slaves or cattle.

All these dangers were foreseen by the political leaders who put our Constitution together after the revolution against England. The Constitution is so built that while we adhere to it we cannot be governed by one man or one faction, and when we have made mistakes we reserve the right to change our minds. The division of powers and the rotation of offices were designed to protect us against dictatorship and arbitrary authority. The fact that there are three branches of government makes for a salutary delay and a blessed inefficiency, the elective rotation makes for a government not by cynical professionals, but by normally honest and fairly incompetent amateurs. That was exactly what the wary old founding fathers wanted, and if we are wise we shall keep it, for no scheme in the history of the world has succeeded so well in maintaining the delicate balance between personal liberty and the minimum of authority which is necessary for the free growth of ideas in a tolerant society. But we shall not keep our Constitution, our freedom, nor our free elections, if we let our government slide gradually into the hands of economic planners who bribe one class of men after another with a state-administered dole.

Since *Knickerbocker Holiday* was written, the power of government in the United States has grown like a fungus in wet weather, price supports and unemployment benefits and farm subsidies are the rule, not the exception, and our government has turned into a giant give-away program, offering far more for votes than was ever paid by the most dishonest ward-healer in the days of Mark Hanna. We march steadily toward the prefabricated state. Yet we see clearly that in England, socialism turns rapidly into communism, and that in Russia and Yugoslavia, communism gives neither freedom nor security. The guaranteed life turns out to be not only not free -it's not safe. Do we want a gangster movement? We're going toward it.

– Maxwell Anderson

> *"The acknowledged aim of socialism is to take the means of production out of the hands of the capitalist class and place them into the hands of the workers. This aim is sometimes spoken of as public ownership, sometimes as common ownership of the production apparatus."*
>
> ... ANTON PANNEKOEK, WESTERN SOCIALIST, NOVEMBER 1947

OWNERSHIP IN COMMON

WHEN the government owns anything-be it a post office, a school, a hydroelectric dam, or whatever-it is called "common ownership" on the theory that it belongs to all of the people. In a discussion of the ideas behind this theory of government or common ownership, it is, of course, unnecessary to examine all the examples of it. The study of a single industry will suffice to illustrate the problem. The example here selected is the electric industry with particular emphasis on the device of river valley development.

Government Electricity

In 1932, the federal government was producing less than one-half of one per cent of all electricity generated in the United States. In 1949, this had increased to more than 13 per cent. If state and local government production is added, this figure rises to almost 20 per cent. Further, it is estimated that federal projects will account for at least 25 per cent of the new production capacity to be constructed in the United States during the next three years. The implications for the future are far more serious than shown by the actual figures of this trend toward government ownership. Here is the reason: When even one government electricity project is built, the result is that private capital for the building and expanding of private power companies in nearby areas tends to become increasingly scarce. Many persons with money to invest are beginning to realize that once the government enters into any area on even a small scale, it will sooner or later control the entire area. So it was in the Tennessee Valley. So it is in the Pacific Northwest. And there is no evidence to indicate a different result in any other section of the country that contains a government electricity plant, regardless of the excuse used by government to build the initial project. As in the past, private competitors will continue to be ruthlessly driven out by such devices as government-created and government-protected cooperatives; by price wars; by the building of duplicate facilities at the taxpayers' expense; and by special elections and referendums where public officials encourage the voters to authorize the government to purchase privately-owned electric systems at fire-sale prices.

Monopoly

In addition to these various methods of discouraging the use of private capital and private ownership, the government has now even gone so far as to actually *forbid* private construction of additional hydroelectric capacity in some instances. The most flagrant example of this is government's refusal to permit the Virginia Electric and Power Company to construct a dam and power plant at Roanoke Rapids, North Carolina. The reason given for this refusal is that government itself may someday decide to build a hydroelectric plant at that location.

Apparently, then, government no longer believes it necessary even to claim that it operates only in areas where private enterprise cannot or will not function. Government now merely issues an edict reserving for it whatever hydroelectric locations and distribution areas it wants-or may want at some time in the future.

Dependent on the State

This evil of government ownership feeds upon itself. Once it starts, there seems no way to confine it to a given area, or even to a given function. The private power companies that are permitted to operate within the area of a government hydroelectric project are soon forced to depend upon government for their own supplies of electricity. This situation should now be obvious to all persons in the Pacific Northwest. For there, many of the owners of private power companies now literally must beg for the "opportunity" to distribute electricity generated by the huge hydro electric dams of government. This same procedure is becoming increasingly obvious in other areas where these grandiose hydroelectric projects have been built by government through its programs for developing the river valleys of the United States. The situation has progressed so far today that we now find some of the owners of private power companies actually praising and encouraging the idea of government electricity production. And many of the private owners, who do not praise the idea, have at least been frightened into silence.

Irrigation Fallacy

These hydroelectric projects usually are first advanced under the guise of the "comprehensive development of an entire river valley-flood control, navigation, irrigation, and any incidental electricity that may result as a byproduct of these other primary aims." But surely no one now believes that the primary purpose of the Tennessee Valley Authority, the Bonneville Administration, and other similar government projects is either flood control or navigation. All of these projects now stand exposed for what they were primarily intended to be in the first place: government ownership of the means of producing electricity. And as for the irrigation features of Bonneville and other similar projects, consider this question: How can government justify the expenditure of public funds to bring new land into agricultural production while, at the same time, it is spending public funds to purchase and store agricultural products and keep them off the market? With one hand the government is trying to force abundance by means of its irrigation programs; with the other hand the government is trying to force scarcity by means of its price support programs. And with both hands the government is bleeding the taxpayers and consumers in the process-all in the beguiling name of irrigation and river valley development.

Source of a False Idea

The advocates of government ownership and operation of the means of producing electricity offer many reasons for their philosophy of common ownership. In the first place, they claim that they can "prove conclusively" that the government can do it better and cheaper than private enterprise. They advance the thesis that no person should be denied the use of electricity merely because he is unable or unwilling to pay the market price for it. They claim that private producers charge "too much," and that such a vital and necessary product as electricity should not be entrusted to misuse and neglect by private owners who are motivated by a desire for profit instead of by patriotism and the unselfish desire for a planned and controlled national prosperity.

Compulsory Investment

The advocates of common ownership who advance these collectivistic arguments are probably sincere. They may honestly believe that their grandiose schemes are best for the people and the nation. But the fact remains that they can put their plans into effect *only* if they can gain control of government to enable them to do so at the forced expense of the taxpayers. This gaining control of government to make the people conform is all-important to the planners. It is necessary because, in advance, they already know that a free people will not voluntarily support, with their own money, what they consider to be uneconomic electric projects and river valley development programs. That is why private enterprise in a free market would not undertake the building of them in the first place. Thus the planners literally have no alternative but to get themselves elected or appointed to public office. They must have the law and the force of government on their side. Only then can they ignore the supply and demand decisions of free people using their own money. Only then can the people's taxes be used to force them to become "investors" in these uneconomic projects which have been repudiated by a free people in a market economy.

Private Enterprise Projects

Contrasted with the TVA and Bonneville method of forced investment, let us now briefly examine an example of the free market approach to river valley development. Probably the most complete project for the integrated development of a river valley by private enterprise is the Wisconsin Valley Improvement Company. The WVIC began its comprehensive development of the 4S0-mile long Wisconsin River in 1907. It has built 21 storage reservoirs for flood control and steadier water flow on the tributaries of the river. There are 24 hydroelectric and hydro-mechanical power plants on the main stream. In addition to flood control, the basic needs for navigation, fish life, elimination of water pollution, and other services are provided-at no cost to the taxpayers. In fact, instead of using the taxpayers' money like TVA and all other government power projects, the WVIC *pays* taxes-local, state, and federal. The WVIC is proud to announce that it was organized to make a profit for its voluntary investors, and that it does so-a current return of 4.4 per cent on its investment.

The Russian Comparison

The political managers of the Tennessee Valley Authority, the Bonneville Administration, and others, generally claim that these various compulsory projects by government also "won't cost the taxpayers a cent; that all of the money, including the equivalent of taxes, interest, and even a profit to the government, will be paid back; that the common owners will then have their original investment, free and clear, plus all the installations and services."

This is essentially the same claim that is advanced by the Russian advocates of common ownership in defense of their river valley programs. For example, the facts and figures issued by the Russians to prove the success of their Dnieper River hydroelectric project are of the same general nature as those issued by the Tennessee Valley Authority and other government power projects. The political managers in both countries issue reports that are designed to prove beyond a shadow of a doubt that government ownership and operation of the means of producing electricity is superior to private ownership. These reports in both countries are designed to show that "unselfish government managers" are more interested in national progress and prosperity than are "selfish private operators who are governed entirely by the profit motive." And the point has now been reached where a person has almost as much difficulty challenging the figures issued by these United States government "authorities" as he has challenging the figures issued by the common-ownership managers in similar electric projects in Russia. In either case, the objector will be called a propagandist, a reactionary, an enemy of the people, a lobbyist, a hireling of Wall Street, a purveyor of half-truths and slanted figures, and the other time-worn and customary epithets that are hurled at those persons who dare challenge the concept of common ownership of the means of production. Yet this concept of government ownership in America must be challenged if freedom is to be revived.

A Cardinal Principle

The supporters of these various hydroelectric projects often advance the argument that they would never be built unless government built them; that the various river valleys would remain "undeveloped" unless government developed them; that all this water would continue to be "wasted" unless government utilized it. Perhaps so. It is also true that a free people have never voluntarily under taken to transport to the tropics all the ice that is "going to waste" around the North Pole. And the reason is simple: A free people do not knowingly support uneconomic expenditures of effort and capital. They will not voluntarily invest their savings in a project where they anticipate that the cost will be greater than the return; where there is no apparent economic demand for the product. That economic concept is the cardinal principle of private ownership. For example, the former owners of private electric companies in Tennessee generally chose to build steam plants instead of hydroelectric dams. Why? Again the reason is simple: In their opinions, it represented the most economic expenditure of capital. If the hydroelectric dam had seemed to be the better choice-as it was in some instances-the private owners would have built them. If this is not true, then the conclusion necessarily follows that the private owners deliberately chose a lesser profit. And no advocate of government ownership can afford to make that statement, because it would eliminate his most effective argument for ownership in common.

A Spurious Claim

The supporters of these government electric projects and river valley development programs sometimes argue that the undertakings are "too big" for private enterprise to finance and build. To see the absurdity of this fallacy, it is only necessary to compare these government hydro electric dams with some of our large private industries in various fields of production, including electricity. Private enterprise could raise the money for any project, if there were sufficient demand for the product or service. And would not the workmen and engineers work just as efficiently-probably more efficiently-for private management than for government management?

Next, the advocates of common ownership will present the facts and the figures to show that government electricity projects have brought prosperity to the various river valleys where they are located. But they seem unaware that the various figures for increased prosperity in the Tennessee Valley since the establishment of TVA can be matched and exceeded by similar figures for many other regions where there is no valley authority. For example, one logical measurement would be the yearly income per person in the various states. Department of Commerce figures show that, relative to all other states, the so-called seven TVA states as a group have lost ground since 1933 in per capita income payments. Tennessee itself was forty second in rank when TVA was begun. And in 1949, Tennessee was still forty-second. Other comparisons, again on a relative or percentage basis, show that while the Southern states as a whole have made great economic gains in the last few years, Tennessee itself has generally lagged behind her neighboring states in these various economic gains.

It is true that there are now more homes and industries in Tennessee and the Pacific Northwest than there were before the advent of TVA and Bonneville. And the officials of those federal agencies do not hesitate to accept full credit for this increased industrial activity. How would they answer this question: Is the privately owned Consolidated Edison Company in New York City primarily responsible for the increased industrial activity there since that company was first established?

Few persons now seem to remember that there were twenty-one private electric companies in the Tennessee Valley before TVA bought them up or otherwise drove them out. Before TVA destroyed the free market in its area, private power companies in Tennessee were producing all the electricity that the people were willing to pay for. If there had been an increased demand for electricity in Tennessee, the private companies in that state would have increased their production to meet it, in the same manner that private electric companies have doubled and trebled their production in many other areas to meet the increased demand from their customers-before TVA, and after TVA.

Tax-Created Prosperity

It is true that the people in Tennessee now have more actual dollars than they had before the advent of TVA. But is this not due in large part to the inflationary schemes of government, and in part to the specific fact that hundreds of millions of dollars were taken in taxes from the people elsewhere and poured into the Tennessee Valley? The cost of TVA, the Oak Ridge atomic project, and the various other government projects in Tennessee, probably runs into the billions of dollars. Any person could create some "prosperity" wherever he wished-including the middle of a desert-if he had that amount of money at his disposal. But in any case, the government cannot create prosperity in Tennessee except at the expense of the prosperity of the taxpayers in other regions who had that much less money to spend on their own welfare and on the private development of their own resources because some of their money was spent in the Tennessee Valley. The advocates of common ownership have still another argument to "prove" that these various government river valley projects that are paid for by all the taxpayers *do* have a beneficial effect for all the people. It is argued that if the people in Tennessee or the Pacific Northwest have more money to spend, this in turn will mean that the spending of this money will create additional prosperity in other sections of the country. This is like saying that a huge national expenditure of tax funds to level all the mountains would create prosperity everywhere on the theory that the mountaineers would then have more flat lands for farming, and thus would soon have more money to spend in this campaign of creating universal prosperity by universal robbery.

The Market Verdict

Again, the advocates of common ownership, with their charts and figures, will "prove conclusively" that it is an economic expenditure of capital and that all the people will prosper if only the government planners are given the power to force all the people to conform to their plans. But, again, not a single one of these political managers is willing-with his own money-to submit his plan to the impartial test of the market place where free people make their voluntary decisions. Since the political managers suspect the market verdict in advance, they by-pass it and resort to the political means. They make all sorts of glowing promises to the people *if only the people will give them power over their actions and their taxes.* It is never stated that honestly, of course, but that is actually what it means.

National Defense

When all other arguments fail, the advocates of common ownership do not hesitate to advance the idea of "national defense" and to play upon a person's love for his country. For example, the Tennessee Valley Authority is generally given credit for supplying the electricity that made the atomic bomb. Yet the truth of the matter is that the Oak Ridge atomic project contained its own steam generating plant when it was first built. Oak Ridge was not designed to be dependent upon TVA for its electricity. The fact that Oak Ridge saves on its fuel costs by using large quantities of TVA "dump power" during the seasonal peak TVA production period, has no bearing whatever on this fact. There have been times when Oak Ridge has supplied electricity to TVA.

It is true that the United States has not lost a war to date. But this has not been due to government ownership of the means of production. On the contrary, our strength has been in the fact that we have had *less* common owner ship and *fewer* government controls than have our enemies. In America, free people-operating in a competitive market over a period of time-have built huge industries for the production of automobiles, nylon hosiery, and aluminum pots and pans *for a profit.* And the necessary electrical capacity to operate these plants has appeared when and where needed. This capacity will continue to be available if the people are free to build the plants with their own money at no expense to the taxpayers. This procedure automatically insures adequate reserve capacities for the building of tanks, uniforms, guns, and airplanes when the need arises.

Erroneous Patriotism

The advocates of common ownership are exceedingly careful to their product in the American flag. They will point out that this is a democracy; that the people can vote for anything that pleases them; that the minority must be forced to conform to the will of the majority.

But the fact that this is the case does not mean that every issue should necessarily be voted upon. For "might" does not make "right" in America, any more than it did in Germany or does in Russia. For example, the issue of what religion a person should follow should never be voted upon-democracy or no democracy. Yet it is true that the citizens of the United States could vote to establish a state religion-and force everyone to follow it-if they so desired. The American people could, if they so desired, also use this "majority rule" principle to divide up all the wealth, to equalize all incomes, to abolish the right of a person to own property, and to endorse the principle of common ownership completely. These measures would, of course, be immoral even though they should come to pass by the democratic process. In truth, the surest way to insure the loss of what most Americans consider to be the real meaning of democracy and right to vote is to vote our destinies into the hands of the advocates of common ownership. For here as in Russia, there would then be no real choice because we would then "own everything in common." And all these common-ownership projects would be "unselfishly" managed in the interest of all the people rather than "for the profit of just a few persons." Or so we would be informed by the political managers who would then control our very lives.

Results of Evil Ideas

We should remember that the Russian people are not innately any more evil than we are; it is just that they have adopted an economic philosophy that necessarily must create evil, and exist upon evil. That economic principle is the theory of government-controlled, compulsory, common ownership of the means of production, be it a complete river valley development or whatever. And what will it profit us even to attempt to stop the world-wide spread of communism-"government ownership of the agents of production"-if in the process we adopt the self same economic principle that we claim to be fighting against?

Freedom will eventually cease to exist in *any* nation that adopts that principle, for the fundamental freedom upon which all other freedoms are based is the economic right of an individual to work, trade, spend, save, and invest as he himself decides is best. The only possible way that this freedom can be expressed is through the voluntary processes of the market economy, leaving each individual responsible for the choice he makes.

– Dean Russell

> *"Democracy and socialism have nothing in common but one word, equality. But notice the difference: while democracy seeks equality in liberty, socialism seeks equality in restraint and servitude."*
>
> ... ALEXIS DE TOCQUEVILLE

A LESSON IN SOCIALISM

As a teacher in the public schools, I find that the socialist communist idea of taking "from each according to his ability," and giving "to each according to his need" is now generally accepted without question by most of our pupils. In an effort to explain the fallacy in this theory, I sometimes try this approach with my pupils:

When one of the brighter or harder-working pupils makes a grade of 95 on a test, I suggest that I take away 20 points and give them to a student who has made only 55 points on his test. Thus each would contribute according to his ability and-since both would have a passing mark-each would receive according to his need. After I have juggled the grades of all the other pupils in this fashion, the result is usually a "common ownership" grade of between 75 and 80-the minimum needed for passing, or for survival. Then I speculate with the pupils as to the probable results if I actually used the socialistic theory for grading papers.

First, the highly productive pupils-and they are always a minority in school as well as in life-would soon lose all incentive for producing. Why strive to make a high grade if part of it is taken from you by "authority" and given to someone else? Why work for something if you know you won't be able to keep it? Second, the less productive pupils – a majority in school as elsewhere – would for a time, be relieved of the necessity for study or to produce. This socialist-communist system would continue until the high had sunk or had been driven the level of the low producers. At that point, in order for anyone to survive, the "authority" would have no alternative but to begin a system of compulsory labor and punishments against even the low producers. They, of course, would then complain bitterly, but without understanding.

Finally I return the discussion to the ideas of freedom and enterprise-the market economy-where each person has freedom of choice, and is responsible for his own decisions and welfare.

Gratifyingly enough, most of my pupils then understand what I mean when I explain that socialism-even in a democracy-will eventually result in a living-death for all except the "authorities" and a few of their favorite lackeys.

– Thomas J. Shelly

ANALYSIS

Thomas Shelly's statements from 60 years ago ring true today and one measure of it is the growth in transfer payments, otherwise known as government payments to individuals either through taxation or debt financing. The growth of the practice is anticipated to surpass $2.4 trillion in 2012.

The first chart shows this in graph form and the second shows the issue according to the county of residence for the individual receiving a government check. How did we let government policymakers channel $2.4 trillion through their hands?

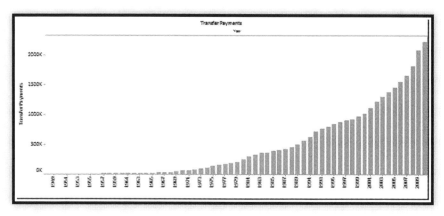

Transfer payments in billions of $ by U.S. County;
source: Moody's Economy.com

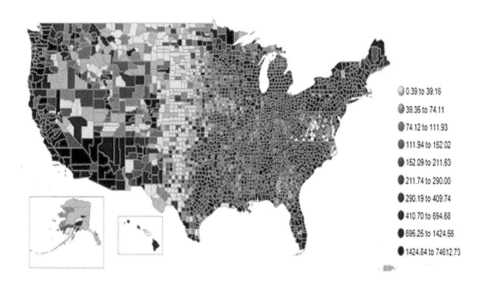

> *Socialism is a philosophy of failure, the creed of ignorance, and the gospel of envy, its inherent virtue is the equal sharing of misery.*
>
> ... WINSTON CHURCHILL

WHY SOCIALISM FAILED

Socialism is the Big Lie of the twentieth century. While it promised prosperity, equality, and security, it delivered poverty, misery, and tyranny. Equality was achieved only in the sense that everyone was equal in his or her misery.

In the same way that a Ponzi scheme or chain letter initially succeeds but eventually collapses, socialism may show early signs of success. But any accomplishments quickly fade as the fundamental deficiencies of central planning emerge. It is the initial illusion of success that gives government intervention its pernicious, seductive appeal. In the long run, socialism has always proven to be a formula for tyranny and misery.

A pyramid scheme is ultimately unsustainable because it is based on faulty principles. Likewise, collectivism is unsustainable in the long run because it is a flawed theory. Socialism does not work because it is not consistent with fundamental principles of human behavior. The failure of socialism in countries around the world can be traced to one critical defect: it is a system that ignores incentives.

In a capitalist economy, incentives are of the utmost importance. Market prices, the profit-and-loss system of accounting, and private property rights provide an efficient, interrelated system of incentives to guide and direct economic behavior. Capitalism is based on the theory that incentives matter!

Under socialism, incentives either play a minimal role or are ignored totally. A centrally planned economy without market prices or profits, where property is owned by the state, is a system without an effective incentive mechanism to direct economic activity. By failing to emphasize incentives, socialism is a theory inconsistent with human nature and is therefore doomed to fail. Socialism is based on the theory that incentives don't matter!

In a radio debate several months ago with a Marxist professor from the University of Minnesota, I pointed out the obvious failures of socialism around the world in Cuba, Eastern Europe, and China. At the time of our debate, Haitian refugees were risking their lives trying to get to Florida in homemade boats. Why was it, I asked him, that people were fleeing Haiti and traveling almost 500 miles by ocean to get to the "evil capitalist empire" when they were only 50 miles from the "workers' paradise" of Cuba?

The Marxist admitted that many "socialist" countries around the world were failing. However, according to him, the reason for failure is not that socialism is deficient, but that the socialist economies are not practicing "pure" socialism. The perfect version of socialism would work; it is just the imperfect socialism that doesn't work. Marxists like to compare a theoretically perfect version of socialism with practical, imperfect capitalism which allows them to claim that socialism is superior to capitalism.

If perfection really were an available option, the choice of economic and political systems would be irrelevant. In a world with perfect beings and infinite abundance, any economic or political system-socialism, capitalism, fascism, or communism-would work perfectly.

However, the choice of economic and political institutions is crucial in an imperfect universe with imperfect beings and limited resources. In a world of scarcity it is essential for an economic system to be based on a clear incentive structure to pro-mote economic efficiency. The real choice we face is between imperfect capitalism and imperfect socialism. Given that choice, the evidence of history overwhelmingly favors capitalism as the greatest wealth-producing economic system available.

The strength of capitalism can be attributed to an incentive structure based upon the three Ps: (1) prices determined by market forces, (2) a profit–and–loss system of accounting and (3) private property rights. The failure of socialism can be traced to its neglect of these three incentive–enhancing components.

Prices

The price system in a market economy guides economic activity so flawlessly that most people don't appreciate its importance. Market prices transmit information about relative scarcity and then efficiently coordinate economic activity. The economic content of prices provides incentives that promote economic efficiency.

For example, when the OPEC cartel restricted the supply of oil in the 1970s, oil prices rose dramatically. The higher prices for oil and gasoline transmitted valuable information to both buyers and sellers. Consumers received a strong, clear message about the scarcity of oil by the higher prices at the pump and were forced to change their behavior dramatically. People reacted to the scarcity by driving less, carpooling more, taking public transportation, and buying smaller cars. Producers reacted to the higher price by increasing their efforts at exploration for more oil. In addition, higher oil prices gave producers an incentive to explore and develop alternative fuel and energy sources.

The information transmitted by higher oil prices provided the appropriate incentive structure to both buyers and sellers. Buyers increased their effort to conserve a now more precious resource and sellers increased their effort to find more of this now scarcer resource.

The only alternative to a market price is a controlled or fixed price which always transmits misleading information about relative scarcity. Inappropriate behavior results from a controlled price because false information has been transmitted by an artificial, non-market price.

Look at what happened during the 1970s when U.S. gas prices were controlled. Long lines developed at service stations all over the country because the price for gasoline was kept artificially low by government fiat. The full impact of scarcity was not accurately conveyed. As Milton Friedman pointed out at the time, we could have eliminated the lines at the pump in one day by allowing the price to rise to clear the market.

From our experience with price controls on gasoline and the long lines at the pump and general inconvenience, we get an insight into what happens under socialism where every price in the economy is controlled. The collapse of socialism is due in part to the chaos and inefficiency that result from artificial prices. The information content of a controlled price is always distorted. This in turn distorts the incentives mechanism of prices under socialism. Administered prices are always either too high or too low, which then creates constant shortages and surpluses. Market prices are the only way to transmit information that will create the incentives to ensure economic efficiency.

Profits and Losses

Socialism also collapsed because of its failure to operate under a competitive, profit-and-loss system of accounting. A profit system is an effective monitoring mechanism which continually evaluates the economic performance of every business enterprise. The firms that are the most efficient and most successful at serving the public interest are rewarded with profits. Firms that operate inefficiently and fail to serve the public interest are penalized with losses.

By rewarding success and penalizing failure, the profit system provides a strong disciplinary mechanism which continually redirects resources away from weak, failing, and inefficient firms toward those firms which are the most efficient and successful at serving the public. A competitive profit system ensures a constant re-optimization of resources and moves the economy toward greater levels of efficiency. Unsuccessful firms cannot escape the strong discipline of the marketplace under a profit/loss system. Competition forces companies to serve the public interest or suffer the consequences.

Under central planning, there is no profit-and-loss system of accounting to accurately measure the success or failure of various programs. Without profits, there is no way to discipline firms that fail to serve the public interest and no way to reward firms that do. There is no efficient way to determine which programs should be expanded and which ones should be contracted or terminated.

Without competition, centrally planned economies do not have an effective incentive structure to coordinate economic activity. Without incentives the results are a spiraling cycle of poverty and misery. Instead of continually reallocating resources towards greater efficiency, socialism falls into a vortex of inefficiency and failure.

Private Property Rights

A third fatal defect of socialism is its blatant disregard for the role of private property rights in creating incentives that foster economic growth and development. The failure of socialism around the world is a "tragedy of commons" on a global scale.

The "tragedy of the commons" refers to the British experience of the sixteenth century when certain grazing lands were communally owned by villages and were made available for public use. The land was quickly over-grazed and eventually became worthless as villagers exploited the communally owned resource.

When assets are publicly owned, there are no incentives in place to encourage wise stewardship. While private property creates incentives for conservation and the responsible use of property, public property encourages irresponsibility and waste. If everyone owns an asset, people act as if no one owns it. And when no one owns it, no one really takes care of it. Public ownership encourages neglect and mismanagement.

Since socialism, by definition, is a system marked by the "common ownership of the means of production," the failure of socialism is a "tragedy of the commons" on a national scale. Much of the economic stagnation of socialism can be traced to the failure to establish and promote private property rights.

As Peruvian economist Hernando de Soto remarked, you can travel in rural communities around the world and you will hear dogs barking, because even dogs understand property rights. It is only statist governments that have failed to understand property rights. Socialist countries are just now starting to recognize the importance of private property as they privatize assets and property in Eastern Europe.

Incentives Matter

Without the incentives of market prices, profit–and-loss accounting, and well-defined property rights, socialist economies stagnate and wither. The economic atrophy that occurs under socialism is a direct consequence of its neglect of economic incentives.

No bounty of natural resources can ever compensate a country for its lack of an efficient system of incentives. Russia, for example, is one of the world's wealthiest countries in terms of natural resources; it has some of the world's largest reserves of oil, natural gas, diamonds, and gold. Its valuable farm land, lakes, rivers, and streams stretch across a land area that encompasses 11 time zones. Yet Russia remains poor. Natural resources are helpful, but the ultimate resources of any country are the unlimited resources of its people-human resources.

By their failure to foster, promote, and nurture the potential of their people through incentive-enhancing institutions, centrally planned economies deprive the human spirit of full development. Socialism fails because it kills and destroys the human spirit-just ask the people leaving Cuba in homemade rafts and boats.

As the former centrally planned economies move toward free markets, capitalism, and democracy, they look to the United States for guidance and support during the transition. With an unparalleled 250-year tradition of open markets and limited government, the United States is uniquely qualified to be the guiding light in the worldwide transition to freedom and liberty.

We have an obligation to continue to provide a framework of free markets and democracy for the global transition to freedom. Our responsibility to the rest of the world is to continue to fight the seductiveness of statism around the world and here at home. The seductive nature of statism continues to tempt and lure us into the Barmecidal illusion that the government can create wealth.

The temptress of socialism is constantly luring us with the offer: "give up a little of your freedom and I will give you a little more security." As the experience of this century has demonstrated, the bargain is tempting but never pays off. We end up losing both our freedom and our security.

Programs like socialized medicine, welfare, social security, and minimum wage laws will continue to entice us because on the surface they appear to be expedient and beneficial. Those programs, like all socialist programs, will fail in the long run regardless of initial appearances. These programs are part of the Big Lie of socialism because they ignore the important role of incentives. Socialism will remain a constant temptation. We must be vigilant in our fight against socialism not only around the globe but also here in the United States.

The failure of socialism inspired a worldwide renaissance of freedom and liberty. For the first time in the history of the world, the day is coming very soon when a majority of the people in the world will live in free societies or societies rapidly moving towards freedom.

Capitalism will play a major role in the global revival of liberty and prosperity because it nurtures the human spirit, inspires human creativity, and promotes the spirit of enterprise. By providing a powerful system of incentives that promote thrift, hard work, and efficiency, capitalism creates wealth.

The main difference between capitalism and socialism is this: Capitalism works.

– Mark J. Perry

At the time of the original publication, Dr. Perry was Director at the Center for World Capitalism of the James Madison Institute, Jacksonville University, Jacksonville, Florida.

Reprinted with permission from The Freeman, a publication of the Foundation for Economic Education, Inc., June 1995, Vol. 45, No. 5.

> *"Socialism is a wonderful idea. It is only as a reality that it has been disastrous. Among people of every race, color, and creed, all around the world, socialism has led to hunger in countries that used to have surplus food to export.... Nevertheless, for many of those who deal primarily in ideas, socialism remains an attractive idea – in fact, seductive. Its every failure is explained away as due to the inadequacies of particular leaders."*
>
> ... THOMAS SOWELL

RIGHTS FOR ROBOTS

I regret that I am unable to come in Britain in person to talk directly to you, but I am not prepared to accept only terms on which my government will allow me to travel.

In the past, I have to meet you on more or less equal terms. I could, for instance, at my own expense offer a handful of roses or a box of candies to a charming hostess. Now I can come to only as a government-created pauper, absolutely barred from securing, of my own right, the dollars or dimes to spend as I myself would like to do. I am not prepared to put myself into this curious and uncomfortable position. Thus my address must be read for me.

Socialism is a disease

I understand that in States there are those who think that the machinery of government can be used as a substitute for personal responsibility on the part of the governed. This idea as we know only too well in Britain is the open road to disaster. It changes persons with responsibilities into robots with rights.

And while you fortunate Americans will last a little longer than the rest of us, your doom is also assured if you, like us, rely upon politics and collective action to relieve you of the normal and natural responsibilities of healthy men. For socialism is not a system; it is a disease. The "something for nothing" mentality is, in fact, an economic cancer.

In England we have suffered nearly five years of effective socialist government. But that is only the end of the story; we are merely completing 50 years of a sloppy sentimentalism in public affairs of which the present socialism is merely the logical outcome. In the process we have murdered old virtues with new deals. Well-meaning, shallow thinking, kindly people, aware of the scriptural injunction that "the greatest of these is charity, have failed to notice the distinction between the real article and the giving away of other people's money. So, having lost our faith, we come to the end of the story; we have accepted false hopes and practiced a charity which is nothing of the kind.

A *Drab Existence*

You will remember that 50 years ago at the end of Victoria's reign; we had achieved in Britain, notwithstanding many shortcomings and blemishes, a high general standard of living. From that proud position we have now descended to the point where American tourists coming to Europe go to the countries conquered by Hitler to escape the drab austerity of utopian Britain.

We have had enough experience to know exactly what "security" means: It is a prior government claim upon salaries and wages. It is austerity rations bought with Marshall Plan aid. It is more and more paper money, and less and less of anything to buy.

This government-guaranteed "security" is steadily reducing output per man in our industries. There are, of course, glorious minority exceptions. But in general, our people have believed the promises of 1945 and have concentrated on their supposed rights and forgotten their responsibilities. Most thinking people among us now realize that while it is easy to make the *rich* poor, it is quite another matter to make the *poor* rich.

The Long View

There is little purpose to be served in wearying you with the details of our life, especially business life, in Britain today. To argue about taxes, pensions, houses, or even groundnuts is merely to scratch the surface. You will be more interested in the longer view and the lessons to be learned from it.

In the short period of 50 years we have traveled the whole road, starting when government had almost nothing to do with trade, and ending where all trade is under the dead hand of the state. America, as I understand, is about halfway along this road to disaster.

Among the disasters resulting from governmental planning in the economic field, I put at the top of the list the loss of the market. We have no such thing that counts for much in England today. Exchange by willing buyers and willing sellers has, for practical purposes, disappeared. Governmental buying, fixed prices, subsidies, and purchase taxes have substituted force for willingness. Goodwill is a thing of the past. Price, properly the result of a compromise between the willing buyer and the willing seller, is now replaced by an official abstraction arrived at for political rather than economic reasons. The word "willing" is not to be found in any official vocabulary.

The sanctity of contract is also a thing of the past, and that again shows how far we have departed from the principles upon which civilization was constructed. Governments, here and elsewhere, fail to set much value on their pledged word.

Perhaps the biggest of all the changes in this connection is the destruction of the price mechanism. Before the politicians usurped the right of the citizen to provide for himself, the price mechanism indicated with speed and certainty the degree of plenty or of scarcity. It did not require committees of experts and official inquirers to discover changes in production and consumption, and the need for adjusting action accordingly. The price mechanism has been put so completely out of action that we now pay a series of varying prices for the same article at the same time.

Freedom of Choice

The natural process, named by economists "the law of supply and demand," insures the freedom of choice that is essential to the worthwhile life of free citizens. Socialism tries to put the matter the other way around. Some authority, claiming to know what the people want, issues orders for supply without being able to know the requirements of the buyers or demanders. This theory ignores completely the forces which govern the ordinary actions of the ordinary man. The natural order of things requires that the maker shall produce his goods and display them for the inspection of the buyer who is, at all times, free not to buy. The right to buy or not to buy is vital to economic well-being and, of course, to personal liberty.

It is only now that we are beginning to reap the inevitable fruits of wrong thinking. Millions of our people now look to the government much in the same fashion that their fathers of Victorian times looked to God. Political authority has taken the place of heavenly guidance.

Herbert Spencer in that wonderful prophecy, *The Man Versus the State,* explained in detail what would happen. He foretold with exactitude the present rush of the weaklings for jobs as planners and permitters, telling other people what *not* to do.

You will have noticed that while we are all under the thumb of authority, authority becomes composed of those who, lacking the courage to stand on their own feet and accept their share of personal responsibility, seek the safety of official positions where they escape the consequences of error and failure. Active, energetic, and progressive persons, instead of leading the rest, are allowed to move only by the grace and favor of that section of the population which from its very nature lacks all the qualities needed to produce the desired results. Authority is the power to say *no,* which requires little or no ability. On a broad view, the all-important issue in the world today is *individualism* versus *collectivism.*

The Individualist thinks of millions of single human souls, each with a spark of divine genius, and visualizes that genius applied to the solution of his own problems. His conception is infinitely higher than that of the politician or planner who at best regards these millions as material for social or political experiment or, at worst, cannon fodder.

The Individualist believes self-help to be twice blest. For not only does it provide the help required, but it also gives a self-respecting satisfaction in accomplishment which can never attach to help that is received.

Character Must Be Earned

When a man is on his own, an individual responsible for himself, he must earn a character-a personal character that is perhaps his first necessity. Others may then learn and imitate his qualities and capabilities. In a planned society he has no need of a character, for no such thing is wanted. No national or universal plan can afford to take the least notice of his personal character.

As an individual responsible for himself, a man must also acquire credit. Others must be convinced that he is credit-worthy; that he can be trusted; that what he under takes he will perform to the limits of his ability. But when he is planned, nothing so troublesome is in the least necessary. The individual responsible for himself must try to avoid the loss that results from mistakes. But if he is the planner or the planned, the loss comes out of the public purse, and he is relieved of personal responsibility. He can then waste and lose just as much as his inherent laziness may dictate.

The individual responsible for himself must strive to do better-better than his previous performance and better than others. But in a planned society, the only upward route available to a person is into the ranks of the planners where he can presume to arrange the affairs of others.

The Socialist advances the supposition that the individual can be so trained and managed as to cause his every act to be performed in the interests of society as a whole. The idea of the Socialist is to substitute for the enormously constructive natural power of the self-interest of each of us, a manufactured force composed of the theoretical interests of the state. To the Individualist this socialist idea is utter nonsense-a view much strengthened by the losses and disasters of the last five years in England alone.

Honesty the Best Policy

Perhaps, above all, I am an Individualist because it makes for honesty. In a society of free men, each acting on his own responsibility, honesty is the best policy. But as we move further from the individualist position into compulsory associations, unions, districts, counties, nations, and states, we tend to lose touch with that essentially personal quality-honesty. Honesty may be described as a force governing dealings between individuals. When the transactions are between masses, they tend to become less honest; when between nations, there is, indeed, little pretense of honesty about them. That simple circumstance arises not from evil intent but from the very nature of man's conduct.

All this concerns a philosophy; a point of view from which to start and if only individualism could get these foundations well laid in the minds of the people, we could then proceed with our voluntary social services and other humanitarian plans for the comfort of the less fortunate minority. As it is-without these foundations - charity, good feeling, desire to help, sympathy, and many other virtues have been brushed aside. And in their place there has been set up the mean, unworthy, degrading, and destructive notion of rights for robots, which is mankind under complete government planning.

You happy people in the comparatively cleaner atmosphere of the United States are better able to recognize these greater, all-pervading considerations. And you are in a better position to reverse this mad rush to turn persons into robots by means of the "planned economy" and the "welfare state." May God guide you in your decision.

– Sir Ernest Benn

> *"Specie {gold and silver coin} is the most perfect medium because it will preserve its own level; because, having intrinsic and universal value, it can never die in our hands, and it is the surest resource of reliance in time of war."*
>
> … THOMAS JEFFERSON TO JOHN WAYLES EPPES, 1813

DOLLARS MAKE POOR EATING

In America today, we are surrendering our basic liberties. The complexity of the daily affairs of 150 million Americans baffles us. Perhaps we can more clearly appraise the danger of economic suicide under the "welfare state" if we think in terms of our own small group.

Imagine, if you can, that those of us gathered here are the only survivors of a thoroughly destructive hydrogen bomb explosion. Gone are our factories, offices, homes. Every product of civilization has been reduced to the natural state which prevailed when Adam first set foot on earth. How shall we proceed under these conditions to solve the problem of survival?

We know, of course, that we must put our minds and our hands to producing food, clothing, and shelter – things we use in our daily living. Represented here in this pile are the raw materials-wood, soil, ore, rocks-from which we may produce finished consumer goods. If each of us were to attack this pile of materials, molding them into finished goods, we could soon demonstrate to our own satisfaction that the supply of finished goods depends entirely upon how hard and how long and how efficiently we work. The more finished goods a person produces, the more there is for him to eat, wear, and enjoy. By hard work, our standard of living can improve; there is no other way.

We know, also, that we face a problem of distribution of these finished goods among ourselves, once they have been produced. Shall each of us retain what he produces for use or exchange or disposal according to his own choice? Or is there a better system?

Few persons enjoy work. Some downright abhor it, and they envy the hard workers who are enjoying a better and better living, and who by saving some of it, have more and more. Suppose these drones call a meeting. Since it is mainly their kind who would attend the meeting, while the others are working, they might vote in a purely democratic way, among those present-to set a limit of 32 hours of work per week, and to compel a minimum wage of $100 per week. And they might also vote unemployment benefits of $98 a week, and vote every citizen a $200 per month pension beginning at age 45. "Why wait," they would argue, "to enjoy old age until you're too old?" All payments would be made in paper money, which they would make the legal and lawful currency.

Under this plan it would be necessary for some of the workers to watch the other workers, and see that they don't do too much work, or accept pay below the legal minimum, or retire too late; and some must handle the pension scheme. The remaining producers will discover the futility of their efforts under these conditions, and the pile of goods will dwindle toward nothing. Why work to produce more if the results of your efforts are taken from you against your will?

Despite little or no production, leaving the pile of wood and soil and rocks untouched, the unemployed and the pensioners could continue to get their weekly checks just the same. They would receive pieces of paper on which the dollar sign is printed, offered with the kindly words: "There you are, my good man; use this to buy things you need to eat, wear, amuse yourself-in fact, and do anything you wish with it."

Dollars make poor eating.
– C.L. Dickinson

> *"Essentially central planning is not about the efficient allocation of economic resources, it is about control. Central planning maximizes the extent of control that the state and the people running the state, exercise. The desire to control others is a constant in history and is part and parcel of the construction of states. If the state can grab all the land and resources and control who and on what terms people get access to them, then this maximizes control, even if it sacrifices economic efficiency.*
>
> *This sort of economic and political control — not Marxist ideology — is what central planning is all about. This is not to deny that Marxist ideology supported and legitimized central planning in several 20th-century societies. But it is to emphasize that the emergence and persistence of central planning is often a solution to the central economic and political problem of many elites: to control and extract resources from society."*
>
> ... QUOTE OF THE DAY - LEVIATHAN EDITION

PRICE SUPPORTS

Stripped to its essentials, the basic objective of the overall price support program for agriculture is to prevent a general collapse in farm prices such as occurred in 1921 and 1929. Few persons disagree with the desirability of the objective; the basic disagreement lies in whether or not price supports are a suitable means to this end.

Prices of goods and services may be compared with water in a lake. Ripples and waves on the surface of the lake correspond to the prices of individual commodities. They rise and fall in varying degrees depending on supply and demand conditions for each commodity, even though the over-all level of the lake may not change. The level of the lake itself rises and falls because of what happens at the inlet and outlet of the lake. A price support or ceiling on one commodity may change the height of that particular ripple, but it is offset by the height of others. It has little or no effect on the over-all level of the lake, the general price level.

Changes in the prices of individual commodities, constantly going on even in a stable economy, serve a useful and important function. We saw this function in operation in the fall of 1948 in the relation of the price of hogs to corn. With a very short corn crop in 1947, corn prices advanced relative to hogs. And farmers economized in the feeding of corn. In 1948, with a very large corn crop, farmers received the signal-cheaper corn-to expand the feeding of corn to hogs and other livestock. These adjustments run all through our economy. In a free market, farmers will constantly shift their production of cabbage, sweet corn and all other crops and livestock products to meet changing demand and supply conditions. When the signals are tampered with, faulty prices may call for too little of this or too much of that so that consumers are unable to satisfy their demands in the market.

It is not denied that the legal price of a single commodity can be maintained above or below where it would be in a free market. The price of potatoes, for example, could be set at 25 cents a bushel or at $25 a bushel and if a large enough number of policemen were assigned to the job of rationing the very small production at 25 cents, or of restricting the very great attempted production at $25, the price might be maintained. But even if this were done for one commodity, or for many commodities, the major problem of preventing general inflation or deflation would not be solved.

The solution of the problem of the giant swings in the general price level lies in the area of the monetary and fiscal policy of the nation and is outside the scope of this discussion.

It might be asserted that price supports or price ceilings on individual commodities are not effective in preventing major inflationary and deflationary swings, and end the discussion here. But it is important to point out some of the harmful effects of such programs.

Price supports are a one-sided form of price control. Price control is a part of the more important question, namely, whether the nation shall have an economy of free markets, or whether it shall be one of price control leading to production control, allocation of labor, and ultimately, socialism. It matters little whether the outcome of the latter choice is called Democratic Socialism, Socialized Capitalism, State Socialism, Social Democracy, Marxian Socialism, Collectivism or just plain Communism.

The Function of the Free Price Mechanism

A free market system is perhaps the most essential ingredient of a voluntary economy. Without this freedom to express his wants-and thus to have a hand in guiding production and consumption-man can hardly be called free.

The sole purpose of economic production is to cater to the wants of consumers and thus to satisfy the wants of both producers and consumers. The most satisfactory method by which consumers can make their preferences known to producers-and thus to guide production-is through the free price system. Millions of consumers are thereby enabled to vote for or against individual products by their acceptance (purchase) or rejection of items of consumption.

Another method of guiding production and consumption is to have the decision of a single individual or of a central bureau substituted for the decisions of millions of individuals interested in that particular or related commodity. There is no third choice. Either the free price system will be permitted to do the job or it will not. The only way in which there is a middle ground is in the sense that not all items of goods and services may be under control. Some may be free while others are controlled. But there is abundant evidence to indicate that, once started, price control spreads because of the complex influence which products have on each other. First, the price of a single item may be controlled. Then it is found desirable to control its substitute and then the substitutes for the substitute, and so on.

It must be assumed that those who favor price control of a commodity-whether it be price supports, price ceilings, subsidies, marketing agreements, forward pricing or other forms-believe that the price should be either higher or lower than it would be if voluntarily arrived at by a willing buyer and a willing seller. Otherwise it would not be price control.

A Delicate Instrument

The free price mechanism is as delicate as a fine precision instrument with millions of moving parts. Each part contributes to the operation of the whole. It operates so smoothly that it is sometimes called automatic. But it is anything but automatic in the sense that it runs without direction.

Consider, for example, some of the factors which, together, make the price of a bushel of wheat. They include the prospects for rain in the wheat country, the amount of snow in the mountains, the amount of insect damage, the availability of harvest help and machinery, the burning of a few thousand bushels in a local elevator, the availability of boxcars for shipping, the amount of wheat fed to livestock, the production of wheat in Canada, China and Russia, and literally thousands of other things that are wrapped up in what we call supply, or prospective supply.

A Variety of Influences

The price of wheat is influenced by the price of oats, corn, potatoes, rye and many other competing crops. The amount of money in the country and the freeness of persons' spending of it, the amount of wheat purchased for foreign account, the price of automobiles and radios, and an unknown number of other factors all have a bearing.

No one person or bureau can possibly know all the contributing reasons why I reject a radio offered at $12.98 and you decide to buy it. Perhaps my wife wants a new hat and yours doesn't. Fortunately it is not necessary that each buyer and seller have all this information. All that is necessary to consummate a sale is for a seller to say, "I am willing to sell," and the buyer to say, "I am willing to buy" at the same price. The seller may say, "I can't continue to sell for that and stay in business," or the buyer may say, "I can't continue to pay that much and stay in business." Suffice it to say, the exchange was made. And in view of the alternatives known to each party, the exchange was agreeable to both. A price set arbitrarily at a point different from where a willing buyer and seller would voluntarily set it, is certain to make one of the parties feel he was cheated. In fact, it does cheat one of them.

Who Should Plan?

The basic question involved here is not whether there should be economic planning, but rather who should do it. Economic planning there will be. It will be done either by millions of individuals who are directly concerned, each making his own independent decisions, or it will be done by a central planning committee, given power to ignore the judgment of these individuals.

A central statistical bureau may assemble volumes of data concerning the demand for and supply of a certain commodity. There is a strong temptation for the bureau then to feel that it knows so much more about conditions than a single producer or consumer can possibly know, that it can therefore decide the price more wisely. Actually, they cannot have all the pertinent facts and certainly not the most important ones which individuals use in deciding on whether or not to buy a certain item.

The delicate free price mechanism works miracles in guiding workers into each branch of the economy and in guiding the use of raw materials and other resources according to the wishes of consumers. Some have argued that our economy has become too complex to let it run without central planning. Actually, the more complex it becomes, the more important it is to have the economic planning done by the individuals concerned; the more important it becomes to have their decisions reported in a free market.

A Personal Guide

The free market serves as a guide to persons in deciding whether they should be dentists, doctors, farmers, lawyers, school teachers, grocery clerks or bank clerks. When this function of price is tampered with, it becomes necessary to dictate to the workers what jobs they shall fill and how and where they shall fill them. England has already discovered this.

The free price system is a guide as to how much steel shall be used for tractors, for automobiles, for housing, for toys, for railroads and for other purposes. It suggests whether oil or gas or coal shall be used for heating a house. It serves as a guide in determining how much feed grain shall be fed to dairy cows, or hens, or hogs. This system tells the users of a commodity whether to economize in its use or to expand it. It tells the potato producer, for example, how many acres to plant and whether to harvest all of his crop or leave the smaller potatoes on the ground at harvest time. It suggests how much fertilizer to use and whether or not it will pay him to put in an irrigation system. It tells him whether he will profit more by packing his crop in wholesale lots or in consumer packages. All this guidance appears almost accidental and without direction, but behind it all is a vast amount of experience, study and thought by all of the persons concerned. The result is that the crop moves to market in an extremely orderly fashion just meeting the demand. All this serves to guide producers of next year's crop.

Costs of Central Planning

It is not denied that a central planning bureau *could* make decisions (disregarding the quality of these decisions) involving the jobs which each person should fill, as well as the amount of production and the distribution of each individual commodity. This, of course, is the design of a planned economy. Space will not permit a complete discussion of the cost of a planned economy. This cost involves the tremendous staff of planners, administrators and policemen who might be otherwise employed in the production and distribution of goods and services. It involves the question of the right of an individual to the product of his own labor; it involves the question of incentives to high production which come with this right. It involves the satisfactions which individuals gain from making decisions in questions involving themselves. In short, the whole question of human liberty and the purpose of life itself is tied up in this one issue.

If the price of a commodity is arbitrarily set by a central bureau, it might conceivably be where it would have been in a free market at some place and at one time. If so, it serves no purpose at that time and place. It is likely to be wrong at all other places and at all other times because no central bureau can possibly master all of the differentials that a free market solves.

There is no one price for a commodity like potatoes. There are literally thousands of different prices, depending on different conditions, making up what we think of as "the market price." And strangely enough, in a free market, each of the many different prices is the "right" price for the given situation.

Price Is a Signal

Price is somewhat like the Signal which the captain on the bridge of a ship sends to the engine room or the instructions he gives to the helmsman. If the signal is right, the ship stays on its course. If it is wrong, the ship cannot go where it is intended it should go. Price is a signal to both producers and consumers of a commodity as well as to all of the agencies involved in distribution. We have had experience with mixing up the signals. We have seen potato prices set too low with a resulting potato famine before a new crop came along. Under the fixed low prices, the Signal to economize in the use of potatoes failed to reach consumers. Had this faulty signal continued, it would also have been interpreted by producers to cut future production. A similar situation has existed in the rents of dwellings which were fixed too low. The signal to renters was not to economize on space but to expand. And they did just that. The signal to build new housing was not given. The result was that we had a housing "famine."

Tampering With the Signal

When the price of a commodity is set lower by controls than the market would set it, the product becomes scarce and its allocation becomes a problem. When a free price is prohibited from rationing a product, some other method must be used. It may be done outside the law in black markets, or with tickets, or special favoritism, or by some other method.

In the other direction, we have had experience with arbitrarily setting the prices of a commodity higher than a free market would set them. Price supports contemplate doing this. In such a situation, a wrong signal is sent to both producers and consumers, with the result that a "surplus" arises. The consumer does not buy the whole supply, because the price is higher than he will pay for the amount offered. The producer is encouraged to expand the production of a commodity already in unsalable supply.

A system of price supports where prices are maintained above the free market level by government is not unlike a system tried by a number of agricultural marketing co operatives some 25 years ago. They found that by keeping prices too high, they were encouraging more and more production and discouraging consumption. They discovered they were building up a larger and larger carry-over from one crop to the next. One after another, cooperatives based on this principle either failed, or changed their policy. An important difference, of course, between the government and a private cooperative following such a policy is that the government can use its taxing power to make up losses and can conceal the error for a longer time by sending the bill for "services rendered" to others.

Whereas "scarcities," due to setting prices too low, require some kind of a rationing system, "surpluses," due to setting prices too high, require some kind of a disposal plan as well as arbitrary production controls. Otherwise, farmers are paid from taxes to expand acreage or to put in irrigation systems, or to use heavy applications of fertilizer to produce potatoes to be used for livestock feed or to be destroyed.

Subsidize: Control

Agricultural leaders, like leaders in other industries, have long been trying to devise some system to raise the price of their products above free market prices, without at the same time exercising some direct control over production. Such a search seems doomed to failure because of the very nature of the price system. If prices of individual commodities are too high, they stimulate too much production and too little consumption at that level of prices; some kinds of production controls thus become necessary unless the government dumps its surplus abroad or gives it away or diverts it into other uses at home. If prices are too low, some other type of stimulus such as subsidies or direct compulsion is required to bring out the production assumed necessary. It is but a short step from there to the British system where prices are guaranteed and producers told what to produce. It is a still shorter step from that to complete nationalization of industry. Our own Supreme Court has stated that government may properly regulate that which it subsidizes.

A Crutch for Inefficiency

Another consequence of a price support which holds a price above where it would be in a free market, is its effect in keeping less efficient producers in business. A competitive economy, based on free market prices, has been an important factor in improving efficiency in all types of business. The market price serves as a signal to the high cost or less efficient producer to use his talents and resources elsewhere. Think what would be the situation in the automobile business today if, through support prices, all of the hundreds of auto manufacturers that have fallen by the wayside had been kept in business at public expense. Suppose we had adopted a system of price supports to keep buggy manufacturers in business.

The New York State College of Agriculture supervises detailed cost accounts on a number of New York farms each year. On those farms in 1946, where potatoes were grown and detailed records of costs were kept, the cost to produce a bushel of potatoes varied from 49 cents for the lowest to $1.92 for the highest cost farm. The average cost was 75 cents a bushel.

Now, suppose in 1946 the predominant judgment of potato growers had been that, for the following year, the potato business didn't appear as attractive as some other crop and some growers decided to reduce potato acreage. Which ones should have reduced? We will probably all agree that it is the high cost producers or those who have a more profitable use of their resources, regardless of their costs, who should drop out. They might better spend their time doing something more profitable. The free market is the guide in this course of action. As a result, the entire economy, as well as individual producers, benefits.

Planning Dilemma

Instead of a free market for potatoes, suppose the price is arbitrarily set above the market at, say, $2.00 a bushel. What happens? Not only are the less efficient producers encouraged to stay in the potato business, but also new producers who are still less efficient may be drawn in. As a result, more potatoes may be produced than can be sold at the designated price. The problem of the planners now is what to do about the surplus production. They may decide that acreage should be reduced or marketing quotas should be established. How will they do it? Your guess is as good as mine because it is now a political football. They may decide to scale down each grower's acreage by the same percentage. It would be virtually impossible to set up a workable formula that would affect nearby areas and areas far from the market, the way a free price would. The method chosen is not likely to be one that will eliminate the less efficient producers.

This illustrates some of the problems involved on the production side when free markets are interfered with. Problems on the consumption side are just as involved and critical. Consumers are prevented from having a hand in directing production according to their wishes. It is self-evident that people can consume no more than what is produced. The free market permits consumers to express a choice for fewer potatoes at a higher price per bushel together with the things produced by those who were formerly potato producers. It permits them to make this choice if they wish, in preference to having more and cheaper potatoes, but without the production of the other things. Certainly, few consumers would voluntarily call for so bountiful a supply of potatoes that they be fed to livestock, used for fertilizer or be destroyed.

Over the years, less efficient farmers have found that they could not meet the competition of more efficient ones. In our expanding economy they have found their services useful elsewhere. This has made it possible for the efficiency of our farms to increase from the point where an average farm produced little more than enough for the farmer and his family to where a farm family now feeds itself and five or six other families. The farmer not only feeds his family better but also gains from the production of automobiles, refrigerators, bathtubs, transportation, entertainment, education, churches and many, many other goods and services produced by non-farmers.

Competition and Progress

This kind of progress will continue only with competition and free markets. It is conceivable that farm efficiency can further develop to a point where only one family in twenty or thirty will be required to raise the nation's food supply. Such progress cannot continue if inefficient production is encouraged.

Efficient farm producers have nothing to fear from competition. It is the lack of competition that they should fear. It has been estimated that one-third of the farmers produce 80 per cent of the nation's food. Price supports will tend to keep in competition the least efficient one-third of the farmers who produce only 4 per cent of the food and who might far better be doing something else.

Another aspect of price supports for agricultural products is the matter of special privileges for minority groups. Under a political system such as ours, there is a tendency for certain groups to seek special privileges at the expense of other groups. If they are strong enough politically, they may be able to obtain them. Agriculture has been and still may be strong politically. But it is rapidly becoming a smaller and smaller minority. In the interest of equal rights for all, it would seem that farmers would gain more in the long run by promoting the idea of no special privilege for any group.

To illustrate the point of what may happen to minority groups, we have only to observe what has been happening to wheat farmers in Canada. The Canadian government has been marketing the farmers' wheat and has been receiving for it a price well over a dollar in excess of what they have paid the wheat producers. This process, Canadian farmers have been forced to subsidize the consumers of Canada and Britain. They have paid what amounts to an occupational tax to their own government. This happened in a country where farming is far less of a minority occupation than it is in the United States.

Two Wrongs

An argument frequently used by agricultural leaders for various farm programs is that labor and other types of business have "enjoyed" advantages in the form of tariffs and other devices, and that therefore agriculture is entitled to a share of "protection." These are exactly the tactics used in a pressure-group economy. Two wrongs do not make a right. And in the end, this process leads to a thoroughly confused situation where vast numbers of persons become willing to turn the whole sorry mess over to government, as they are rapidly doing in England and have done in other nations of the world.

Summarizing briefly, price supports, like other forms of price control, are not an answer to the important problem of bringing reasonable stability to our economy-of eliminating major swings in our general price level caused by monetary inflation and deflation. In addition to their failure to reach this objective, price supports rob us of the most important function of free prices-the guiding of production and consumption of goods and services in accordance with the wishes of those directly concerned.

Finally-and this is most important-price controls must be accompanied by controls of production and consumption. It cannot be otherwise. Such controls lead to complete economic domination of citizens by agents of the State.

– W.M. Curtiss

ANALYSIS

How does Curtiss' price level discussion relate to today's economic environment?

Well, in fact, it is very relevant given that America has shifted responsibility to one group of individuals – the Board of Governors of the Federal Reserve – to manipulate the price level to a politically acceptable range.

Although a number of factors are outside of the federal government's control (thank goodness), such as the price of oil, the Federal Reserve attempts to control the price level through use of monetary policy instruments, such as manipulating short term or long term interest rates, changing the supply of money, or altering banking regulations.

Has it worked? In general no, the Federal Reserve has a poor record of manipulating interest rates and other factors to control economic activity and the economy's price level.

How bad of a failure? Overall, the price level has risen about 2,200% over the past 95 years, while absent the Federal Reserve; the price level likely would have raised more along the lines of a reasonable 200%.

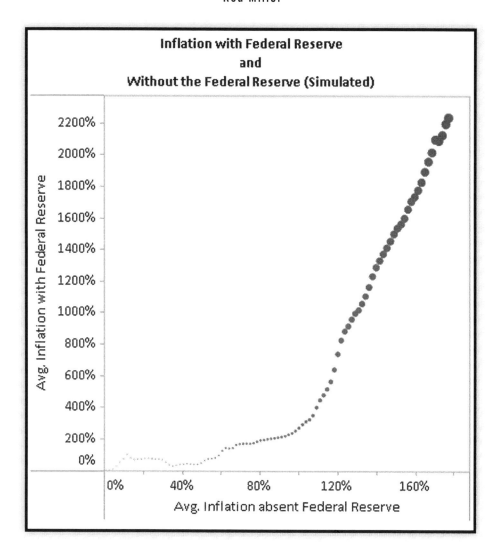

> *"Very simply, we subsidize high-fructose corn syrup in this country, but not carrots. While the surgeon general is raising alarms over the epidemic of obesity, the president is signing farm bills designed to keep the river of cheap corn flowing, guaranteeing that the cheapest calories in the supermarket will continue to be the unhealthiest."*
>
> ... Michael Pollan, The Omnivore's Dilemma: A Natural History of Four Meals

The Other Side Of The Subsidy

From MONTHLY ECONOMIC LETTER, Northeast Farm Foundation, Ithaca, New York, October 1, 1949

WE are this fall beginning to feel more of the iron fist beneath the velvet glove.

. . . Farmers have been forced to sow winter wheat this month in accordance with permission granted by the United States government. One, reading the official document giving a certain farm owner in the Genesee Valley, for instance, permission to sow 13 acres of wheat on his 200 acre farm for the year 1950, cannot help but wonder....

When the farmer applies for a larger allotment he is informed that he can have five minutes on a certain Tuesday afternoon to present his case ....

"Failure to appear at this hearing may be considered a waiver of your right in connection with such appeal."

An insidious part of this system is that it makes use of local committees to harness the farmers in every county. The allotment is issued in the name of the local county ... committee, but in fact it is sent out by a bureaucrat in the Federal Building at the county seat. The original idea of having local committees do the hatchet work was borrowed from Russia. It works well and helps to silence opposition.

It is hardly lack of due process for the government to regulate that which it subsidizes.

UNITED STATES SUPREME COURT
Wickard v. Filburn, 317 U.S. Ill, p.131, Oct. 1942

This court decision shocked many persons who believed that they could have both liberty and subsidies. But the government must of necessity control the spending of money collected from taxpayers.

Avoiding control requires avoiding a subsidy, whether it be as a wheat payment or in any other form. A person cannot be both dependent and independent.

> *"Suppose that you want to destroy a city. Should you bomb it, or would it be sufficient just to impose rent control?"*
>
> ... ART CARDEN, THE UNINTENDED
> CONSEQUENCES OF RENT CONTROL.

NO VACANCIES

A DOLLAR a month will pay a wage-earner's rent in Paris. Our authority for this assertion is the Communist-dominated Federation of Labor Unions, the CGT. In setting forth its demands for a minimum wage to insure a decent living, it produced a worker's budget where the expenditure for rent was put at 316 francs. (In this analysis, all figures will be stated in dollars at the rough valuation of 300 francs to the dollar.)

Against this figure one may set the estimate of the conservative Union of Family Associations. Thinking in terms of families, this source sets the expenditure on rent, providing adequate space, at a dollar and a half for a man and wife with a child and an infant; for a family of six the expenditure on rent should go up to a little less than two dollars.

Such cheapness is amazing. In the CGT budget, rent is reckoned as equal in cost to transportation to and from work. To put it otherwise, a month's rent for an individual worker costs little more than six packages of the cheapest cigarettes. For a large family of six it costs as much as eleven packages of cigarettes (cigarettes, now uncaptioned in France, cost 15 cents a package).

Even in a worker's very modest budget such an expenditure absorbs but a small part of the income, 2.7% of the minimum income demanded by the

CGT; as little as 1.2% of the income of a six-member family as calculated by the Union of Family Associations.

Against such estimated blueprint budgets we can resort to actual declarations of wage-earners canvassed by the French statistical services. It appears from their budgets that, on an average, rent makes up 1.4% of wage-earners' expenses; for white-collar workers rent goes up to 1.7% of total expenses.

In fact there are many rents lower than a dollar a month, rents of half-a-dollar are not uncommon, nor should it be believed that the lodgings are necessarily worse, for price and comfort, as we shall see, are unrelated.

Such low rents are not a privilege of wage-earners only. Middle-class apartments of three or four main rooms will frequently cost from a dollar and a half to two dollars and a half per month. Rents paid by important officials or executives range from $3.50 a month to $8 or $10 a month. There is no regular relation between income and rent. Rent seldom rises above 4% of any income; frequently it is less than 1%.

It is then not surprising that the Parisians spend on shows every month far more than they pay for three months' rent.

This may seem a very desirable state of affairs. It has, of course, its drawbacks.

While you pay no more than these quite ridiculous prices if you are lucky enough to be in possession, on the other hand if you are in search of lodgings you cannot find them at any price. There are no vacant lodgings, nor is anyone going to vacate lodgings which cost so little, nor can the owners expel anyone. Deaths are the only opportunity.

Young couples must live with in-laws, and the wife's major activity consists in watching out for deaths. Tottering old people out to sun themselves in public gardens will be shadowed back to their flat by an eager young wife who will strike a bargain with the janitor, the *concierge,* so as to be first warned when the demise occurs and to be first in at the death. Other apartment-chasers have an understanding with funeral parlors.

Bootleg Housing

There are two ways of obtaining an apartment which death has made available. Legally, if you fulfill certain conditions which give you a priority, you may obtain from a public authority an order of requisition; you will usually find that the same order for the same apartment has been given to possibly two or three other candidates. The illegal method is the surest. It is to deal with the heir, and with his complicity to immediately carry in some pieces of your furniture. As soon as you are in, you are the king of the castle.

Buying one's way into an apartment will cost anywhere from $500 to $1,500 per room. At such prices you may also share flats which the tenants will agree to divide. As for wage-earners, they may as well give up the hope of setting up house; they have to stay with their families or live in very miserable hotels by the month.

In short, rents are very low but there are no lodgings available. Nor are any being built. And practically none have been built for the last twelve years.

There are some 84,000 buildings for habitation in Paris. 27.2% of these were built before 1850; 56.9% of the total was built before 1880. Almost 90% of the total was built before the First World War. Most of the supplementary building occurred immediately after that war; then it slackened, and by 1936 had practically stopped.

Parisian Plight

Even a very lenient officialdom estimates that there are about 16,000 buildings which are in such a state of disrepair that there is nothing else to do with them than pull them down. Nor are the others quite satisfactory.

To go into sordid details, 82% of the Parisian population have no bath or shower, more than half the population must go out of their lodgings to find a lavatory, and a fifth do not even have running water in the lodgings.

Little more than one in six of the existing buildings is pronounced satisfactory and in good condition by the public inspectors. Disrepair is spoiling even these.

Owners can hardly be blamed. They are not in a financial position to allow them to keep up their buildings, let alone improve them. The condition of the owners can hardly be believed. To take an example of a very common situation, here is a lady who owns three buildings containing thirty-four apartments, all inhabited class families. Her net loss from the thirty-four apartments, taxes and repairs taken care of, is eighty dollars per year. Not only must her son put her up and take care of her, but he must also payout the eighty dollars. She cannot sell; there are no buyers.

When the owner tries to milk a little net income from his property by cutting down the repairs, he runs great risks. Another person postponed repairs on his roofs; rain filtering into an apartment spoiled a couple of armchairs. He was sued for damages and condemned to pay a sum amounting to three years of the tenant's paltry rent.

The miserable condition of owners is easily explained. While rents since 1914 have been at the outside multiplied 6.8 times, taxes have been multiplied 13.2 times and the cost of repairs has been multiplied from 120 to 150 times the 1914 price!

By Easy Stages

The position is, of course, as absurd as it is disastrous. An outsider may be tempted to think that only an incredible amount of folly can have led us to this. But it is not so. We got there by easy, almost unnoticed stages, slipping down on the gentle slope of rent control. And this was not the work of the Reds but of succeeding parliaments and governments, most of which were considered to be rather conservative.

The story starts with World War One. It then seemed both humane and reasonable to preserve the interests of the families while the boys were in the army or working for victory. So existing situations were frozen. It was also reasonable to avoid disturbances at the end of the war. The veterans' homecoming should not be spoiled by evictions and rent increases. Thus prewar situations were hardened into rights. The owner lost-"temporarily," of course-the disposition of his property, and the stipulations of law superseded agreement between the parties. This was only for a time.

But by the time the situation was reviewed in 1922, retail prices had trebled with rents still at their prewar level. It was then plain that a return to liberty would imply huge increases, an index to them being provided by rents in the smallish free sector, which hovered around two and a half times the 1914 rents. The legislator shrank from this crisis. Wages were by then three and a half times what they had been in 1914, and the expenditure for rent in the worker's budget had shrunk from something like 16% before the war to around 5%. In our times habits grow up rapidly: Instead of regarding rent as constituting normally one-sixth of one's expenditures, one took it now as being normally one-twentieth. Also, a "right" had developed, the "right" to dig in. Always very sedentary, the French now had struck roots in their rented lodgings.

The legislator decided to deal with this matter in a prudent, statesmanlike manner. So the tenant's right to stay in possession was confirmed but the rent was slightly raised. Successive increases were granted in further laws, all warmly debated. A new owner-tenant relationship thus took shape. The owner was powerless either to evict the tenant or debate the price of rent with him, the State took care of that price. The price rose but slowly, while in the meantime the field of regulation was successively enlarged to bring in such flats as had not been previously regulated. New buildings put up since 1915 were alone left unregulated to stimulate construction. This exception was not to endure for long.

The Fear of Liberty

No systematic view inspired this policy. It just grew from the fear of a sudden return to liberty which seemed ever more dangerous as prices stepped up. And, of course, if one must control the price of rent, one could not allow the owner to dismiss tenants, because in that case he might so easily have stipulated secretly with the new tenant; so rent control implied necessarily the denial of the owner's right to dismiss.

What then happened to rents under this regime? In 1929, with retail prices more than six times what they had been in 1914, rents had not yet doubled; the real rents, the rents in terms of buying power, were less than a third of what they had been before the war.

Lawmaking went on; no single subject has taken up so much of the time and energy of Parliament. But the improvement in the condition of the owners, when it occurred, was not the work of the lawmakers. It was brought about by the economic crisis which lowered retail prices. Thus by 1935, rents then being up to almost three times their prewar level, retail prices were down and the owners obtained almost two-thirds of their prewar real income. Or they would have obtained it had not the Laval government then decided on a cut of 10% in rents as one of the measures designed to bring down the cost of living and implement a policy of deflation.

When the Popular Front came in, in 1936, the process of devaluations started again, retail prices soared, and the real income from buildings crumbled from year to year.

Then came World War Two. The return to liberty which had been devised for 1943 was, of course, dismissed, and all rents were frozen, including this time those of recent buildings which had till then escaped.

Since the Liberation, an order in council of 1945 and two laws in 1947 have intervened, bringing up to 119 the number of laws or quasi-laws on the subject since 1918. The new laws have provided for increases jacking up rents. The lodgings built before 1914 can now be rented at prices 70% above the 1939 price. But while rents increased 1.7 times, retail prices increased more than fourteen times. In other terms, the buying power of rents was set at 12% of its 1939 level, already greatly depressed as we have seen. The buildings put up since 1914 were more severely treated on the assumption that the ruling rents in 1939 had been more adequate. The permissible increase was set at 30% as against 1939, thus keeping the buying power of rents at 9% of what it was before World War Two. It was further specified for the buildings dating back to 1914 or earlier, which comprise as we have noted nine out of ten buildings, that their rent should in no case be more than 6.8 times the 1914 rent. This in spite of the fact that retail prices were then 99.8 times as high as in 1914.

In short, owners of new buildings have been allowed to get in terms of real income less than a tenth of what they got before World War Two.

Owners of old buildings, that is, nine-tenths of all buildings, have been allowed to get in terms of real income either 12% of what they got in 1939 or a little less than 7% of what they got in 1914-whichever is least, the law took care to specify.

The Price Predicament

If on the other hand a builder were now to put up apartments similar to those in existence, these new apartments would have to rent for prices representing from ten to thirteen times present rent ceilings, in order to reward the costs of construction and the capital invested. According to an official source, a report of the Economic Council, a wage-earner's apartment of three small rooms and a kitchen now renting for $13 to $16 a year (!) would have to be rented for $166 to $200 a year; and a luxury apartment of 1600 square feet floor space would have to be rented for $55 to $70 a month, comparing with a present price of $14 to $17 a month. Quite obviously, as long as the buildings in existence are as low priced as they are, it will be psychologically impossible to find customers at prices ten or twelve times higher, and hence construction will not be undertaken.

Such is the spread between the legal and the economic price of lodgings that even the most fervent advocates of freedom are scared at the prospect of a return to freedom; they shudder at the thought of a brutal return to reality. They feel that if the right to dismiss tenants and the right to bargain and contract with them were restored, evictions could not be executed, the whole nation of tenants sitting down to nullify the decision. The thing, they say, has now gone too far, the price of rent is too far removed from the cost.

Hence the strange plans which are now being considered by the French Parliament. It is proposed to maintain a right of occupation, a right to retain one's lodgings, and it is proposed to come to a "fair price-fixing." That is, the true service value of every flat would be fixed according to floor space, the value of the square meter being multiplied by a coefficient according to the amenities, situation and so forth. Thus the "fair rent" would be ascertained. But it would not be wholly paid by the tenant. He would benefit by a special subsidy, an inflationary measure of course, as are all subsidies. Nor would the greater part of this fair rent be paid to the owner. It would be divided in slices. A slice to correspond with the cost of upkeep would be paid in to the owner, but to a blocked account to make sure it did go for repairs. A much bigger slice for the reconstitution of the capital would not go to the owner at all, but to a National Fund for Building. Thus the dispossession of the owners would be finally sanctioned. They would be legally turned into the janitors of their own buildings, while on the basis of their dispossession a new State ownership of future buildings would rear its proud head.

Road to Ruin

Possibly the French example may prove of some interest and use to our friends across the sea. It goes to show that rent control is self-perpetuating and culminates in both the physical ruin of housing and the legal dispossession of the owners. It is enough to visit the houses in Paris to reach conclusions. The havoc wrought here is not the work of the enemy but of our own measures.

– Bertrand de Jouvenel

ANALYSIS

What would happen to the U.S. economy today if a mandatory maximum rent of $1 per dwelling unit was implemented?

We simulated the effects of decreased home construction on the overall labor market, assuming 700,000 fewer multifamily housing units are built annually. Overall, the results are not pretty, with a decrease in annual employment of 8.2 million workers in the areas of construction, food services and drinking places, real estate establishments, whole trade, physician offices, and retail stores, among many other affected industries.

Rent control was a terrible idea when de Jouvenel wrote about it, and it is still a terrible idea today. So, next time someone talks about decreasing rent price inflation, just mention the industries hurt the most. It's never worth it over the long haul.

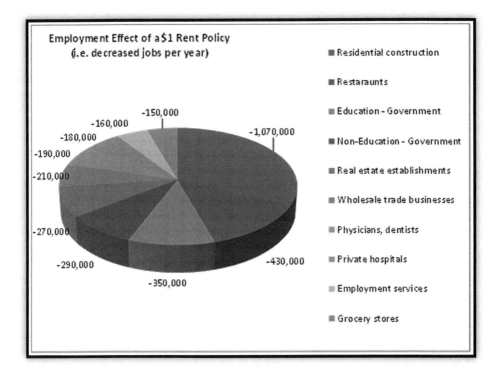

> *"The only way that has ever been discovered to have a lot of people cooperate together voluntarily is through the free market. And that's why it's so essential to preserving individual freedom."*
>
> ... MILTON FRIEDMAN

THE FREEDOM TO COMPETE

It is recognized that aggressive competition may result in a virtual identity of prices. It is also suggested that an unlawful price conspiracy will achieve price identity. Yet the Committee will discover that a considerable part of the present uncertainty flows from the insistence of government and particularly administrative officials in assuming that where substantial price identity is found there must have been a conspiracy in fact.

This is sometimes put in terms of saying that where competitors sell at about the same prices the result is the same as though there had been a conspiracy and that there must be some illegality. Any such theory is not only a calumny on American business; it is also a conclusion contrary to fact. It assumes without realism that the lower price level produced by competition would be identical with the higher price level produced by collusion.

No one can assume -the lawyers prefer to say infer that the competitive hammering of prices to a common level betokens conspiracy instead of competition, any more than the fact that most men wear collars and ties is the basis for a proper inference that they have conspired to do *so*. ... The lawful conduct of one businessman may be made unlawful by the independent acts of his competitors over whom he has no control. This is no more realistic than to say that all of the citizens of one community are either righteous or criminal, depending upon what people in other towns in the same state might do.

Editorial Comment: Apparently, a seller now: 1) is guilty of *collusion* if he sells at the same price as competitors, in recognition of the fact that consumers in a free market will refuse to pay more to one seller than to another for virtually the same thing; 2) is guilty of *profiteering* if he raises his price to avoid the charge of collusion and 3) is guilty of *"cut-throat competition"* if he lowers his price to avoid the charge of collusion.

– John M. Hancock

"When unions get higher wages for their members by restricting entry into an occupation, those higher wages are at the expense of other workers who find their opportunities reduced. When government pays its employees higher wages, those higher wages are at the expense of the taxpayer. But when workers get higher wages and better working conditions through the free market, when they get raises by firm competing with one another for the best workers, by workers competing with one another for the best jobs, those higher wages are at nobody's expense. They can only come from higher productivity, greater capital investment, more widely diffused skills. The whole pie is bigger - there's more for the worker, but there's also more for the employer, the investor, the consumer, and even the tax collector.

That's the way the free market system distributes the fruits of economic progress among all people. That's the secret of the enormous improvements in the conditions of the working person over the past two centuries."

... MILTON FRIEDMAN, FREE TO CHOOSE: A PERSONAL STATEMENT

"... The record of history is absolutely crystal clear. That there is no alternative way, so far discovered, of improving the lot of the ordinary people that can hold a candle to the productive activities that are unleashed by a free enterprise system".

... MILTON FRIEDMAN

> *"All, too, will bear in mind this sacred principle, that though the will of the majority is in all cases to prevail, that will to be rightful must be reasonable; that the minority possess their equal rights, which equal law must protect, and to violate would be oppression."*
>
> ... THOMAS JEFFERSON

FREEDOM & MAJORITY RULE

The publisher of the London Times came to this country a few years after World War I. A banquet in his honor was held in New York City, and at the appropriate time Lord Northcliffe rose to his feet to propose a toast. Prohibition was in effect, you will recall, and the beverage customarily drunk by Northcliffe in his homeland was not available here. So Northcliffe raised his glass of water and said: "Here's to America, where you do as you please. And if you don't, they make you!"

Here, in this land of the free, "we" as voters had amended the Constitution to punish conduct which "we" - as consumers - had been enjoying. If you point out that the Eighteenth Amendment had been inserted into the Constitution by majority vote, and that therefore "we" had done it to "ourselves," you need to be reminded that the "we" who did it were not the same people as the "ourselves" to whom it was done!

The Eighteenth Amendment was annulled in 1933. Shortly thereafter another prohibition law was passed, this one a prohibition against owning gold. Under the earlier dispensation you could walk down the street with a pocketful of gold coins without breaking the law; but if you were caught carrying a bottle of whiskey you might be arrested.

Then the rules were changed, and you could carry all the whiskey you wanted, but if you had any gold in your pocket you could be thrown in jail!

Our scientists are exploring outer space looking for intelligent life on other planets. I hope they find some, because there's none to spare on planet earth! With how little wisdom do we organize our lives, especially in the areas of government and the economy!

The fundamental issue in political philosophy is the limitation of governmental power; it is to determine the role of law, the functions appropriate to the political agency. The basic question may be phrased in a variety of ways: What things belong in the public domain? And what things are private? What tasks should be assigned to Washington or some lesser governmental agency, and in what sectors of life should people be free to pursue their own goals? When should legal coercion be used to force a person to do something against his will? In view of government's nature, what is its competence? What are the criteria which enable us to distinguish a just law from an unjust law?

These are questions we cannot avoid. It is true that we don't have to debate them, or even think about them; but we cannot help acting on them. Some theory about government is the hidden premise of all political action, and we'll improve our action only as we refine our theory.

What Functions Are Appropriate?

In the light of government's nature, what functions may we appropriately assign to it? This is the question, and there are two ways to approach it. The approach favored today is to count noses - find out what a majority of the people want from government, and then elect politicians who will give it to them! And believe me; they've been giving it to us! The party that wins an election is "swept into office on a ground swell of public opinion," as popular mythology has it; and of course the winners have "a mandate from the people." That's spelled Peepul.

I do not accept this approach to political philosophy, and will offer some reasons for rejecting it. Neither did our forebears accept this approach. Every political thinker in the West from Plato down to modern times has taken a different tack. Now the mere fact that something is enshrined by tradition is no reason for accepting it; we accept something because we believe it to be true. But anything which is both tried and true has a lot going for it. Let me try to sketch briefly the way our forebears went about the intellectual and moral problem of trying to figure out what government should do, and how we determine whether or not a law is just.

The backbone of any legal system is a set of prohibitions. The law forbids certain actions and punishes those who do them anyway. The solid core of any legal system, therefore, is the moral code, which, in our culture is conveyed to us by the Mosaic Law. The Sixth Commandment of The Decalogue says: "Thou shalt not commit murder," and this moral imperative is built into every statute which prescribes punishment for homicide. The Eighth Commandment forbids stealing, and this moral norm gives rise to laws punishing theft. There is a moral law against murder because each human life is precious; and there is a moral law against theft because rightful property is an extension of the person. "A possession," Aristotle writes, "is an instrument for maintaining life." Deprive a person of the right, to own property and he becomes something less than a person; he becomes someone else's man. A man to whom we deny the rights of ownership must be owned by someone else; he becomes another man's creature-a slave. The master-slave relation is a violation of the rightful order of things, that is, a violation of individual liberty and voluntary association.

The Gift of Life

Each human being has the gift of life and is charged with the responsibility of bringing his life to completion. He is also a steward of the earth's scarce resources, which he must use wisely and economically. Man is a responsible being, but no person can be held responsible for the way he lives his life and conserves his property unless he is free. Liberty, therefore, is a necessary corollary to Life and Property. Our forebears regarded Life, Liberty and Property as natural rights, and the importance of these basic rights was stressed again and again in the oratory, the preaching, and the writings of the Eighteenth Century. "Life, Liberty and Property are the gifts of the Creator," declared the Reverend Daniel Shute in 1767 from the pulpit which I occupied some 200 years later. Life, Liberty and

Property are the ideas of more than antiquarian interest; they are potent ideas because they transcribe into words an important aspect of the way things are.

Our ancestors intended to ground their legal and moral codes on the nature of things, just as students of the natural sciences intend their laws to be a transcription of the way things behave. For example: Physical bodies throughout the universe attract each other, increasing with the mass of the attracting body and diminishing with the square of the distance. Sir Isaac Newton made some observations along these lines and gave us the law of gravity. How come gravitational attraction varies as the inverse-square of the distance, and not as the inverse-cube? One is as thinkable as the other, but it just happens that the universe is prejudiced in favor of the inverse-square in this instance; just as the universe is prejudiced against murder, has a strong bias in favor of property, and wills men to be free.

Immanuel Kant echoed an ancient sentiment when he declared that two things filled him with awe; the starry heavens without, and the moral law within. The precision and order in nature manifest the Author of nature. The Creator is also the Author of our being and requires certain duties of us, his creatures. There is, thus, an outer reality joined to the reality within, and this twofold reality has an intelligible pattern, a coherent structure.

This dual arrangement is not made by human hands; it's unchangeable, it's not affected by our wishes, and it can't be tampered with. It can, however, be misinterpreted, and it can be disobeyed. We consult certain portions of this pattern and draw up blueprints for building a bridge. If we misinterpret, the bridge collapses. And a society disintegrates if its members disobey the configuration laid down in the nature of things for our guidance. This configuration is the moral order, as interpreted by reason and tradition.

We're in fairly deep water here, and this is as far into theology as I shall venture.

The point, simply put, is that our forebears, when they wanted to get some clues for the regulating of their private and public lives, sought for answers in a reality beyond society. They believed in a sacred order which transcends the world, an order of creation, and believed that our duties within society reflect the mandates of this divine order.

Take a Poll

This view of one's duty is quite in contrast to the method currently popular for determining what we should do; which is to conduct an opinion poll. Find out what the crowd wants, and then say "Me too!" This is what the advice of certain political scientists boils down to. Here is Professor James MacGregor Burns, a certified liberal and the author of several highly touted books, such as The Deadlock of Democracy and a biography of John F. Kennedy. Liberals play what Burns calls "the numbers game." "'As a liberal I believe in majority rule," he writes. "I believe that the great decisions should be made by numbers." In other words, don't think; count!" What does a majority have a right to do?" he asks. And he answers his own question. "A majority has the right to do anything in the economic and social arena that is relevant to our national problems and national purposes." And then, realizing the enormity of what he has just said, he backs off: "except to change the basic rules of the game."

Burns' final disclaimer sounds much like an afterthought, for some of his liberal cohorts support the idea of unqualified majority rule. The late Herman Finer, in his anti-Hayek book entitled Road to Reaction, declares "For in a democracy, right is what the majority makes it to be." (p. 60.) What we have here is an updating of the ancient "might makes right" doctrine. The majority does have more muscle than the minority, it has the power to carry out its will, and thus it is entitled to have its own way. If right is whatever the majority says it is, then whatever the majority does is O.K., by definition. Farewell, then to individual rights, and farewell to the rights of the minorities; the majority is the group that has made it to the top, and the name of the game is winner take all.

The dictionary definition of a majority is 50% plus 1. But if you were to draw up an equation to diagram modern majoritarianism it would read:
$50\% + 1 = 100\%; 50\% - 1 = \text{ZERO}!$

Amusing confirmation comes from a professor at Rutgers University, writing a letter to the Times. Several years ago considerable criticism was generated by the appointment of a certain man to a position in the national government. Such criticism is unwarranted, writes our political scientist, because the critics comprise "a public which, by virtue of having lost the last election, has no business approving or disapproving appointments by those who won." This is a modern version of the old adage, "To the victor belong the spoils." This Rutgers professor goes on to say, "Contrary to President Lincoln's famous but misleading phrase, ours is not a government by the people, but government by government." So there!

The Nature of Government

What functions may we appropriately assign to the political agency? What should government do? Today's answer is that government should do whatever a majority wants a government to do; find out what the People want from government, and then give it to them. The older and truer answer is based upon the belief that the rules for living together in society may be discovered if we think hard and clearly about the matter, and the corollary that we can conform our lives to these rules if we resolve to do so. But I have said nothing so far about the nature or essence of government.

Americans are justly proud of our nation, but this pride sometimes blinds us to reality. How often have you heard someone declare, "In America, 'We are the government." This assertion is demonstrably untrue; "We" are the society, all 215 million of us; but society and government are not at all the same entity. Society is all-of-us, whereas government is only some-of-us. The some-of-us who comprise government would begin with the President, Vice-president, and Cabinet; it would include Congress and the bureaucracy; it would descend through governors, mayors and lesser officials, down to sheriffs and the cop on the beat.

A Unique Institution

Government is unique among the institutions of society, in that society has bestowed upon this one agency exclusive legal control over the weaponry, from clubs to hydrogen bombs. Governments do use persuasion, and they do rely on authority, legitimacy and tradition - but so do other institutions like the Church and the School. But only one agency has the power to tax, the authority to operate the system of courts and jails, and a warrant for mobilizing the machinery for making war; that is government, the power structure.

Governmental action is what it is, no matter what sanction might be offered to justify what it does. Government always acts with power; in the last resort government uses force to back up its decrees.

Society's Power Structure

When I remind you that the government of a society is that society's power structure, I am not offering you a novel theory, nor a fanciful political notion of my own. It is a truism that government is society's legal agency of compulsion. Virtually every statesman and every political scientist - whether Left or Right - takes this for granted and does his theorizing from this as a base. "Government is not reason, it is not eloquence;" wrote George Washington, "it is force."

Bertrand Russell, in a 1916 book, said, "The essence of the State is that it is the repository of the collective force of its citizens." Ten years later, the Columbia University professor, R. M. MacIver spoke of the state as "the authority which alone has compulsive power." The English writer, Alfred Cobban, says that "the essence of the state, and of all political organizations, is power."

But why labor the obvious except for the fact that so many of our contemporaries - those who say "we are the government" overlook it? What we are talking about is the power of man over man; government is the legal authorization which permits some men to use force on others. When we advocate a law to accomplish a certain goal, we advertise our inability to persuade people to act in the manner we recommend; so we're going to force them to conform! As Sargent Shriver once put it, "In a democracy you don't compel people to do something unless you are sure they won't do it."

In the liberal mythology of this century, government is all things to all men. Liberals think that government assumes whatever characteristics people wish upon it - like Proteus in Greek mythology who took on one shape after another, depending on the circumstances. But government is not an all-purpose tool; it has a specific nature, and its nature determines what government can accomplish. When properly limited, government serves a social end no other agency can achieve; its use of force is constructive. The alternatives here are law and tyranny - as the Greeks put it. This is how the playwright, Aeschylus, saw it in The Eumenides: "Let no man live uncurbed by law, nor curbed by tyranny."

The Moral Code

If government is to serve a moral end it must not violate the moral code. The moral code tells us that human life is sacred, that liberty is precious, and that ownership of property is good. And by the same token, this moral code supplies a definition of criminal action; murder is a crime, theft is a crime, and it is criminal to abridge any person's lawful freedom. It becomes a function of the law, then, in harmony with the moral code, to use force against criminal actions in order that peaceful citizens may go about their business. The use of legal force against criminals for the protection of the innocent is the earmark of a properly limited government.

This is an utterly different kind of procedure than the use of government force on peaceful citizens - whatever the excuse or rationalization. People should not be forced into conformity with any social blueprint; their private plans should not be overridden in the interests of some national plan or social goal. Government - the public power - should not be used for private advantage; it should not be used to protect people from themselves.

Well, what should the law do to peaceful, innocent citizens? It should let them alone! When government lets John Doe alone, and punishes anyone who refuses to let him alone, then John Doe is a free man.

In this country we have a republican form of government. The word "republic" is from the Latin words, res and publica, meaning the things or affairs which are common to all of us, the affairs which are in the public domain, in sharp contrast to matters which are private. Government, then, is "the public thing," and this strong emphasis on public serves to delimit and set boundaries to governmental power, in the interest of preserving the integrity of the private domain.

What's in a name? You might be thinking. Well, in this case, in the case of republic, a lot. The word "republic" encapsulates a political philosophy; it connotes the philosophy of government which would limit government to the defense of life, liberty and property in order to serve the ends of justice. There's no such connotation in the word "monarchy," for example; or in aristocracy or oligarchy.

A monarch is the sole, supreme ruler of a country, and there is theoretically no area in the fife of his citizens over which he may not hold sway. The king owns the country and his people belong to him.

Monarchical practice pretty well coincided with theory in what is called "Oriental Despotism," but in Christendom the power of the kings was limited by the nobility on the one hand, and the Emperor on the other; and all secular rulers had to take account of the power of the Papacy. Power was played off against power, to the advantage of the populace.

Individual Liberty

The most important social value in Western civilization is individual liberty. The human person is looked upon as God's creature, gifted with free will which endows him with the capacity to choose what he will make of his life. Our inner, spiritual freedom must be matched by an outer and social liberty if man is to fulfill his duty toward his Maker. Creatures of the state cannot achieve their destiny as human beings; therefore, government must be limited to securing and preserving freedom of personal action, within the rules for maximizing liberty and opportunity for everyone.

Unless we are persuaded of the importance of freedom to the individual, it is obvious that we will not structure government around him to protect his private domain and secure his rights. The idea of individual liberty is old, but it was given a tremendous boost in the sixteenth century by the Reformation and the Renaissance.

The earliest manifestation of this renewed idea of liberty was in the area of religion, issuing in the conviction that a person should be allowed to worship God in his own way. This religious ferment in England gave us Puritanism, and early in the seventeenth century Puritanism projected a political movement whose members were contemptuously called Whiggamores - later shortened to Whigs - a word roughly equivalent to "cattle thieves." The king's men were called Tories - "highway robbers." The Whigs worked for individual liberty and progress; the Tories defended the old order of the king, the landed aristocracy, and the established church.

One of the great writers and thinkers in the Puritan and Whig tradition was John Milton, who wrote his celebrated plea for the abolition of Parliamentary censorship of printed material in 1644, Areopagitica. Many skirmishes had to be fought before freedom of the press was finally accepted as one of the earmarks of a free society. Free speech is a corollary of press freedom, and I remind you of the statement attributed to Voltaire: "I disagree with everything you say, but I will defend with my life your right to say it."

Adam Smith extended freedom to the economic order, with The Wealth of Nations, published in 1776 and warmly received in the thirteen colonies. Our population numbered about 3 million at this time; roughly one third of these were Loyalists, that is, Tory in outlook and besides, there was a war on. Despite these circumstances 2,500 sets of The Wealth of Nations were sold in the colonies within five years of its publication. The colonists had been practicing economic liberty for a long time, simply because their governments were too busy with other things to interfere - or too inefficient - and Adam Smith gave them a rationale.

The Bill of Rights

Ten amendments to the Constitution were adopted in 1791. Article the First reads: "Congress shall make no law respecting the establishment of religion, or prohibiting the free exercise thereof ... "The separation of Church and State enunciated here was a momentous first step in world history. Religious liberty, freedom of the press, free speech and the free economy are four departments of the same liberating trend - the Whig movement.

The men we refer to as the Founding Fathers would have called themselves Whigs. Edmund Burke was the chief spokesman for a group in Parliament known as The Rockingham Whigs. In 1832 the Whig Party in England changed its name to one which more aptly described its emphasis on liberty. It became the Liberal Party, standing for free trade, religious liberty, the abolition of slavery, extension of the franchise, and other reforms.

Classical Liberalism is not to be confused with the thing called "liberalism" in our time! Today's "liberalism" is the exact opposite of historical Liberalism - which came out of the eighteenth-century Whiggism - which came out of the seventeenth-century Puritanism. The labels are the same; the realities are utterly different. Present day liberals have trouble with ideas, as ideas, so they try to dispose of uncomfortable thoughts by pigeonholing them in a time slot. The ideas of individual liberty, inherent rights, limited government and the free economy are, they say, eighteenth-century ideas. What a dumb comment! The proper test of an idea is not the test of time but the test of truth!

You may be wondering why I have not yet used the word "democracy," although I've spoken of monarchy, oligarchy, and liberalism. Well, I'll tell you. Our discussion has focused on the nature of government, and we have discovered that the essence of government is power, legal force.

Once this truth sinks in we take the next step, which is to figure out what functions may appropriately be assigned to the one social agency authorized to use force. This brings us back to the moral code and the primary values of life, liberty and property. It is the function of the law to protect the life, liberty and property of all persons alike in order that the human person may achieve his proper destiny.

Voting Is Appropriate for Choosing Officeholders

There's another question to resolve, tied in with the basic one, but much less important: How do you choose personnel for public office? After you have employed the relevant intellectual and moral criteria and confined public things to the public sector, leaving the major concerns of life in the private sector ... once you've done this there's still the matter of choosing people for office.

One method is choice by bloodline. If your father is king, and if you are the eldest son, why you'll be king when the old man dies. Limited monarchy still has its advocates, and kingship will work if a people embrace the monarchical ideology. Monarchy hasn't always worked smoothly, however, else what would Shakespeare have done for his plays? Sometimes your mother's lover will bump off the old man, or your kid brother might try to poison you.

There's a better way to choose personnel for public office; let the people vote. Confine government within the limits dictated by reason and morals, lay down appropriate requirements, and then let voters go to the polls. The candidate who gets the majority of votes gets the job. This is democracy, and this is the right place for majority action. As Pericles put it 2,500 years ago, democracy is where the many participate in rule.

Voting is little more than a popularity contest, and the most popular man is not necessarily the best man, just as the most popular idea is not always the soundest idea. It is obvious, then, that balloting - or counting noses or taking a sampling of public opinion - is not the way to get at the fundamental question of the proper role of government within a society. We have to think hard about this one, which means we have to assemble the evidence; weigh, sift, and criticize it; compare notes with colleagues, and so on. In other words, this is an educational endeavor, a matter for the classroom, the study, the podium, the pulpit, the forum, the press. To count noses at this point is a cop out; there's no place here for a Gallup Poll.

To summarize: The fundamental question has to do with the scope and functions of the political agency, and only hard thinking - education in the broad sense - can resolve this question. The lesser question has to do with the choice of personnel; and majority action - democratic decision - is the way to deal with it. But if we approach the first question with the mechanics appropriate to the second, we have confused the categories and we're in for trouble.

"Democratic Despotism"

We began to confuse the categories more than 140 years ago, as Alexis de Tocqueville observed. His book, Democracy in America, warned us about the emergence here of what he called "democratic despotism," which would "degrade men without tormenting them." We were warned again in 1859 by a professor at Columbia University, Francis Lieber, in his book, On Civil Liberty and Self-government: "Woe to the country in which political hypocrisy first calls the people almighty, then teaches that the voice of the people is divine, then pretends to take a mere clamor for the true voice of the people, and lastly gets up the desired clamor." Getting up the desired clamor is what we call "social engineering," or "the engineering of consent."

What is called "a majority" in contemporary politics is almost invariably a numerical minority, whipped up by an even smaller minority of determined and sometimes unscrupulous men. There's not a single plank in the platform of the welfare state that was put there because of a genuine demand by a genuine majority. A welfarist government is always up for grabs, and various factions, pressure groups, special interests, causes, ideologies seize the levers of government in order to impose their programs on the rest of the nation.

Let's assume that we don't like what's going on today in this and other countries; we don't like it because people are being violated, as well as principles. We know the government is off the track, and we want to get it back on; but we know in our bones that Edmund Burke was right when he said, "There never was, for any long time ... a mean, sluggish, careless people that ever had a good government of any form." Politics, in other words, reflects the character of a people, and you cannot improve the tone of politics except as you elevate the character of a significant number of persons. The improvement of character is the hard task of religion, ethics, art, and education. When we do our work properly in these areas, our public life will automatically respond.

Large numbers are not required. A small number of men and women whose convictions are sound and clearly thought out, who can present their philosophy persuasively, and who manifest their ideas by the quality of their lives, can inspire the multitude whose ideas are too vague to generate convictions of any sort. A little leaven raises the entire lump of dough; a tiny flame starts a mighty conflagration; a small rudder turns a huge ship. And a handful of people possessed of ideas and a dream can change a nation - especially when that nation is searching for new answers and a new direction.

– Edmund A. Opitz

At the time of the original publication, The Reverend Mr. Opitz was a member of the staff of the Foundation for Economic Education, a seminar lecturer, and author of the book, Religion and Capitalism: Allies, Not Enemies.

Reprinted with permission from The Freeman, a publication of The Foundation for Economic Education, Inc., Vol. 27, No. 1, January 1977.

> *"What you give for the cause of charity in health is gold; what you give in sickness is silver; what you give after death is lead."*
>
> ... JEWISH PROVERB

CHARITY: BIBLICAL AND POLITICAL

CHARITY is defined as an "act of loving all men as brothers because they are sons of God." This is a purely personal matter; an act voluntarily performed by one person for another; an act of faith in God and His commandments for governing our relationships with our fellow men. When we keep this concept in mind, it becomes a simple matter to distinguish between true charity and the spurious schemes that now masquerade under its name.

Charity Debased

The original concept of charity as an expression of love now appears to have been largely replaced by a concept of government-guaranteed security. One possible explanation for the development of this concept of charity may be that so many people felt that personal responsibility in the dispensing of charity was too slow and inadequate. Thus they chose to move into the speedier method of the use of public funds.

Admittedly, the motives of these people were probably good and charitable. But the method chosen was uncharitable because love was replaced by force. The spirit of charity was debased to "public welfare," and the shift from personal responsibility to grants by the state was on. The flow of state funds for relief and rehabilitation has become greater and greater, and the part that personal responsibility can play has necessarily become less and less.

The element which gives meaning to charity is personal consideration and responsibility, but that element is lost when the edicts of the state are substituted for the voluntary decisions of persons. The means have destroyed the ends.

Double Responsibility

There are two areas in which this sense of personal responsibility comes home to us. One is the person's responsibility for himself, and the other is in the person's responsibility to his fellow men. Both of these lie in the area of religion, and of them the Judeo-Christian religion has something definite to say. It states, unequivocally, that man himself is responsible both for his personal life and for his social relations.

This is one of the first lessons taught in the Bible. In the drama with which the Bible opens, there is the picture of God as One who is walking in the cool of the evening in the Garden of Eden, and He calls out to Adam: "Where art thou?" And Adam replies: "I heard Thy voice in the garden, and I was afraid." It was the picture of man being afraid of what God would ask of him. But then God puts responsibility upon the man and the woman, and sends them forth out of the ease and the luxury of Eden into the reality of the world God had formed, in which man was to find himself through the acceptance of his personal responsibility.

The Teachings of Jesus

This was also the theme of the Hebrew prophets. And in the teachings of Jesus Christ we find this concept of personal responsibility emphasized over and over again. Jesus faced all kinds and conditions of men and women, but He never allowed anyone to escape the sense of responsibility for his own life, and for the needs of others. The parable of the talents is set in the midst of the teachings of Jesus, and each person, no matter whether he is endowed with ten or five talents-or even one-is responsible for the preservation of them, and also for the development of them.

The Good Samaritan

So it is concerning the need of others. The one story which best exemplifies all the teachings of Jesus regarding our relationship to the need of others are the story of the Good Samaritan. There was a man who was beaten by robbers and left to die. A priest, and then a Levite, came along. As it should be, the choice of helping the man was left with each of them. Both chose not to help. Then a Samaritan came by. He personally and voluntarily accepted responsibility for the man who was in need. *He* knelt down and bound up the man's wounds, took him to the nearest inn, and paid for having him cared for until he could return and pay the full bill. In accepting his personal responsibility for the need of his neighbor, he acted in accord with God's commandments.

But in this immortal story, we should remember that Christ did not say that part of the duty of the charitable man was to levy a tax upon the priest and the Levite so that they would *be* forced to pay two-thirds of the cost of helping the wounded man, even against their will, while he would pay the other third, which would be his share under such an arrangement. The Bible confronts each with his responsibility. But in addition to being purely personal, it is also completely voluntary. And the excuse of "good motives" in voting to confiscate another's money will hardly be adequate. For how can charity-the love of a person for his fellow men-ever *be* connected with force and compulsion in any form? Are not these two concepts-the voluntary law of love of person for person, and the compulsory law of force of person against person -irreconcilable in all respects?

Christian Philosophy

Over and over again Jesus emphasized this teaching. Always He spoke of what one does with his personal life, with the responsibilities which are the cost of his being a person. With love and understanding and example, *He* explained that there can be no escape from personal responsibility by taking refuge in customs and in laws and in subservience to the state.

In fact, in His condemnation of the tradition or law of "corban," Christ specifically stated that no person could use the law to relieve himself of the responsibility of caring for the aged and dependent members of his family. He said that this denial of responsibility was a rejection of God's commandments even though the excuse for denying such responsibility was "corban"-a dedicating of one's resources since Jesus would not accept even this as sufficient excuse for rejecting personal responsibility for the maintenance and welfare of one's kindred, how do you suppose He would react to our present-day mania for turning this responsibility over to the secular state? What does the future hold for a nation wherein parents have come to believe that the purpose of government is to relieve them of the responsibility for their children, and wherein in turn demand government relieve them of the responsibility for their parents?

Equality

This Christian philosophy of freedom of choice and personal responsibility for one's own actions was men who were steeped in totalitarianism. It is not surprising that it was difficult for them to understand this concept. And even today, many persons are still to reconcile communistic methods-public control of land and resources, equalization of property by force for "the good of all"-with the teachings of Christ.

But the parable of the talents teaches that equalitarianism is not a Christian concept. In truth, God has designed each person to be an individual; except in value before God and before the law, no person is identical or equal to any other person. And as for the references in the New Testament that allegedly advocate some equalization or common ownership of resources, they are *always* on a voluntary basis among persons who wish to participate. They are *never* advanced in the form of a commandment or a law. Compulsory collectivism, on the contrary, takes both responsibility and resources from the individual and places them in the secular state. This is a denial of the rights of the individual, as well as a denial of his duty, for then the individual ceases to be a person who must make account for his stewardship of the gifts granted by God. As a collectivized member of the state, man is held accountable to the state for his every thought or action, and so the collectivization has deprived him of his birthright as a personality accountable only to God.

Disasters

Now many persons will agree that aid to the unfortunate should theoretically be voluntary and a purely personal matter and that the state should not enter into the process. But then they will recall various natural and man-made disasters-such as floods, droughts, depressions, explosions, and earthquakes-and claim that the economic problems then involved are too great for strictly private solution. This, of course, is a legitimate question. Let us examine it.

First, where is the proof that the children of God will refuse to voluntarily help their brothers who are victims of *any* disaster, however great? An examination of the evidence reveals that-as any Christian would expect-the necessary voluntary aid through private organizations soon makes its appearance wherever disaster strikes. Persons do not starve-or even for long remain ill fed, ill housed, or ill clothed-in a free, Christian nation. Starvation is found only in countries where God is denied and where persons are fed and controlled by their governments. If this voluntary aid is now less than what could ordinarily be expected, is it not due solely to the fact that the force of government has entrenched itself in this area of love which, by its very nature, can apply only to individuals acting alone or through their voluntary organizations?

Eternal Principles

And as for the governmental controls that have been perpetuated upon us on a "temporary" basis during an alleged national emergency, we must remember that the Christian philosophy deals with eternal or timeless principles. Is a thing right or wrong? If it is wrong, then reject it; if it is right, then accept it-regardless of the temporary opposition and the shallow arguments of political expediency that will surely appear. For example, must we continue the evil of governmental "charity" merely because so many people-those who receive it and those who have the political jobs of dispensing it-now have a vested interest in its continuance? If governmental control over people's lives is us abolish it now before this evil consumes us.

Jesus Did Not Compromise

The proponents of social control by the state collide as directly with the teachings of Christ as would two trains upon the same track. Jesus was so uncompromising in his insistence that responsibility be placed upon the individual for both his personal attitude toward others that Jesus never suggested an institution of any kind that could take the place of individual responsibility. Nor did He ever mention an institution or a power to which an individual could transfer such responsibility, either by acquiescence, force or plunder.

Nevertheless, this fatal temptation-the temptation to that functions are spiritual can be transferred to the secular state because it possesses the necessary power to "get things done" -continues to confront both religious and social effort. This temptation shows itself in our modern mood of believing that it is the function of religion to force a change in the spirit of people law, by the naked power of the state. In socialist democracies this *is* done by the due process of law; in more realistic totalitarian states the naked power is used. But both take away the resources of those who do not contribute willingly to whatever the government may currently designated as "social need." The Soviet system, which is the ultimate development of socialism, this by killing many millions of farmers who resisted the collectivization of all the farms of Russia. The state owned all the land and the resources, so it could do what it wanted with them, and personal decisions were no longer permitted.

Good Intentions Not Enough

Such action rudely shocks the well-intentioned people who believe in what they call the welfare provisions of the socialist state, but who deplore police-state methods. But though the words describing the welfare state methods are more honey-covered, the results are the same. That is, the laws of the welfare state are imposed to plunder the resources-and control the actions-of the farmer or the businessman to the same extent as does the dictate of the totalitarian state. In either case, the objector is either fined or jailed or liquidated, if he refuses to conform.

Not a Christian Idea

There is no Christianity in the concept that pressure groups, desiring material benefits, have the right to use the power of the state to take property from some individuals for the material gain of those who have the political power. That is plunder, and it is still plunder even if Robin Hood declares that he is robbing the rich to help the poor.

It is strange that even many of our churchmen should trust neither themselves nor others to do the right and the good thing about the need of the world. But we can see that they lack faith when churchmen themselves advocate these civil laws to take money away from people by force to give it to those who demand material benefits. This procedure may be a way to distribute money, but it is as far from being a spiritual experience as anything in this world could be.

Who Will Refuse?

We need new recognition of the power which lies within us. We need to know that the life of God is within us in far greater measure than we now believe. We turn despairingly to the state, which is the vainest of hopes, because we do not believe enough in either God or man. Let us lift up our hearts. For which one of us is it that will refuse his help in a case of real human need? You? I? Or is the finger to be pointed again at that nebulous scapegoat "someone else"?

I write as a minister, and I want to attest that through an experience of thirty years I have never seen a church member fail to respond to an authentic case of human need. And from those who could and did help when I have described such a case, I have invariably received expressions of gratitude that the opportunity was presented.

It is that faith which we need restored today. If we will only believe that such is the spirit of man we will not only be believing more in God, but we shall receive a response from the people of God that no one has yet dreamed of. We act as though the opposite were true that men are not really like God and are unable and reluctant to be moved by Him.

If we need laws to make people treat men of other faiths and races as friends; if we need the police power of the secular state to take money from men for human need; if it is believed that the only hope of a city of God is to seek the alternative of a collectivized mass leveled to the lowest common denominator of mentality and ability-if all this be the limit of our hope for mankind, then even such activity is sheer futility, for even if such an effort could be achieved it would have no meaning at all for mankind. This rejection of personal responsibility would prove only that it is possible to make men live like whipped dogs, and the proving of it would be hell.

Two Vital Questions

There are two questions in the beginning of Genesis that illustrate the God-given personal responsibility of man. The first is the question of God to Adam: "Where art thou?" The second is the question of God to Cain: "Where is Abel thy brother?" In both questions the Bible goes to the heart of man's being and meaning. He is to make a response to the personal search of God, and he is to bear a personal responsibility for his brother. Man could not evade his personal response to God by saying that the woman tempted him, and he could not evade his personal responsibility for his brother by saying that such responsibility was not his and could be turned over to any other power. When God raises such questions as those-and He raises them to every man and woman in every generation as He did in the Garden of Eden-God is not speaking to a community. He is alone with a man. And in that moment man cannot excuse himself by saying that his community is immoral and has corrupted him, any more than Adam could transfer his responsibility to a temptress, or any more than Cain could transfer his responsibility to the community.

The concept that the community is a moral object which can accept such responsibility is utterly absurd. Only persons are moral or immoral; responsible or irresponsible. Society and community are secular in form and substance; they are terms describing social units which are without moral significance at all. There is no more of a moral sense, good or bad, about a state or a community than there is about a crowd at a game. One would not dream of saying that he could give over his responsibility for himself, or for his brother, to the crowd in the bleachers. And no more can a Christian believe that he can do so with the state.

Charity Is Secret

Finally, we must remember one other biblical principle when we are considering the plight of the poor and unfortunate: "Take heed that ye do not your alms before men, to be seen of them: Otherwise ye have no reward of your Father which is in heaven. Therefore when thou doest thine alms, do not sound a trumpet before thee, as the hypocrites do in the synagogues and in the streets, that they may have glory of men. Verily I say unto you, they have their reward. But when thou doest alms, let not thy left hand know what thy right hand doeth: That thine alms may be in secret; and thy Father which seeth in secret Himself shall reward thee openly."

How can *any* attempt at governmental alms giving be in harmony with this Christian principle? Do the advocates of social security legislation, relief laws, United Nations rehabilitation programs, Point Four, and other compulsory governmental schemes to aid poor and unfortunate people "do their alms in secret"? Or do they "sound their trumpets before them" in order "that they may have glory of men"? Is it their own money, or is the money taken from others without their consent? Are their theory and practice of "police-grants from the state" in harmony with the teachings of Christ? If so, then are our voluntary social and missionary societies really in accord with the mind of Christ?

Christ Rejected

In defense of their acts, some of these legislators point out that they-like Christ-have distributed food to those who were hungry, and clothed those who were naked, and housed those who were cold. This is a true statement. But, nevertheless, they have rejected Christ in the process. They have introduced the evil principle of force into an arrangement that should be voluntary. They have made a Roman holiday out of a responsibility that is essentially spiritual, both for the giver and the receiver. These rulers of men have rejected the spiritual, and have made this stated or implied compact with their supporters: Elect me to a position of power and I will then reward you-or others designated by you-with special privileges and the money that I will legally take from others.

Robbery is thus legalized. Equality before the law is thus denied. Personal responsibility is thus rejected. Freedom is thus destroyed.

This political approach to charity may or may not be effective strategy for winning elections, but let us never inject the name of Christ or the principles of Christianity into this sordid bargain. Rather let us hang our heads in shame at the evil we have done or tolerated in the name of charity-especially to the very ones we have claimed to be helping. Let us search for the lesson to be found in this statement by the Apostle Paul: "And though I bestow all my goods to feed the poor ... and have not charity, it profiteth me nothing."

Let us render unto the state that which belongs to the state, and unto God that which belongs to God. It is God's commandment that there must be a personal concern, as well as a personal sharing, with those in need. The use of the force of government in this area of compassion and charity precludes any personal expression of Christianity. It becomes a mechanistic and secular thing, devoid of feeling. So let us return to the teachings of the Gospels, and render unto God our willing response to those of His children who need our help and ourselves.

– Russell J Clinchy

> *"You don't need to pray to God any more when there are storms in the sky, but you do have to be insured."*
>
> ... BERTOLT BRECHT

INSURING YOUR INSURANCE

THE life insurance business was founded and has existed on faith in the validity of certain economic principles. One of them has been that only through investment in productive enterprise could real earning power and true prosperity be achieved, and that only through thrift and conservation of resources could it be maintained.

We have believed that prosperity could not long continue under a system whereby one man reaped what another had sown; that it could not be increased by wars, trade barriers, artificial or natural famines, high taxes, restraints of trade or production, special-privilege legislation, currency debasement-the very obstacles to progress against which our forefathers tried to protect us when they set up our Constitution and form of government.

The trust that our policyholders have in us depends on a confidence that when we repay our obligations in dollars, those dollars will have a commensurate exchange value for something else. It is our unwritten, but nevertheless moral, obligation to do all we can to repay value with value.

But we must now frankly face the fact that our own government has become predatory. As long as we had government which performed the functions of protecting us against those who would seek to take our money or possessions without compensation, this tendency to take advantage of the belongings of others was held in check. But now that our government itself has become predatory, a good part of this protection has vanished.

If we include the foreign aid grants with the costs of preparation for future wars, then almost one-half of our 40-odd billion dollar budget is being spent presumably to fight off foreign collectivist threats to our security, our liberty, and our way of life. And yet a vast part of the rest of it is being spent right here at home to promote steps which are leading us inexorably toward exactly the same kind of collectivism-the same fallacies, the same delusions.

The life insurance companies of America have 78 million policyholders. What efforts have we made, let us ask ourselves, to convey to them any idea of the damage the something-for-nothing policies of government have done to their savings and to their future?

It seems to me that the only hope for our economic salvation must lie in a determined expansion of an informational program. This is a good time to start. We must all of us turn salesmen for this, the most important sales campaign we have ever conducted. We must be fighters in the most important war we have ever fought-a war once again for American independence.

– Asa V. Call

UPDATE:

Sadly, 47 percent of all Americans – at least 122 million people – have NO life insurance coverage at all. This life insurance need was at one time estimated to be nearly $5 trillion and the number of uninsured individuals and households has only grown. Michael White's Bank Insurance & Investment Fee Income Report, 2001

America's population is now over 300 million less the 122 million uninsured leaves a policyholder base of about 178 million. Since 1950, America has added another 100 million policyholders.

> *"The first panacea for a mismanaged nation is inflation of the currency; the second is war. Both bring a temporary prosperity; both bring a permanent ruin. But both are the refuge of political and economic opportunists."*
>
> ... ERNEST HEMINGWAY

INFLATION

INFLATION can be prevented. Failure to do so is purely and simply a matter of negligence.

Inflation is a trick done with money. Suppose that the government were to provide vending machines all over the country where persons could deposit each dollar they now have and get two in return, by merely pressing a button. If everyone were to use this gadget, each person could then pay twice as much as before for everything he buys. That would be inflation in a clear and simple form.

People could, of course, put away some of this new money in "a sock" or otherwise hide it from circulation and use. But with this inflation gadget operating, there would be less incentive than before to keep the money in hiding, because it would become worth less and less with passing time. So the hoarding of money isn't likely to solve the present inflation problem, if it persists.

Inflation means too much money. The way to prevent inflation, then, is to close down the money factory. It is just that simple. All the complicated gibberish one hears and reads about inflation simply blocks an understanding of the essentials of the problem-though it may impress the ignorant, or hide the negligence of those who are responsible for inflation by making the task of preventing inflation seem hopelessly complicated.

The Money Factory

Where is the money factory? Who operates it?

The money factory in our present money system is operated by the federal government, either directly or by farming it out to sub-contractors under the control of government.* It makes paper money to replace that which has become dirty or worn out. It makes new paper money to increase the supply. It makes pennies, nickels, and the silver coins. It permits the banks to grant credit to borrowers, which becomes money that is interchangeable with any of the other forms of money in use.

But for purposes of seeing where responsibility lies in the inflation problem, we need not concern ourselves with all these different kinds of money. It is necessary only to say that at present all forms of money come out of the government factory, or are controlled by the government, under a complete monopoly.

If anyone doubts the existence of this money monopoly by the government, he can test it by manufacturing some money himself-even one cent. He would then be charged with counterfeiting, and be given a penitentiary sentence for having infringed on the monopoly. The policeman in this instance is the one who holds the monopoly.

The money monopoly is a strange one. We usually think of a monopoly as restricting output, which can then be sold at a much higher price. But in the money monopoly, the government can force the citizens to take the entire output of its product.

*Beyond the scope of this analysis is the important question of alternative money systems, with advantages or disadvantages so far as the danger of inflation is concerned.

A Highly Profitable Monopoly

Not only that, but the operation is highly profitable nearly 100 per cent, or almost the entire price of the product. This is one clear case of an "excess profit" which the victimized customers are forced to pay.

If the money monopoly were not so profitable, there would be no inflation problem at this time. The profit incentive works with money and stimulates its production, just as it does with anything else. In olden days when some otherwise useful commodity like gold, for instance, was used as money, anyone who wished could produce as much of it as he liked. The production of money was then legal and competitive, rather than being a crime as it is now. Its production was so costly in time and expense that the inefficient producers were crowded out, just as they are crowded out of the production of brooms or mouse traps.

But it is not so with present-day money, with the paper bills and deposits that makes up most of our money of exchange. It doesn't cost much for the paper and ink and printing needed to make a $100 bill. It is probably the most profitable monopoly that ever existed, and the entire force of the federal government is available to protect its monopoly against the infringement of private counterfeiting.

When a private citizen counterfeits money, the wrath of other citizens is aroused and they say: "He did no useful work to get that money, and yet he spends it in the market place, taking food, clothing, and other things away from those of us who have earned our money by working for it. He takes useful things out of the market without producing other useful things to go into the market, as we do. The effect of his chicanery is that prices go up and the rest of us receive less and less for our money."

This is a correct statement of what happens under counterfeiting. It is the reason for objecting to counterfeiting, because the counterfeiter gets something for nothing. And it is the reason for objecting to legal counterfeiting, too. If everybody tried to live off counterfeit money, one would at once discover its effect in the extreme. There would be nothing to buy with the money and it would be completely worthless.

When the government makes new money and spends it, the effect on the supply of things in the market to be bought by people with their earnings-and the effect on prices-is exactly the same as when any private counterfeiter does so. The only difference between the two is whether it is a private counterfeiter that gets benefits looted from others, or whether it is a counterfeiting government spending it on pet projects-projects that the citizens are unwilling to finance either by private investment or by tax payments.

Counterfeit money affects what you can get for your money in the market much like water affects the punch at a bring-your-own party. Each in attendance is to be allowed to dip into the punch bowl in proportion to the quantity of ingredients he has brought and dumped into it. All bring some pure ingredient wanted in the mixture.

Now suppose that one person brings water, and dumps it in. This dilutes the punch, but the person who does it is permitted to drink of the mixture the same as those who are being cheated. He gets something for nothing, and the rest get nothing for something by an equal amount. If everyone were to do the same as he has done, it would be perfectly clear what the adding of water does to the taste of the punch. So it is with counterfeit money, whether done privately or by the government.

Why Government Inflates Money

The government makes this new money in order to cover what it spends in excess of its income-its costs in excess of its tax revenues. The government makes up the shortage with the new money made in its monopolistic money factory. For our present purposes, it makes no difference whether this is done with paper bills directly, or with bills which it obtains by issuing another form of paper money government bonds-which are forced upon the banking system.

What the government does is like a counterfeiter who continuously spends more than his earnings, and who goes to his basement print shop each evening and makes enough counterfeit money to balance the shortage. His print shop might put out either paper money direct or counterfeit bonds which he sells to the banks in exchange for the money; the effect would be the same in either of the two instances.

Living within Income

The way-the only way-to stop this form of inflation is for the government to live within its income. This can be done either by raising enough in taxes to meet its costs, Or by paring down its costs to equal its income.

In a family, the housewife may try the former method nudging the husband to ask for a raise, or to hustle for more sales-but in the end the family must always resolve the problem by spending less than it would like to spend, and living within its income.

The government holds unlimited power to tax every family in the nation and for two decades has been raising more and more taxes, but it has never resolved the problem that way. It appears to have forgotten the possibility of reducing expenses as the means of living within its income and avoiding inflation. So we have had inflation almost continuously for twenty years, and are now faced with its acceleration.

The only way to prevent inflation is to prevent these governmental deficits; to pay currently and in full all the expenses of government that we either demand or tolerate. To do this it is necessary either to increase taxes or to cut down the costs of government. We are only kidding ourselves if we say that we can avoid both taxes and governmental frugality, by inflation-financing of the excess of its costs over its income.

Inflation a Form of Tax

Inflation of the type we are discussing is in reality a form of tax, not an alternative to taxes. It is, in fact, perhaps the most pernicious form of tax, for the reason that it is not recognized as such. It can ply its evil way under cover of this ignorance, and without the resistances and disciplines of a tax that is open and recognized.

We speak of direct and indirect taxes. Property taxes or income taxes which are paid by individuals are direct taxes; only about one-third of all taxes are of this type where we can see them clearly. Indirect taxes, making up the other two-thirds, are collected at some point away from the consumer, and become buried in the prices of the things we buy and the services we employ. All these direct and indirect taxes are at specific rates which are set by a governmental body charged with that responsibility. They decide what will be taxed, and how much.

But with inflation, which is in reality also a tax, it is not these taxing bodies which designate the tax. It is a tax created by default. When the spending part of government outruns the taxing part, the difference is financed by governmental counterfeit, by inflation which falls as a tax on each person in the market place in the form of higher prices for what he buys. Everyone who uses money for buying in the market pays some of this form of tax. It is the close equivalent of a sales tax on everything. One who favors deficit spending-the inflation tax-should not be opposed to a sales tax imposed on all purchases of goods and services, without exception. The only important difference is that the sales tax is known to be a tax, but the inflation tax is thought to be avoidance or postponement of the tax.

Postponed Taxes a Myth

This makes clear, I believe, why inflation is such a pernicious form of tax. People who would otherwise protest and curb the extravagances of government are lulled by the foolish notion that inflation is a means of postponing payment of some of the current costs of government.

It is especially tempting to try to avoid taxes when the government is spending with abandon for a "national emergency." It is then argued that "since the expensive projects of government are largely for the benefit of later generations," why shouldn't part of the costs be left for them to pay? This notion, as has been said, has become a steady habit in the United States, especially during the past two decades.

The truth is, however, that if the government this year dips into the national punch bowl of goods and services that are produced and available, what it takes out and squanders this year is not there for others this year. The more government takes and squanders this year, the less someone will get back this year compared with what he produces.

Why, if we ignore the minor item of foreign trade balances, is it believed that a nation can postpone this year's cost of government? Probably it is the presence of money that confuses us. If we were to think only of punch and potatoes and things-exchanged by barter-we would not be confused, because we would then realize that we cannot eat potatoes this year which are to be grown next year.

A whole nation of persons can't go on year after year consuming more than it has to consume. It can't do it for one year, or even for one day. It can't do it by allowing inflation, or by any other means. Failure to realize that inflation is a form of tax leads to the false belief that inflation affords a means of postponing some of the costs of government. But it can't be done.

If it were possible for a whole nation to postpone one third of this year's cost of government until next year, why not postpone half of it? All of it? And if it is possible to postpone it until next year, why not postpone it for two years? Ten? Forever? If this were possible, we would not need to wait for Utopia. We could have it now!

Guns and Butter

The error in this line of thinking leads us to false hopes about what the preparation for war will do to our living. We are being told that both guns and butter are possible, and that we can add the cost of a military machine without sacrifice in our civilian welfare.

We find these promises either stated or implied in statements given out by government and by various other "leaders." People are to be protected, they tell us, against suffering any decline in their living. They are to continue to receive incomes about as high as before, after taxes. Wage rates are being increased by about as much as the prospective increase in personal taxes. The price control program is offered as a promise to hold prices down. This amounts to a promise that each dollar of wages will buy as much as before the war program started. A promise of the same take-home pay, with a promise that each dollar will continue to buy as much as before, means a promise of no decline in consumption.

Four minus One Is *Four*

It has been claimed that the economy of the United States was running full blast-"full employment"-prior to going on a wartime basis. Now a part of the national output is to be absorbed into the military machine and its operation. One qualified economist estimates that in 1951 about one fourth of the output will be drained off for that purpose, leaving three-fourths for civilian goods and services.

If one-fourth of our national effort is to be drained from consumer living into military use, then one who believes all these promises about no decline in consumer living must believe that 4 minus 1 is 4. He should have learned the error of this in first grade arithmetic. But apparently he did not-not in a form that prevents his becoming a dupe for all these dishonest promises.

A comprehensive survey shows that about half the people believe we can keep up our previous living standards, without any sacrifice, during this war effort. One person in six expects that living standards will even be increased!

There is much talk about suddenly increasing production to meet this added burden, by more output from no more employed persons. Small increases may be possible, of course, but an increase of such proportions cannot be accomplished merely by somebody ordering it to be done. One who believes that must be obsessed with the authoritarian idea. If it were that easy, why haven't the orders accomplished it long ago? There has never been any shortage of the wish for more things, even in peacetime. If it could be done that way, why is the output per man hour in Russia one-sixth below what it was in the pre-revolution days of 1913, and even below that of 50 years ago? If it could be done that way, why was the output per man-hour in manufacturing in the United States in 1945-46 lower than in 1940?

It is a terrible disservice to these persons to lead them into this trap of expectations. One might as well try to do a person a service by convincing him that if he walked off a cliff he would not fall and hurt himself. Such an illusion might be pleasant before its truth is tested, but it cannot cushion the fall.

Our present situation comes into clearer focus when it is realized that inflation is a form of tax. A part of the cost of government is paid for by what is commonly called taxes, in both direct and hidden forms, levied by the taxing part of government. The remainder of the cost of government is paid for by the inflation tax, which is in reality levied by the appropriations part of government over the protest of the taxing part of government, which has refused to raise all the taxes needed to cover all appropriations. This results in inflation, and prices rise.

There then is said to arise "need" for another big project in government, the "inflation fighters." A big force of lawyers, economists, and policemen is hired. They organize the citizens into community inflation-fighting gangs, to lend an appearance of local respectability to the endeavor. These local organizations also insure that neighbors will be enrolled to serve as policemen over their neighbors, in the front line trenches where the fiercest fighting is most likely to occur.

Why does all this new machinery seem to be necessary? What are they doing? The new branch of government is set up for the purpose of fighting the payment of the inflation tax that has been assessed, by another branch of government-the appropriations division. It would be as logical to have the government set up a big unit in Washington, with citizens' committees and all that, to conduct a tax revolt against the payment of income taxes-to fight the Internal Revenue branch of the Treasury Department.

Economic Quackery

Every illusion floats on a plausibility.

Quack medical doctors attack the most vivid symptom with something that is plausible to the suffering patient. The treatment may be to throw cold water on a fevered patient, or to throw hot water on one with chills. The quack doctor may use two thermometers-one that does not rise above 98.6 degrees which he uses for fever patients, and another that does not fall below that point which he uses for chill patients-to "prove" that his "cure" has been effective.

A quack engineer might try to prevent an explosion by adjusting the pressure gauge downward or closing the safety valve. Or a quack railroad engineer might try to prevent a wreck by adjusting the speed gauge downward instead of reducing the speed.

All these are silly, indeed, but no more silly than their equivalents in the economic field. "Price control to prevent inflation" is also silly. The only reason why the medical plausibility's seem sillier than these economic ones is that medicine is further advanced and more widely understood. The economic mistakes we are now bringing upon ourselves may one day appear to our descendants to be just as foolish as the medical superstitions of old now appear to us.

Freezing the Price Thermometer

When there is inflation, prices rise. It would appear, then, that inflation is caused by rising prices. And this is the weapon of plausibility selected by the price-control part of government to justify its fight against the appropriations part: "The way to fight inflation is simple-just establish price controls, and prohibit prices from rising."

There are two ways, in general, to test the truth of a proposal like this, and to prevent the practice of quackery: (1) judging from experience, and (2) reasoning to the right answer. By both of these tests, price control is shown to be economic quackery.

Lessons from History

There has been a wealth of historical experience with price controls. In fact, a recent archaeological discovery reveals that the oldest known laws in the world were price control laws-3,800 years ago in ancient Babylonia.

One of the best summaries of historical experience with price controls is easily accessible to governmental officials and others. In 1922, Mary G. Lacy, Librarian of the government's Bureau of Agricultural Economics, addressed the Agricultural History Society under the title, *Food Control during Forty-six Centuries.* She pointed out how her search of history over this entire period revealed repeated attempts in many nations to curb by law the inflationary rises of price. She said:

The results have been astonishingly uniform.... The history of government limitation of price seems to teach one clear lesson: That in attempting to ease the burdens of the people in a time of high prices by artificially setting a limit to them, the people are not relieved but only exchange one set of ills for another which is greater. ... The man, or class of men, who controls the supply of essential foods is in possession of supreme power. ... They had to exercise this control in order to hold supreme power, because all the people need food and it is the only commodity of which this is true.

But we need not go so far back into history, and to a foreign land, for evidence. Five short years ago we were experiencing some of the vivid consequences of these controls in the form of the "meat famine." It was not a time shortage of meat at all. The trouble was that controls were preventing its exchange, all along the lines of trade from producer to consumer. This was only one small sample of the consequences of those wartime controls. How short are our memories?

Free Price Is Economic Governor

Some may be tempted to ignore this long history of failure of price controls on grounds that "conditions are now different." Then they evidently do not understand the reasons why price controls must always fail. These reasons are perhaps the best test of whether they are likely to fail of their avowed purpose this time.

It is impossible to consume something that has not been produced, and it is foolish to produce something that is not going to be consumed-to throw it away, or let it rot. It follows, then, that a balance between what is produced and what is consumed is the most desirable condition-if, in fact, it is not economically imperative to have this balance. How is this balance of "supply" and "demand" to be attained?

Under a condition of price freedom, those who produce and those who consume will resolve this problem peace fully. This means... price and quantities differ from one product or service to another and change with passing time. The principles… apply whether the price is controlled directly by government or by any other form of monopoly.

These are the principles of price-free and controlled:

- Reductions in price cause increased in quantities wanted.
- Reductions in price cause decreases in the quantities offered.
- Supply and demand are equal at only one point - the free market price. Higher prices always cause surpluses - lower prices always cause shortages.
- Trading and the economic welfare of both producers and consumers are greatest at the free market price, and are prevented as prices are forced either higher or lower.
- The only instance in which "price fixing" fails to have these consequences is where it is set at the free market level in which event the governmental edict is a sham because that is where the price would be in the absence of this pointless edict. This is the point where people are freely acting in response to the inexorable signals of the market place. Yet, doing business at this price becomes "lawlessness" and "irresponsibility" by edict when price control sets it elsewhere.

Prices that are rigged very high or very low will kill off practically all trading. Attempts to stimulate production, consumption, and trading by forced labor, socializing of property, and subsidies to producers and consumers are all awkward attempts to replace the performance of people in a free market.

Under controls, those near the source of supply get most of it, and those at a distance have to go without. Black markets spring up. Distant consumers try to get some of the supply. Confusion increases and tempers mount. More and more price policemen are hired who, instead of producing useful things, try to quell the confusion and chaos. The bill for their salaries and other costs is sent to the unfortunate victims of the controls…

Will price control stop inflation? All history has shown it to have failed. There is only one point of price where supply and demand are in balance, where both shortage and surplus are avoided, where trade is most peaceful, and where welfare is at a maximum. If this incontestable fact is understood, the belief that we can escape reality by enacting price control laws must be dispelled as an illusion.

From Price Lies To Rationing

Price control really means that laws are passed to make official prices tell lies. One of the penalties for the lying is the creation of shortages that cannot be peacefully resolved.

The shortage, once created, must be dealt with by further powers of government and law. There must be "rationing"-rationing by the government of the shortage it has created by law, rationing of goods and services to individuals because the government failed to limit the output of its money factory.

When the free market is allowed to operate and to set the price at a point where supply and demand will equate, each person will have purchase tickets in the market which correspond to the supply of something he puts into the market. Gifts, of course, are an exception; but in the case of gifts, the rights to draw on the market are still given by the person who supplied the market with something to be bought. These purchase rights are tickets of merit based on production. And the whole thing balances out, as we have said, peacefully.

When the government intervenes with price control laws, this balance is no longer maintained. There are now more tickets for things than there are things to redeem. There are shortages created by law. Then governmental rationing seems to be needed, whereby government officials are empowered to decide who shall get the short supplies. This substitutes political considerations for the merit of production under a free price in a free market.

Laws That Promote Dishonesty

Not only do government-controlled prices lie, but the process also rapidly promotes dishonesty among all groups-merchants, producers, consumers, government employees, everybody. The temptation of bribery of government officials becomes great. Late during World War II, a grocer of extremely high integrity and wide experience told me that it was absolutely impossible for anyone to practice honesty according to the law and still stay in that business under price controls. The reason for this should be clear when we consider the legislated falseness and interference with business operations that become involved.

If this nation is to carry a role of moral leadership in the world, it will have to be founded on the morality of individual persons. And this base is destroyed by such laws.

The shortages that result from price and wage controls are purely a legal creation, created by the price control law and nothing else. *In an otherwise free economy, the "success" of any price control law can be measured by the extent of the shortage it creates, or the decline in production which it causes. And if such controls were complete and effective, they would probably stop all production for trade, which uses money.* This conclusion is inescapable.

Under present conditions of inflation, caused by rampant governmental spending-with laws aimed at the symptoms of inflation rather than dealing with its cause the time is short for making an important choice. Its nature is indicated by what Lenin allegedly said in 1924: "Someday we shall force the United States to spend itself into destruction." And Lord Keynes reports: "Lenin is said to have declared that the best way to destroy the Capitalist System was to debauch the currency. By a continuing process of inflation, governments can confiscate, secretly and unobserved, an important part of the wealth of their citizens." Lenin probably knew that price and other controls-one of the main objectives of the system he favored -would then be imposed.

Unless the price control law is rescinded, its disrupting influence will lead to governmental enslavement of all labor and confiscation of all production facilities-to adopt, in other words, a completely socialist-communist system which we are presumably opposing.

The only escape from the consequences of these laws would seem to be for the citizens to ignore them. This means lawlessness, technically, in the form of black market operations and all the other forms of evasion. This places the honest citizen who favors human liberty in a strange dilemma. He must choose between practicing lawlessness in this technical sense, and supporting a socialist communist regime.

A Sobering Thought

If we add to a moral breakdown of the people the confusion that is created when illusions and wishful thinking bump up against economic laws which cannot be revoked by man-made laws, and add to this the animosity that grows under these conditions and the utter distrust of one another that is aroused, then the prospect is too sobering to be ignored.

A step in the direction of taking away the government's monopoly in the production of money, and restricting government to the judicial aspects of exchange, would be to compel the government to live within its income. This means limiting government expenditures, strictly and absolutely, to taxes that are openly acknowledged to be taxes. It means prohibition of the concealed and deceptive tax of inflation.

If this were to be done, there no longer would be an inflation problem of the type we now have. If this were to be done, there no longer would be any excuse for the enactment of socialist-communist measures-these deceptive processes of legalized price fictions and interference with exchange. If this were to be done, it no longer would be "necessary" to give up our liberty under futile controls aimed at the consequences of inflation rather than at its cause.

Ruthless measures are called for after the citizens have allowed their servant-government-to become their master. But it is better to be ruthless and successful in preventing inflation than to become the victims of both ruthlessness and failure.

– F. A. Harper

ANALYSIS

As is the case throughout this work, Harper's thoughts are certainly applicable in today's world. The largest taxpayer in the United States, the Federal Reserve System, will likely contribute about $70 billion to the Treasury's coffers in calendar year 2012. Additionally, the inflation tax and the lower than market interest rates, both influenced to a large degree by the Federal Reserve and the Department of the Treasury, will likely tax away from American families in 2012 over $3 trillion in what would be real wealth creation.

When one takes a step back and thinks about the tentacles of the government bureaucrats involved in almost every aspect of our lives, one has to be sickened.

How do we get the mammoth ship moving in a direction more inclined toward personal responsibility and individual initiative? Well, this is where it gets tricky. The meshing of monetary and fiscal policy involves various powers that will not easily give in, but one real possibility is for the public to move towards greater acceptance of a private supplier of the money supply.

Instead of the United States requiring all citizens use dollars, banks and other currency issuers would compete for the business of supplying individuals and businesses the means of purchase. It's certainly more complicated than a paragraph's worth of explanation, but it's doable.

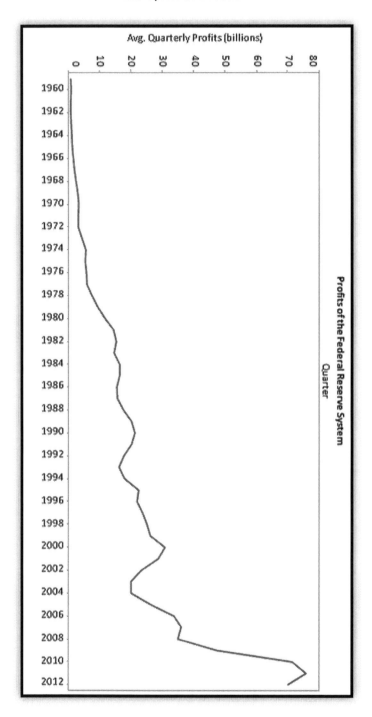

Avg. Quarterly Profits (billions)

Profits of the Federal Reserve System

Quarter

> *"Inflation is when you pay fifteen dollars for the ten-dollar haircut you used to get for five dollars when you had hair."*
>
> ... SAM EWING

ATHLETES, TAXES, INFLATION

Williams Signs with Red Sox for Record Baseball Pay of $125,000

BOSTON, Feb. 7 (AP) - Ted Williams, the Red Sox slugger signed the highest salaried contract in baseball history – for an estimated $125,000.

Babe Ruth's $80,000 salary in 1930 and '31 was tops in the old days. *The New York Times, February* 8, *1950.*

Dollar Salaries

This is a comparison of Ruth's and Williams' dollar salaries.

RUTH (1931) $80,000; WILLIAMS (1950) $125,000

1931 1950

Take-Home Pay

But after federal income taxes, this is a comparison of their take-home pay.

RUTH (1931) $68,535; WILLIAMS (1950) $62,028

What the Take Home Will Buy

Inflation has shrunk the buying power of the dollar since 1931, so Williams' real take-home pay is only a little over half of Ruth's-57 per cent.

If Ted Williams were to have as much buying power in 1950 as Babe Ruth had in 1931, he would have to be paid $327,451.

–W.M Curtiss

"...Inflation had risen to the unimaginable figure of just over 100,000 percent by the end of 1947–and it was to go to 2,870,000 percent by the end of 1948..."

... JUNG CHANG, WILD SWANS: THREE DAUGHTERS OF CHINA

UPDATED 2012:

Babe Ruth, considered by many to be the greatest baseball player of all time, earned $80,000 as a member of the New York Yankees in 1930. At the time this was an incredible sum (he earned more than then-President Hoover), but compared to today's baseball player his salary looks like chump change. Here's how some of baseball's most-beloved players would have stacked up if their salaries were updated to 2010 dollars:

Ted Williams

The left fielder was a 19-time All-Star player with 521 career home runs and a .344 lifetime batting average. He had a total of 2,654 hits and an impressive 1,839 runs batted in (RBIs).

Highest salary: $125,000 (1959)
Adjusted salary (2010): $935,000

Hank Aaron

"Hammerin' Hank" was a 25-time All-Star. He set the MLB record for the most career home runs with 755 and had a .305 lifetime batting average. The outfielder's career RBIs were 2,297.

Highest salary: $250,000 (1976)
Adjusted salary (2010): $960,000

Willie Mays

Considered by many to be the greatest all-around player of any era, Mays was a 24-time All-Star who knocked out 660 home runs. He earned a .302 lifetime batting average, a whopping 3,283 hits, and 1,903 RBIs.

Highest salary: $180,000 (1971)
Adjusted salary (2010): $965,000

Joe DiMaggio

The New York Yankees center fielder was a 13-time All-Star, the only player to play in the All-Star Game in every season he played. His career stats include 361 home runs, a .325 lifetime batting average, 2,214 hits and 1,537 RBIs.

Highest salary: $100,000 (1949)
Adjusted salary (2010): $900,000

Mickey Mantle

Legendary National Baseball Hall of Famer Mickey Mantle was a 20-time All-Star who tallied 536 home runs, a .298 lifetime batting average, 2,415 hits and 1,509 RBIs.

Highest salary: $100,000 (1963)
Adjusted salary (2010): $710,000

Babe Ruth

"The Bambino" hit 714 home runs and finished with a .342 lifetime batting average. Arguably the most famous player to have ever played the game, Ruth totaled 2,873 hits and 2,217 RBIs.

Highest salary: $80,000 (1930)
Adjusted salary (2010): $1,050,000
Adjusted for inflation, Ruth's salary would be a little over $1 million.

By comparison, the top five base-ball salaries in 2010 were held by

Alex Rodriguez ($33 million, or 33 times Ruth's salary),

CC Sabathia ($24.3 million),

Derek Jeter ($22.6 million),

Mark Teixeira ($20.6 million)

And,

Johan Santana ($20.1 million).

ANALYSIS

Curtiss' example of early 20th Century superstar baseball players is applicable to today's typical office worker. Suppose you are just starting your first job out of college and your initial starting salary is $50,000 per year. Because of such things as unemployment insurance, health care costs, and other taxes, your final cost to your employer is probably around $77,000.

Presuming you get a raise of 5% per annum for 30 working years, how much of your lifetime income ends up in bureaucratic hands? Working through averages, the figures comes out to be about $1.3 million. Anyone that hasn't been desensitized to social planners' arguments that this is fairness, must certainly hear the large sucking sound every month when the government takes its share. How did it get this way? Slow, but steady steps towards greater dependence on government programs.

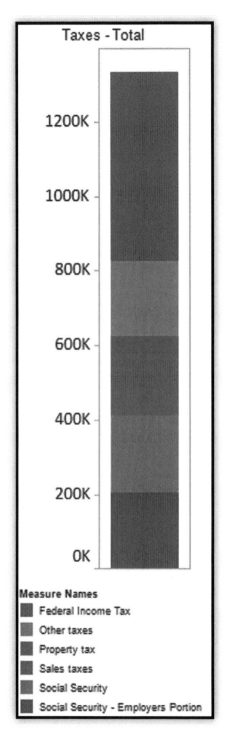

Taxes - Total

1200K

1000K

800K

600K

400K

200K

0K

Measure Names

- Federal Income Tax
- Other taxes
- Property tax
- Sales taxes
- Social Security
- Social Security - Employers Portion

How do we start moving in the freedom direction? An answer to this question largely requires more in-depth discussions on every topic with a future of greater dependence on one's self or the private sector overall. One good starting point is the Spirit of Freedom Foundation (sprt76.org) and the Foundation for Economic Education (FEE.org), each with a plethora of articles addressing real action points for economic success.

> *"The name of American, which belongs to you, in your national capacity, must always exalt the just pride of Patriotism.... It should be the highest ambition of every American to extend his views beyond himself, and to bear in mind that his conduct will not only affect himself, his country, and his immediate posterity; but that its influence may be co-extensive with the world, and stamp political happiness or misery on ages yet unborn."*
>
> ... GEORGE WASHINGTON

ON BEING AN AMERICAN

All the while I have been forgetting the third of my reasons for remaining so faithful a citizen of the Federation, despite all the lascivious inducements from expatriates to follow them beyond the seas, and all the surly suggestions from patriots that I succumb. It is the reason which grows out of my mediaeval but unashamed taste for the bizarre and indelicate, my congenital weakness for comedy of the grosser varieties. The United States, to my eye, is incomparably the greatest show on earth. It is a show which avoids diligently all the kinds of clowning which tire me most quickly — for example, royal ceremonials, the tedious hocus-pocus of haut politique, the taking of politics seriously — and lays chief stress upon the kinds which delight me unceasingly — for example, the ribald combats of demagogues, the exquisitely ingenious operations of master rogues, the pursuit of witches and heretics, the desperate struggles of inferior men to claw their way into Heaven. We have clowns in constant practice among us who are as far above the clowns of any other great state as a Jack Dempsey is above a paralytic — and not a few dozen or score of them, but whole droves and herds. Human enterprises which, in all other Christian countries, are resigned despairingly to an incurable dullness — things that seem devoid of exhilarating amusement, by their very nature — are here lifted to such vast heights of buffoonery that contemplating them strains the midriff almost to breaking. I cite an example: the worship of God. Everywhere else on earth it is carried on in a solemn and dispiriting manner; in England, of course, the bishops are obscene, but the average man seldom gets a fair chance to laugh at them and enjoy them. Now come home. Here we not only have bishops who are enormously more obscene than even the most gifted of the English bishops; we have also a huge force of lesser specialists in ecclesiastical mountebankery — tin-horn Loyolas, Savonarolas and Xaviers of a hundred fantastic rites, each performing untiringly and each full of a grotesque and illimitable whimsicality. Every American town, however small, has one of its own: a holy clerk with so fine a talent for introducing the arts of jazz into the salvation of the damned that his performance takes on all the gaudiness of a four-ring circus, and the bald announcement that he will raid Hell on such and such a night is enough to empty all the town blind-pigs and bordellos and pack his sanctuary to the doors. And to aid him and inspire him there are travelling experts to whom he stands in the relation of a wart to the Matterhorn — stupendous masters of theological imbecility, contrivers of doctrines utterly preposterous, heirs to the Joseph Smith, Mother Eddy and John Alexander Dowie tradition — Bryan, Sunday, and their like. These are the eminences of the American Sacred College. I delight in them. Their proceedings make me a happier American.

Turn, now, to politics. Consider, for example, a campaign for the Presidency. Would it be possible to imagine anything more uproariously idiotic — a deafening, nerve-wracking battle to the death between Tweedledum and Tweedledee, Harlequin and Sganarelle, Gobbo and Dr. Cook — the unspeakable, with fearful snorts, gradually swallowing the inconceivable? I defy anyone to match it elsewhere on this earth. In other lands, at worst, there are at least intelligible issues, coherent ideas, salient personalities. Somebody says something, and somebody replies. But what did Harding say in 1920, and what did Cox reply? Who was Harding, anyhow, and who was Cox? Here, having perfected democracy, we lift the whole combat to symbolism, to transcendentalism, to metaphysics. Here we load a pair of palpably tin cannon with blank cartridges charged with talcum powder, and so let fly. Here one may howl over the show without any uneasy reminder that it is serious, and that someone may be hurt. I hold that this elevation of politics to the plane of undiluted comedy is peculiarly American, that no-where else on this disreputable ball has the art of the sham-battle been developed to such fineness...

... Here politics is purged of all menace, all sinister quality, all genuine significance, and stuffed with such gorgeous humors, such inordinate farce that one comes to the end of a campaign with one's ribs loose, and ready for "King Lear," or a hanging, or a course of medical journals.

But feeling better for the laugh, Ridi si sapis, said Martial. Mirth is necessary to wisdom, to comfort, above all to happiness. Well, here is the land of mirth, as Germany is the land of metaphysics and France is the land of fornication. Here the buffoonery never stops. What could be more delightful than the endless struggle of the Puritan to make the joy of the minority unlawful and impossible? The effort is itself a greater joy to one standing on the side-lines than any or all of the carnal joys it combats. Always, when I contemplate an uplifter at his hopeless business, I recall a scene in an old-time burlesque show, witnessed for hire in my days as a dramatic critic. A chorus girl executed a fall upon the stage, and Rudolph Krausemeyer, the Swiss comedian, rushed to her aid. As he stooped painfully to succor her, Irving Rabinovitz, the Zionist comedian, fetched him a fearful clout across the cofferdam with a slap-stick. So the uplifter, the soul-saver, the Americanizer striving to make the Republic fit for Y.M.C.A. secretaries. He is the eternal American, ever moved by the best of intentions, ever running a la Krausemeyer to the rescue of virtue, and ever getting his pantaloons fanned by the Devil. I am naturally sinful, and such spectacles caress me. If the slap-stick were a sash-weight, the show would be cruel, and I'd probably complain to the Polizei. As it is, I know that the uplifter is not really hurt, but simply shocked. The blow, in fact, does him good, for it helps get him into Heaven, as exegetes prove from Matthew v, 11: Hereux serez-vous, lorsqu'on vous outragera, qu'on vous persecutera, and so on. As for me, it makes me a more contented man, and hence a better citizen. One man prefers the Republic because it pays better wages than Bulgaria.

Another because it has laws to keep him sober and his daughter chaste. Another because the Woolworth Building is higher than the cathedral at Chartres. Another because, living here, he can read the New York Evening Journal. Another because there is a warrant out for him somewhere else. Me, I like it because it amuses me to my taste. I never get tired of the show. It is worth every cent it costs.

That cost, it seems to me is very moderate. Taxes in the United States are not actually high. I figure, for example, that my private share of the expense of maintaining the Hon. Mr. Harding in the White House this year will work out to less than 80 cents. Try to think of better sport for the money: in New York it has been estimated that it costs $8 to get comfortably tight, and $17.50, on an average, to pinch a girl's arm. The United States Senate will cost me perhaps $11 for the year, but against that expense set the subscription price of the Congressional Record, about $15, which, as a journalist, I receive for nothing. For $4 less than nothing I am thus entertained as Solomon never was by his hooch dancers. Col. George Brinton McClellan Harvey costs me but 25 cents a year; I get Nicholas Murray Butler free. Finally, there is young Teddy Roosevelt, the naval expert. Teddy costs me, as I work it out, about 11 cents a year, or less than a cent a month. More, he entertains me doubly for the money, first as a naval expert, and secondly as a walking attentat upon democracy, a devastating proof that there is nothing, after all, in that superstition. We Americans subscribe to the doctrine of human equality — and the Rooseveltii reduce it to an absurdity as brilliantly as the sons of Veit Bach. Where is your equal opportunity now? Here in this Eden of clowns, with the highest rewards of clowning theoretically open to every poor boy — here in the very citadel of democracy we found and cherish a clown dynasty!

– H.L. Mencken (1922)

ANALYSIS: Mencken is a legendary writer whose style is sure to be refreshingly humorous at this point. In any event, we needed a break.

> *"It is amazing that people who think we cannot afford to pay for doctors, hospitals, and medication somehow think that we can afford to pay for doctors, hospitals, medication and a government bureaucracy to administer it."*
>
> ... THOMAS SOWELL

WARDS OF THE GOVERNMENT

THE constitutions of former American slave states generally specified that the masters must provide their slaves with adequate housing, food, medical care and old-age benefits. The Mississippi Constitution contained this additional sentence:

The legislature shall have no power to pass laws for the emancipation of slaves ... [except] where the slave shall have rendered the State some distinguished service;

The highest honor that Mississippi could offer a man for distinguished service to his country was personal responsibility for his own welfare! His reward was freedom to find his own job and to have his own earnings, freedom to be responsible for his own housing, freedom to arrange for his own medical care, freedom to save for his own old age. In short, his reward was the individual opportunities -and the personal responsibilities-that have always distinguished a free man from a dependent.

What higher honor can any government offer?

But many present-day Americans are trying to avoid this personal responsibility that *is* freedom. They are voting for men who promise to install a system of compulsory, government-guaranteed "security" -a partial return to the old slave laws of Georgia that guaranteed to all slaves "the right to food and raiment, to kind attention when sick, to maintenance in old age ...." And the arguments used to defend this present-day trend toward the bondage of a Welfare State are essentially the same arguments that were formerly used to defend the bondage of outright slavery.

For example, many of the slave-holders claimed that they knew what was "best for the slaves." After all, hadn't the masters "rescued" the slaves from a life of savagery? The advocates of government-guaranteed "security" also claim that they know what is best for the people. Many of them argue in this fashion: "After all, haven't the American people conclusively shown that they are in capable of handling the responsibility for their own welfare?"

Many of the slave-holders sincerely believed that the "dumb, ignorant slaves" would starve to death unless their welfare was guaranteed by the masters. And the advocates of compulsory "security" frequently say: "Are you in favor of letting people starve?"

Most Precious of All

But as proof of the fact that personal responsibility for one's own welfare brings increased material well-being, consider the emancipated slaves. Among them, there were old and crippled and sick people. They had no homes, no jobs, and little education. But-most precious of all-the former slaves were responsible for their own welfare. They were *free*. They had the privilege of finding their own security.

Now compare the remarkable progress of those former slaves to the lack of progress of the American Indians who were made wards of the government; who were given state-guaranteed "security" instead of freedom with responsibility. In 1862, most American Negroes were slaves. Today they are about as self-supporting and responsible as other American citizens. Meanwhile the Indians as a group have become less self-supporting and more dependent on government aid. It has been claimed that many thousands of Indians will actually die of starvation unless the government feeds them. If this is true-why?

Caretakers

There seems to be no scientific basis for calling the Indians an innately inferior race. As has been proved by the success of many individual Indians, they have just as much capacity for understanding and advancement as the Negroes and the so-called Nordics. But today there are more than 12,000 federal employees directly "taking care" of the 233,000 reservation Indians who are still classified as wards of the government. The number of government caretakers for the Indians has been steadily increasing over the years. As a result, the reservation Indian is becoming less self-sufficient and more dependent upon what he calls "the Great White Father in Washington."

Instead of freedom, the Indian has government-guaranteed "security." Instead of individual responsibility, he has a government bureau to handle his personal affairs. There are special laws governing his right to own land and to spend tribal money. Under that system of bondage it should surprise no one to find that many thousands of Indians have remained uneducated, hungry, diseased, and mismanaged.

The only *lasting* solution is for the Indians themselves to handle their own affairs on the basis of individual freedom and personal responsibility. If this is not true, then the blessings of freedom would appear to be fanciful myths. But for some queer reason, we Americans seem to believe that just because our pioneer fathers once subjugated the Indians, we in turn are obligated to keep them in the bondage of government "security." As a result, the Indian has the status of a *ward* instead of a citizen. Instead of being a responsible person, he is a dependent.

And in a like manner, if we free Americans continue to turn to government for our security, we too will surely become dependent wards instead of responsible citizens. There will be a Commissioner to control our personal affairs and our individual responsibilities. Instead of calico and blankets, we may be promised a hundred dollars every month. But since the *principle* is the same in both cases, the results will also eventually be the same.

A *Return to Bondage*

The advocates of this compulsory "security" honestly seem to believe that most Americans-including the Indians are too ignorant, or lazy, or worthless to be trusted with their own destiny; that they will literally starve in the streets unless their welfare is guaranteed by a "benevolent" government. However good their intentions may be, these disciples of a Relief State are demanding that they be given the power to *force* mankind to follow their plans. In the name of liberty they advocate bondage!

This is true because the persons who receive support from the state are thereby led to expect-and then to demand-more support from the state. They become dependents. Thus they enter into a form of bondage. They lose their individual freedom of choice to whatever extent the state assumes responsibility for their personal welfare. In time, as is now the case in the Welfare State of Russia, the people become completely subservient to the state. In effect, they become slaves of the "benevolent" government that has promised to solve all of their personal problems for them!

Admittedly, this is not the intent of the planners. Apparently, most of the advocates of government paternalism really believe that they are able to know and to do what is "best" for all of the people. Most of them may honestly desire to help the people. But their efforts *always* result in some form of bondage. For example, the leaders of the Labor government in Britain probably never even dreamed of bringing compulsory labor to its supporters. Yet that is what they did. In England today the democratically elected leaders can-and do-force persons to work where the government decrees they are most needed. And if the person objects to his government's decision, force is used to make him conform.

The Road to Hell

In Russia we find another example of the fact that good intentions are no guarantee of freedom. For instance, in the beginning Lenin and Stalin probably had no desire whatever to bring slavery to Russia. Their announced plan was to free the Russian people *from* the slavery of an all-powerful government. But look what happened!

We Americans of today are following this same path toward the bondage of a Welfare or Slave State. Just as the law once guaranteed "adequate" medical care for American slaves, so a law to guarantee adequate medical care for all Americans is being demanded today. And who will determine what adequate medical care is for a person? Not the person, but the government official who has the *authority*.

And jobs? Of course the government can guarantee every man a job-just as every slave was "guaranteed" a job; just as every Russian is "guaranteed" a job. But it is impossible, of course, for the government to guarantee everyone a job of his own choosing. Some persons must be guaranteed the scavenger jobs. They may not like it, but dependents have little choice.

The Only Hope

It is true that many citizens in this country are old and crippled and sick and homeless. Possibly some of them are jobless through no fault of their own. The same conditions existed during our Revolutionary War. But our ancestors knew that their only hope for permanent security lay in their own individual efforts. They knew that the main purpose of government should be to *protect* whatever security the people were able to attain individually or in voluntary cooperation. They knew that electing or appointing a man to public office cannot endow him with wisdom; it can endow him only with *power.* Thus they took no chances on this power of government being used to encroach upon their individual liberties and their personal responsibilities. In advance, they put positive restrictions on all office-holders. And as a final guarantee of freedom, they specified that any powers not expressly given to the federal officials were to remain with the individual citizens and their local governments.

The Use of Force

The American Constitution naturally did not list virtues such as compassion, charity, and respect for one's fellow man-as functions of government. The statesmen who founded our government knew that *all* virtues are purely personal and voluntary. It is utter nonsense to imagine that a person can be *forced* to be good. Government can and should use force to punish a person who commits a crime. But this same force *cannot* be used to create kindness and compassion within the mind and heart of any person.

Thus the authors of our Constitution left compassion and charity-aid to the unfortunate-on a strictly voluntary basis. They designed a form of government based on individual freedom, personal responsibility, and equality before the law for all citizens. Wisely, they made no attempt whatever to separate freedom of choice from the resulting reward or punishment, success or failure. Since they recognized the absurdity of passing laws to protect a person from himself, they left all citizens free to make their own decisions concerning their own personal welfare. From all viewpoints, including that of material security for the so-called common man, those decisions concerning the proper functions of government proved to be the most effective that the world has ever known in this field.

Bread and Circus

If this state-guaranteed "security" idea were new, it might help explain why so many people insist on trying it. But it is not new. It was written into the Code of Hammurabi over 4,000 years ago. In one form or another, it has been tried time and again throughout history-always with the same result. In the Roman Empire it was called "bread and circus." More recently, Karl Marx called it socialism. He believed that the state should take "from each according to his abilities" and "give to each according to his needs."

Marx said that it was the duty of government to provide all people with adequate housing, medical care, jobs and social security. Word for word, the advocates of government "security" in this country is saying the same thing today.

And just as the Russians are enslaved to a 'Welfare State, so this country is being carried into bondage by accepting the same false principle, just as force is used in Russia to make the people conform to the security laws designed "for their own good," so we also are now forced to submit to American security laws designed "for our own good." And just as the Russian state punishes any objector, so the American state will now imprison us if we refuse to conform.

Enemy of the State

If you doubt that compulsory socialism has gone to that extreme in this country, just test it, for instance, by refusing to pay the social security tax that is taken from your salary. The government will do the same thing to you that it did to the owner of a small battery shop in Pennsylvania who balked at the idea of compulsory social security. First, the state confiscated his property. Still he refused to obey. Then the state preferred *criminal* charges against him. And in January of 1943, the government gave him the choice of conforming or going to prison as a criminal-an enemy of the state because he refused to pay social security! He paid. And his six-month' prison sentence was suspended.

Next may come total government housing-"for our own good," of course. Then the state will assign us so many square feet of "adequate" living space. This is true because, under complete state ownership of housing, there is no other way that government can do it. We may ask for more space, a different location, better service, or a choice of neighbors. But we already know the government's answer. Even today, a person has no real choice when he lives in government housing.

Next may come full employment with government guaranteed jobs for everyone. A person will say: "I don't want this job." And as happened under England's program of government-guaranteed full employment, the American Welfare State will also answer: "We will put you in jail unless you work at your assigned task."

Along about then, the advocates of government-guaranteed "security" may begin to understand the inevitable results of their ideas. They may realize that it is *power* that makes a dictator, and not what he's called or how he's elected. When that fact has become obvious to everyone, the advocates of compulsory "security" will then exclaim: "But we didn't mean this" It will be too late to turn back at that point. Just as the night follows the day, so government aid *to* the individual is followed by government control *of* the individual, which necessarily means government force *against* the individual.

No Easy Way

Fortunately, it is not yet too late for America to turn away from the evil that is a Welfare State; a Slave State. But, unfortunately, there is no simple or easy way to do it. Both major political parties-along with the smaller ones -seem to be trying to outbid each other by promising more government housing, more social security, more "free" medical care, more government "welfare" projects, and more special privileges to various groups and interests.

Most of our movies, magazines, newspapers and radio programs generally endorse-directly or indirectly-the idea of some form of government-guaranteed "security." Even the few objections seem to be aimed mostly at poor administration instead of recognition that the theory is wrong in principle.

And, whether we like it or not, many of the instructors in our schools and colleges are teaching the desirability of the Relief State, the "planned economy" and government ownership in general.

Golden Rule Rejected

Finally, even some of our church leaders are teaching that the force of government should be used to make people charitable and good. Some of these Christian leaders seem to have forgotten that the principles of the Good Samaritan and each individual doing unto others as he would have others do unto him are voluntary principles. In many cases, these principles have now been discarded for this evil slogan: "It is the duty of government to care for the sick, to feed the hungry, to aid the unfortunate, and to build houses for those who need them." Probably one of the main reasons for the declining influence of the church is that the church is defaulting on many of its own responsibilities by turning them over to government. Many of our church leaders are rendering unto Caesar that which does not belong to Caesar.

But the politicians, periodicals, schools and churches generally reflect the opinions of the persons who support them. Thus the final decision rests on the attitude of each individual American. If enough of us accept the degrading idea of a Welfare State-a Relief State, a Slave State-the process will soon be completed. But if enough individual Americans desire a return to the personal responsibility that *is* freedom, we can have that too.

The Choice Is Ours

Before choosing, however, consider this: When one chooses freedom-that is, personal responsibility-he should understand that his decision will not meet with popular approval. It is almost certain that he will be called vile names when he tries to explain that compulsory government "security" -jobs, medicine, housing, and all the rest-is bad in principle and in its total effect; it saps character and strength by encouraging greed and weakness; it destroys the individual's God-given responsibility for self-help, respect, compassion and charity; in some degree, it automatically turns all who accept it into wards of the government; it will eventually turn a proud and responsible people into cringing dependence upon the whims of an all-powerful state; it is the primrose path to serfdom.

No, the choice is not an easy one. But then, the choice of freedom never has been easy. It never will be easy. Since this capacity for personal responsibility-freedom is God's most precious gift to mankind, it requires the highest form of understanding and courage.

– *Dean Russell*

> *"Almost any sect, cult, or religion will legislate its creed into law if it acquires the political power to do so."*
>
> … ROBERT A. HEINLEIN

POWER CORRUPTS

WHEN a person gains power over other persons-the political power to force other persons to do his bidding when they do not believe it right to do so-it seems inevitable that a moral weakness develops in the person who exercises that power. It may take time for this weakness to become visible. In fact, its full extent is frequently left to the historians to record, but we eventually learn of it. It was Lord Acton, the British historian, who said: "All power tends to corrupt; absolute power corrupts absolutely."

Please do not misunderstand me. These persons who are corrupted by the process of ruling over their fellow men are not innately evil. They begin as honest men. Their motives for wanting to direct the actions of others may be purely patriotic and altruistic. Indeed, they may wish only "to do good for the people." But, apparently, the only way they can think of to do this "good" is to impose more restrictive laws.

Now, obviously, there is no point in passing a law which requires people to do something they would do anyhow; or which prevents them from doing what they are not going to do anyhow. Therefore, the possessor of the political power could very well decide to leave every person free to do as he pleases so long as he does not infringe upon the same right of every other person to do as he pleases. However, that concept appears to be utterly without reason to a person who wants to exercise political power over his fellow man, for he asks himself: "How can I 'do good' for the people if I just leave them alone?" Besides, he does not want to pass into history as a "do nothing" leader who ends up as a footnote somewhere. So he begins to pass laws that will force all other persons to conform to *his* ideas of what is good for *them*.

A Strain on Morality

That is the danger point! The more restrictions and compulsions he imposes on other persons, the greater the strain on his own morality. As his appetite for using force against people increases, he tends increasingly to surround himself with advisers who also seem to derive a peculiar pleasure from forcing others to obey their decrees. He appoints friends and supporters to easy jobs of questionable necessity. If there are not enough jobs to go around, he creates new ones. In some instances, jobs are sold to the highest bidder. The hard-earned money of those over whom he rules is loaned for questionable private endeavors or spent on grandiose public projects at home and abroad. If there is opposition, an emergency is declared or created to justify these actions.

If the benevolent ruler stays in power long enough, he eventually concludes that power and wisdom is the same thing. And as he possesses power, he must also possess wisdom. He becomes converted to the seductive thesis that election to public office endows the official with both power and wisdom. At this point, he begins to lose his ability to distinguish between what is morally right and what is politically expedient.

– Ben Moreell

> *Freedom is never more than one generation away from extinction. We didn't pass it to our children in the bloodstream. It must be fought for, protected, and handed on for them to do the same.*
>
> ... RONALD REAGAN

SURVIVAL OF THE SPECIES

When Charles Darwin's book, *On the Origin of Species,* appeared in 1859 it was strongly condemned by those who believed that his theory of evolution contradicted the thesis that man is a creature of God. But now it is generally accepted that the theory of evolution is not a contradiction of God's designs for mankind.

Today I want to discuss with you not the *origin* of species, but the *survival* of species; and I want to discuss this subject in terms of faith in my fellow man, which stems from a faith in God. I might have chosen a shorter title-a single word-liberty. For I believe that the key to the survival of civilization is human liberty. When our liberty is gone-whether because some aggressor takes it from us by force, or because we ourselves willingly vote it away-civilized man will die. Men will become robots, machines without minds, controlled and driven by godless masters.

God and Freedom

I believe that God intended men to be free to make their own decisions and to be responsible for the consequences of those decisions. Thus it seems to me that it is an act against God for men to pass laws which destroy individual liberty; which deprive persons of the responsibility for their own acts or for their own welfare. Such laws are advocated by persons who lack faith in God and in their fellow men!

It seems to me that there is convincing evidence to support my beliefs on this subject. And the basic evidence is found in the fact that no person is physically or mentally or morally identical to any other person. For example, everyone knows that the fingerprints of all persons are different. And these differences-these individualities, these inequalities-carry through all the physical, mental, and moral characteristics of mankind. It seems to me that if we have faith in God, we must realize that He had a purpose in designing us so that no person is like any other person; that is to say, so that each person is an individual. Let us examine this God-given individuality of men and speculate upon its relationship to liberty and responsibility and survival.

The Right to Choose

It must be obvious that liberty necessarily means freedom to choose foolishly as well as wisely; freedom to choose evil as well as good; freedom to enjoy the rewards of good judgment, and freedom to suffer the penalties of bad judgment. If this is not true, the word "freedom" has no meaning. Yet there are persons in America who wish to pass laws to force people to do only "good," or at least their concept of what is good. These would-be dictators are not content with a preventive law which punishes a person who deliberately chooses to injure his neighbor; a law which prevents any person from forcing his viewpoint upon any other person; a law which penalizes the person who interferes with the liberty of others. On the contrary, these persons who arrogate to themselves the functions of God demand a *positive* law to compel others to do as they wish them to do. And-for some reason which I cannot understand-these same people use the words "liberty" and "democracy" to justify their plans to deprive other men of freedom.

These proposed laws are frequently justified on the ground that there are physical and mental inequalities in the world; that those inequalities result in economic in equalities; and that the primary function of government is to pass laws that will tend to equalize such inequalities. Is not this concept of government a rather brazen indictment of God? Is not this an acceptance of the communistic theory of using force to take "from each according to his abilities" and to give "to each according to his needs"? It is true that no two persons are equal, and that some persons receive more pay for their services than do other persons. But my faith in God makes me insist that there is a logical and good reason for this fact. And I believe that this is the reason:

This inequality among persons is a law of nature, a law which is just as unchangeable and just as necessary to understand as is any other natural law, as, for example, the law of gravity. This particular law is known as the "law of variation," and from the unrestricted operation of this law of nature comes all human progress. The law of variation permits children to be different from their parents. It permits brothers to think differently and to act differently. It permits the existence of both misers and philanthropists; saints and sinners; rich and poor. It permits inventors to invent, managers to manage-and purchasing agents to purchase. It permits each person to seek a job or profession which is most suited to his inherent talents and his desires. It encourages a voluntary division of labor, with resulting maximum efficiency and greater prosperity for all. Without this variation-this-unequalness-our social structure would be similar to that of an anthill or a bee hive, where each member is born to do a certain predetermined job which he does with blind allegiance to his society and with no consideration of personal interests or preferences.

Unfortunately there are many persons in the world who hate variations and inequalities, who admire the type of society developed by the ants and bees. These people see that variation among human beings has allowed one person to produce more than another, with resulting differences in material possessions and comforts. And then these self-appointed supervisors of human destiny, who cannot tolerate variation, begin to agitate for a law to take away from the high producer and give to the low producer. They want to use the force of government to repeal the law of variation; to redesign mankind; to force their concepts of morality and economics on all other persons; in short-to play God.

Masterminds at Work

And in this process they deny to every person the right to dispose of the products of his own labor as *he* chooses. On the contrary, it must be as *they,* the "masterminds," decree! These so-called do-gooders and benevolent legislators deny this right of choice to the producer because they fear that other people will spend their earnings in a pattern different from that which they would plan for them. They have no faith in the voluntary decisions of free persons!

For example, the person who earns the money might want to endow a college or a hospital or a summer camp for poor children; but the planner wants to take the money away from him and use it to subsidize "cheap" electricity for the people who live in Tennessee or in the Pacific Northwest. The person with a good income might want to spend some of his money for a trip around the world, but the planner calls this "social inequality," and he pro poses a law whereby the government may take the individual's money, by force, and use it for some so-called socially-useful purpose like encouraging the growth of surplus potatoes, for which there is no market, in order that they may be destroyed. Or the planner may propose to deprive the producer of his money and apply it to some alleged "social good" like government ownership of housing, or a government steel plant, or govern-ment-controlled education, or some similar project which gives to govern-ment the power to tell the people what they must or must not do; how they must or must not live.

Enemies of Liberty

I am willing to concede that the do-gooder may have the best intentions in the world. But it cannot be denied that the laws he proposes always involve more government, more government ownership and operation of the means of production, more government interferences in the distribution of what individuals have produced, more power for government and less freedom of choice for individuals. I hold that the people who advocate these positive laws against freedom of choice are-knowingly or unknowingly-the enemies of freedom and progress. They themselves have lost all faith in liberty and in the ability of free persons to care for themselves and voluntarily to extend a helping hand to their neighbors in need. Thus they band together to advocate laws antagonistic to humanity; laws which restrain liberty, thwart variation, belie inequalities, and defy God's design!

Against the background of my many years of service in the Navy, I make this declaration: I do not fear the Russian Army, or the atom bomb, or the hydrogen bomb, nearly so much as I fear this concept of using the law to relieve individuals of the responsibility for their own welfare and to deprive them of their freedom of choice. We can all see the danger of a military threat to our freedom. If we are attacked we will fight, and we will win! But few of us appear to understand this insidious process whereby we use our own laws and our own government to destroy our own liberties just as surely as if some foreign conqueror had power over us.

Here is an example of how we are deceiving ourselves: Let us suppose that some foreign power could confiscate the incomes of persons in America; and let us suppose, further, that this foreign power were to confiscate 89% of the income of our most efficient producer. Would this producer continue to produce abundantly under such circumstances, or would he not soon relax and begin producing only enough to subsist himself and those dependent upon him? This situation is easy enough to understand when we visualize the confiscator as a foreigner. But we do not seem to understand it when the confiscator is a combination of fellow citizens. For we ourselves have voted to confiscate 89% of the income of our best producers!

The Way to Communism

When will this confiscation of an individual's income rise to 100%? Do you believe that ambitious men who are hungry for power would stop short of this complete communism if, by going on, they could achieve their aims? Let us consider this question: Just how much liberty does a person *really* have when more than half of his earnings are taken from him without his consent and are spent for purposes distasteful to him?

Not satisfied with taking this high percentage of a person's income, we Americans have also voted to confiscate 38% of the earnings of our most successful industries even before the owners of the income get it. And our representatives in Congress are now considering the possibility of raising the take to 41%. Even in conquered Germany and Japan, we would not dare to take 38% of the industrial earnings, because we know that the results would be disastrous. And yet, in the face of this knowledge, we are seriously considering taking 41% of the earnings of all successful American industries. Unless we change the present course of our thinking in America, the next step will be 50%-and then more!

The End of the Road

It makes one wonder whether we are deliberately trying to destroy ourselves. All along this course our liberties begin to slip away from us. In the beginning this happens slowly and almost unnoticed. The "emergency" and "temporary" restrictions and compulsions by government are not generally recognized as lost liberties. But the end result of this procedure-a procedure that always comes neatly wrapped in the American Hag and labeled "social justice"-is complete government control, complete loss of liberty, and the extinction of civilized man as we know him. Why should this confiscation-a percentage of our production that even a conqueror would not dare to take be called liberty? Why should the word "freedom" be used to describe these government compulsions and restrictions? Certainly the founders of this republic had no such concept of freedom.

Now I know that those who disagree with me will say that this is a democracy and that we can vote for anything we please; that, in fact, we can vote to turn all industry and all income over to the government, if we so desire.

That is true; but consider this: It is also true that we could vote to re-establish slavery in America. "Would that make slavery "right" or "democratic"? We could democratically vote to have a state religion and to force everyone to conform to the majority decision; but that would make a mockery of democracy and the right to vote. We could democratically vote to print enough money to give every person a million dollars; but would such exercise of the franchise help anyone except those who wish to destroy America?

Inalienable Rights

All these measures-and others of a similar nature-could be enacted legally and democratically under the concept of majority rule. But would any person be so foolish as to say that they *should* be enacted? Will any thinking person say that a law is "right" merely because a majority has voted for it?

We must always remember that our Constitution was designed to protect the freedom of the smallest possible minority-one person-against the demands of the greatest possible majority-all other persons combined.

That single idea of inalienable rights of the individual person is-or, at least, was-the fundamental spirit of the American tradition of government. And if we lose that concept of government, by force or by our own votes, the American dream of liberty will be ended.

I am very glad that we have a form of government that requires voting, because so long as this condition exists, there is nothing to prevent us from voting against these immoral laws that are leading the American people into bondage to their own government. It is still possible to turn back; and it is not yet too late to turn back. If we really want to face the responsibility, to pay the price, of a return to freedom, we 'can still have it.

How to Destroy Progress

Let us speculate on the price which we must pay for liberty. First and foremost, all so-called welfare schemes must go; for dependence upon government will destroy progress and production in two ways: First, the high producers will not continue to do their best if most of the product of their labor is taken from them. Second, the low producers will not be eager to work harder if they know that government will guarantee to them the security of housing, food, medical care, old age benefits, and the other necessities of life. If we continue along this path to the misnamed welfare state, we must soon find ourselves in the position of our reservation Indians, who have had a system of government-guaranteed "security" for the past hundred years.

The inevitable result of such "security" -to the Indians or to any other people who try it-is dramatically told in a report from a young minister, R. J. Rushdoony, who is now a missionary to the Indians on one of our American reservations:

One of the surest consequences of a government of "welfare" and "security" is the rapid decline and death of responsibility and character.

Whatever the pre-reservation Indian was, and his faults were real, he was able to take care of himself and had a character becoming to his culture and religion. He was a responsible person. Today he is far from that. The wretched security he has had, beginning with the food and clothing dole of early years, designed to enforce the reservation system and destroy Indian resistance, has sapped him of character. The average Indian knows that he can gamble and drink away his earnings and still be sure that his house and land will remain his own, and, with his hunting rights, he can always eke out some kind of existence.

Government men too often hamper and impede the man with initiative and character. This is because their program inevitably must be formulated in terms of the lowest common denominator, the weakest Indian. In addition, the provisions of the government for the "welfare" and "security" of the Indians remove the consequences from their sinning and irresponsibility. The result is a license to irresponsibility, which all the touted government projects cannot counteract.

And I believe the results would be no better for the best hundred or thousand persons selected from any society, after a generation or so of the same kind of "welfare" and "security" government....

Slavery in America

Let us look at another example from our own history. Here is a statement from a recently-published article called *Wards of the Government* by Dean Russell:

The constitutions of former American slave states generally specified that the masters must provide their slaves with adequate housing, food, medical care, and old-age benefits. The Mississippi Constitution contained this additional sentence: "The legislature shall have no power to pass laws for the emancipation of slaves ... [except] where the slave shall have rendered the State some distinguished service;"

The highest honor that Mississippi could offer a man for distinguished service to his country was personal responsibility for his own welfare! His reward was freedom to find his own job and to have his own earnings, freedom to be responsible for his own medical care, freedom to save for his own old age. In short, his reward was the individual opportunities -and the personal responsibilities-that have always distinguished a free man from a dependent.

What higher honor can any government offer?

But many present-day Americans are trying to avoid this personal responsibility that is freedom. They are voting for men who promise to install a system of compulsory, government-guaranteed "security"-a partial return to the old slave laws of Georgia that guaranteed to all slaves "the right to food and raiment, to kind attention when sick, to maintenance in old age...." And the arguments used to defend this present-day trend toward the bondage of a Welfare State are essentially the same arguments that were formerly used to defend the bondage of outright slavery.

For example, many of the slave-holders claimed that they knew what was 'best for the slaves." After all, hadn't the masters "rescued" the slaves from a life of savagery? The advocates of government-guaranteed "security" also claim that they know what is best for the people. Many of them argue in this fashion: "After all, haven't the American people conclusively shown that they are incapable of handling the responsibility for their own welfare?"

Many of the slave-holders sincerely believed that the "dumb, ignorant slaves" would starve to death unless their welfare was guaranteed by the masters. And the advocates of compulsory "security" frequently say: "Are you in favor of letting people starve?"

But as proof of the fact that personal responsibility for one's own welfare brings increased material well-being, consider the emancipated slaves. Among them were old and crippled and sick people. They had no homes, no jobs, and little education. But-most precious of all-the former slaves were responsible for their own welfare. They were free. They had the privilege of finding their own security.

Now compare the remarkable progress of those former slaves to the lack of progress of the American Indians who were made wards of the government; who were given state-guaranteed "security" instead of freedom with responsibility. In 1862, most American Negroes were slaves. Today they are about as self supporting and responsible as other American citizens. Mean while the Indians as a group have become less self-supporting and more dependent on government aid. It has been claimed that many thousands of Indians will actually die of starvation unless the government feeds them. If this is true, why is it so?

How to Destroy a Person

To those two reports on the results of government-guaranteed "security" I desire to add this thought: If I should want to destroy you, I would try to relieve you of the responsibility for your own welfare and to make you dependent upon me for food, clothing, housing, medical care, and the other necessities of life. After a few years of such dependence you would be helpless, subject to my every command-in effect, a slave.

But in spite of the two cases I have noted above, and many similar ones which can be cited from the long record of history, there are well-intentioned but misinformed persons who still insist that unless government supports its citizens they will be ill-clothed, ill-housed, and ill-fed. This belief is often expressed by the question: "Would you let them starve?"

Freedom Rejected

Do the people who utter such nonsense understand the meaning of their proposals? In effect they are saying that a free person in a free society cannot support himself; that a free American cannot or will not support his own family; that free Americans will permit their less fortunate neighbors to starve; that our American doctors will not aid a sick person who has no money; that persons with freedom of choice will choose to let homeless people sleep in the streets; that a free people will reject their responsibilities to their fellow men; and that we have renounced Christ's commandments on love and charity.

I refuse to concede that we Americans have sunk so low. If we have, then liberty is dead, and we are taking part in its interment. If we cannot and will not accept the responsibilities of liberty and a voluntary society of free men, then indeed is civilized man at the end of his rope. If I had any thought that this is the case, I would not be speaking to you today. For I believe that we Americans want liberty, and that we are willing and able to pay the price for it.

This price which we must pay is the abolition of *all* special laws for *all* special groups and interests. Subsidies to businessmen as well as to farmers must stop. Special privileges and preferences for able-bodied veterans must be ended. There must be an end to special laws which exempt labor groups from the consequences of their actions. The special tax privileges for producer and consumer cooperatives must be repealed, or extended to all corporate business. The law which gives tenants special treatment at the expense of home owners must be abolished. Whatever the sacrifice, our government must live within its income; and the amount of that income which is taken from the people must be drastically reduced. We must abolish all privileges and ask of government the only equality which can possibly exist-equality before the law. In short, we must demand that government confine itself to the primary functions of protecting the life, liberty, and property of the individual-all individuals. Then each person will be free to do as he pleases so long as he does not interfere with the right of any other person to do as *he* pleases. Then each person will enjoy as much equality and security as it is possible for him to have in a world of admitted inequality and insecurity.

Liberty the Key to Survival

I am aware that this price for liberty may seem high to some people. I know that those groups and persons who now enjoy those special privileges will do all in their power to keep them-and to extend them. Even so, I have faith that the vast majority of the American people want liberty and am willing to accept the personal responsibility which liberty requires. I believe that the only requirement for the return to liberty is an understanding of what it is. I believe that we will understand it and that we will then return to it. I have this faith in my fellow Americans because I believe they will know that upon liberty and *upon liberty alone depends* the survival of the species!

    – Ben Moreell

'If you control the oil you control the country; if you control food, you control the population."

… HENRY KISSINGER DECLARATION IN THE 1970's

FOOD CONTROL DURING FORTY-SIX CENTURIES

… A Contribution to the History of Price Fixing

THE man, or class of men, who controls the supply of essential foods is in possession of the supreme power. The safe guarding of the food supply has therefore been the concern of governments since they have been in existence. They had to exercise this control in order to hold the supreme power, because all the people need food and it is the only commodity of which this is true.

In connection with this control it would seem that every possible expedient and experiment had been tried. One of the most frequent methods of control used has been the limitation of prices by legal enactment. The results have been astonishingly uniform considering the variety of conditions and circumstances under which the experiments have taken place. They make an interesting record and one which contains food for thought. ...

****

The history of government limitation of price seems to teach one clear lesson: That in attempting to ease the burdens of the people in a time of high prices by artificially setting a limit to them, the people are not relieved but only exchange one set of ills for another which is greater.

Among these ills are:

1. The withholding of goods from the market, because consumers being in the majority price fixing are usually in their interest;
2. The dividing of the community into two hostile camps, one only of which considers that the government acts in its interest;
3. The practical difficulties of enforcing such limitation in prices which in the very nature of the case requires the cooperation of both producer and consumer to make it effective. — *Mary G. Lacy*

> *"Socialism never took root in America because the poor see themselves not as an exploited proletariat but as temporarily embarrassed millionaires."*
>
> ... JOHN STEINBECK

ON THAT DAY BEGAN LIES

> *"From the day when the first members of councils placed exterior authority higher than interior, that is to say, recognized the decisions of men united in councils as more important and more sacred than reason and conscience; on that day began lies that caused the loss of millions of human beings and which continue their unhappy work to the present day."*
>
> ... LEO TOLSTOY*

THIS is a striking statement. Is it possible that there is something of a wholly destructive nature which has its source in councilmanic, or in group, or in committee-type action? Can this sort of thing generate lies that actually cause the loss of "millions of human beings"?

Any reasonable clue to the unhappy state of our affairs merits investigation. Two world wars that settled nothing except adding to the difficulties of avoiding even worse ones; men lacking in good character rising to positions of power over millions of other men; freedom to produce, to trade, to travel, disappearing from the earth; everywhere the fretful talk of security as insecurity daily becomes more evident; suggested solutions to problems made of the stuff that gave rise to the problems; the tragic spectacle, even here in America, of anyone of many union leaders being able, at will, to control a strategic part of the complex exchange machinery on which the livelihood of all depends; these and other perplexities of import combine to raise a tumultuous "why," and to hasten the search for answers.

The Search for Answers

Strange how wide and varied the search, as though we intuitively knew the cause to lie in some elusive, hidden, unnoticed error; tens of thousands of not too well tutored folks trying to find light in Toynbee's difficult and erudite *A Study of History,* other thousands desperately groping through the pages of Du Nouy's *Human Destiny,* and *The Big Fisherman* by Lloyd Douglas maintaining week after week its best-seller position.

Yes, the search is on for the errors and their answers. These are definitely not being sought from the comics, from advertisements, or from over-simplified screeds prepared for the "Mortimer Snerd" trade. The affair is serious. The stake is life itself. And the error or errors, it is agreed at least by the serious-minded, may well be found deep in the thoughts and behaviors of men, even of well-intentioned men. Anyway, everything and everyone is suspect. And, why not? When there is known to be a culprit and the culprit is not known, what other scientifically sound procedure is there?

"... on that day began lies ...." That is something to think about. Obviously, if everything said or written were lies, then truth or right principles would be unknown. Subtract all knowledge of right principles and there would not be even chaos among men. Quite likely there would be no men at all.

If half of everything said or written were lies....

Human life is dependent not only on the knowledge of right principles but dependent, also, on actions in accordance with right principles. Admittedly there are wrong principles and right principles. However, the nearest that any person can get to right principles-truth-is that which his highest personal judgment dictates as right. Beyond that one cannot go or achieve. *Truth, then, as nearly as any individual can express it, is in strict accordance with this inner, personal dictate of rightness.*

The accurate representation of this inner, personal dictate is intellectual integrity. It is the expressing, living, acting of such truth as any given person is in possession of. Inaccurate representation of what one believes to be right is untruth. It is a lie.

Attaining knowledge of right principles is an infinite process. It is a development to be pursued but never completed. Intellectual integrity, the accurate reflection of highest personal judgment, on the other hand, is within the reach of all. Thus, the best we can do with ourselves is to represent ourselves at our best. To do otherwise is to tell a lie. To tell lies is to destroy such truth as is known. To deny truth is to destroy ourselves.

It would seem to follow, then, that if we could isolate anyone or numerous origins of lies we might put the spotlight on the genesis of our troublous times. This is why it seems appropriate to accept Tolstoy's statement as a hypothesis and examine into the idea that lies begin with "decisions of men united in councils as more important and more sacred than reason and conscience." For, certainly, today, much of the decision that guides national and world policy springs from "men united in councils."

In what manner then do "the decisions of men united in councils" tend to initiate lies? Experience with these arrangements suggests that there are several ways.

The Spirit of the Mob

The first has to do with a strange and what in most instances must be an unconscious behavior of men in association. Consider the mob. It is a loose-type association. The mob will tar and feather, burn at the stake, string up by the neck, and otherwise murder. But dissect this association, pull it apart, investigate its individual components. Each person, very often, is a God-fearing, home-loving, wouldn't-kill-a-fly type of individual.

What happens, then? What makes persons in a mob behave as they do? What accounts for the distinction between these persons acting as responsible individuals and acting in association?

Perhaps it is this: These persons, when in mob association, and maybe at the instigation of a demented leader, remove the self-disciplines which guide them in individual action; thus the evil that is in each person is released, for there is some evil in all of us. In this situation, no one of the mobsters consciously assumes the *personal* guilt for what is thought to be a collective act but, instead, puts the onus of it on an abstraction which, without persons, is what the mob is.

There may be the appearance of unfairness in relating mob association to association in general. In all but one respect, yes. But in one respect there is a striking similarity.

Persons advocate proposals in association that they would in no circumstance practice in individual action.* Honest men, by any of the common standards of honesty, will, in a board or a committee, sponsor, for instance, legal thievery-that is, they will urge the use of the political means to exact the fruits of the labor of others for the purpose of benefiting themselves, their group, or their community.

These leaders, for they have been elected or appointed to a board or a committee, do not think of themselves as having sponsored legal thievery. They think of the board, the committee, the council or the association as having taken the action. The onus of the act, to their way of thinking, is put on an abstraction which is what a board or an association is without persons.

Imagine this: Joe Doakes passed away and floated up to the Pearly Gates. He pounded on the Gates and St. Peter appeared.

"Who are you, may I ask?"

*It is acknowledged that most of us acting in association do not consciously regard any of our acts as bad. Yet, the fact remains that we persist in doing things in this circumstance that we would not do on our own responsibility. Actually, involved is a double standard of morality. Morality is exclusively a personal quality. Any action not good enough to be regarded as attached to one's person is, *ipso facto,* bad.

"My name is Joe Doakes, sir,"

"Where are you from?"

"I am from Updale, U.S.A."

"Why are you here?"

"I plead admittance, Mr. St. Peter."

St. Peter scanned his scroll and said, "Yes, Joe, you are on my list. Sorry I can't let you in. You stole money from others, including widows and orphans."

"Mr. St. Peter, I had the reputation of being an honest man. What do you mean; I stole money from widows and orphans?"

"Joe, you were a member, a financial supporter and once on the Board of Directors of The Up dale Do-Good Association. It advocated a municipal golf course in Updale which took money from widows and orphans in order to benefit you and a hundred other golfers."

"Mr. St. Peter, that was The Up dale Do-Good Association that took that action, not your humble applicant, Joe Doakes."

St. Peter scanned his scroll again, slowly raised his head, and said somewhat sadly, "Joe, The Updale Do-Good Association is not on my list, nor any foundation, nor any chamber of commerce, nor any trade association, nor any labor union, nor any P.T.A. All I have listed here are persons, *just persons.*"

It ought to be obvious that we as individuals stand responsible for our actions regardless of any wishes to the contrary, or irrespective of the devices we try to arrange to avoid personal responsibility. Actions of the group character heretofore referred to are lies for in no sense are they accurate responses to the highest judgments of the individuals concerned.

The Spirit of the Committee

The second way that lies are initiated by "the decisions of men united in councils" inheres in commonly accepted committee practices. For example: A committee of three has been assigned the task of preparing a report on what should be done about rent control. The first member is devoted to the welfare-state idea and believes that rents should forever be controlled by governmental fiat. The second member is a devotee of the voluntary society, free market economy and a government of strictly limited powers and, therefore, believes that rent control should be abolished forthwith. The third member believes rent controls to be bad but thinks that the decontrol should be effected gradually, over a period of years.

This not uncommon situation is composed of men honestly holding three irreconcilable beliefs. Yet, a report is expected and under the customary committee theory and practice is usually forthcoming. What to do? Why not hit upon something that is not too disagreeable to anyone of the three? For instance, why not bring in a report recommending that landlords be permitted by government to increase rents in an amount not to exceed 15%? Agreed?

In this hypothetical but common instance the recommendation is a fabrication, pure and simple. Truth, as understood by anyone of the three, has no spokesman. By any reasonable definition a lie has been told.

The Lowest Common Denominator

Another example: Three men having no preconceived ideas are appointed to bring in a report. What will they agree to? Only that which they are willing to say in concert which, logically, can be only the lowest common denominator opinion of the majority! The lowest common denominator opinion of two persons cannot be an accurate reflection of the highest judgment of each of the two. The lowest common-denominator opinion of a set of men is at variance with truth as here defined. Again, it is a fabrication. Truth has no spokesman. A lie has been told.

These examples (numberless variations could be cited) suggest only the nature of the lie in embryo. It is interesting to see what becomes of it.

Not all bodies called committees are true committees, a phase of the discussion that will be dealt with later. However, the true committee, the arrangement which calls for resolution in accordance with what a majority of the members are willing to say in concert, is but the instigator of fabrications yet more pronounced. The committee, for the most part, presupposes another larger body to which its recommendations are made.

These larger bodies have a vast, almost an all-inclusive, range in present-day American life. The neighborhood development associations; the small town and big city chambers of commerce; the regional and national trade associations; the P.T.A.'s; labor unions organized vertically to encompass crafts and horizontally to embrace industries; farmers' granges and co-ops; medical and other kinds professional societies; ward, precinct, county, state and national organizations of political parties; governmental councils from the local police department board to the Congress of the United States; the United Nations; thousands and tens of thousands of them, every citizen embraced by several of them and millions of citizens embraced by scores of them; most of them "resoluting" as groups, deciding as "men united in councils."

These associational arrangements divide quite naturally into two broad classes, (1) those that are of the voluntary type, the kind to which we pay dues if we want to, and (2) those that are a part of government, the kind to which we pay taxes whether we want to or not.

For the purposes of this critique, emphasis will be placed on the voluntary type. In many respects criticisms applying to the former are valid when applied to the latter*; nonetheless, there are distinctions between the way one should relate oneself to a voluntary association and the way one, for the sake of self-protection, is almost compelled to relate himself to a coercive agency.

*The common political idea that a member of Congress, for instance, must "compromise," that is, must on some issues vote contrary to his convictions in order to effect a greater good on some subsequent issue, or to keep himself in office that he may insure The public good, leaves shattered and destroyed any moral basis of action. If each member of Congress were to act in strict accordance with his inner dictate of what is right, the final outcome of Congressional action would, of course, be a composite of differing convictions. But the alternative of this is a composite of inaccurate reflections of rightness.

Now, it is not true, nor is it here pretended, that every associational resolution originates in distortions of personal conceptions of what is right. But anyone of the millions of citizens who participates in these associations has, by experience, learned how extensive these fabrications are. As a matter of fact, there has developed a rather large acceptance of the notion that wisdom can be derived from the averaging of opinions, providing there are enough of them. The quantitative theory of wisdom, so to speak!

A Lie Compounded

If one will concede that the aforementioned committee characteristics and council behaviors are perversions of truth, it becomes interesting to observe the manner of their extension-to observe how the lie is compounded.

Analyzed, it is something like this: An association takes a stand on a certain issue and claims or implies it speaks for its 1,000,000 members. It is possible, of course, that each of the 1,000,000 members agrees with the stand taken by the organization. But, in all probability, this is an untruthful statement, for the following possible reasons:

(1) If every member was actually polled on the issue, and the majority vote was accepted as the organization's position, there is no certainty that more than 500,001 persons agreed with the position stated as that of the 1,000,000.

(2) If not all members were polled, or not all were at the meeting where the voting took place, there is only the certainty that a majority of those voting favored the position of the organization-still claimed to be the belief of 1,000,000 persons. If the quorum should be 100, there is no certainty that more than 51 persons agreed with that position.

(3) It is still more likely that the opinion of the members was not tested at all. The officers, or some committee, or some one person may have determined the stand of the organization. Then there is no certainty that more than one person (or a majority of the committee) favored that position.

(4) And, finally, if that person should be dishonest-that is, untrue to that which he personally believed to be right, either by reason of ulterior motives, or by reason of anticipating what the others will like or approve-then, it is pretty certain that the resolution did not even originate in honest opinion.

An example will assist in making the point. The economist of a national association and a friend were breakfasting one morning, just after V-J Day. Wage and price controls were still in effect. The conversation went something as follows:

"I have just written a report on wage, and price controls which I think you will like." "Why do you say you *think* I will like it? Why don't you say you *know* I will like it?"

"Well, I-er-hedged a little on rent controls."

"You don't believe in rent controls. Why did you hedge?"

"Because the report is as strong as I think our Board of Directors will adopt."

"As the economist, isn't it your business to state that which you believe to be right? If the Board Members want to take a wrong action, let them do so and bear the responsibility for it."

Paying For Misrepresentation

Actually, what happened? The Board did adopt that report. It was represented to the Congress as the considered opinion of the constituency of that association. Many of the members believed in the immediate abolishment of rent control. Yet, they were reported as believing otherwise-and paying dues to be thus misrepresented.

By supporting this procedure with their membership and their money they were as responsible as though they had gone before the Congress and told the lie themselves.

To remove the twofold dishonesty from such a situation, the spokesman for that association would have to say something like this to the Congress:

"This report was adopted by our Board of Directors, 35 of the 100 being present. The vote was 18 to 12 in favor of the report, 5 not voting. The report itself was prepared by our economist, *but it is not an accurate reflection of his views.*" *

*It is evident that any such report as this is worthless. Yet, a more pretentious report would be a lie, a thing of positive harm. If a procedure can result only in worthlessness or harm, the procedure itself should be in question.

Such honesty or exactness is more the exception than the rule as everyone who has had experience in associational work can attest. What really happens is a misrepresentation of concurrence, a program of lying about how many of who stands for what. Truth, such as is known, is seldom spoken. It is warped into a misleading distortion. It is obliterated by this process of the majority speaking for the minority, more often by the minority speaking for the majority, sometimes by one dishonest opportunist speaking for thousands. Truth, such as is known-the best judgments of individuals-for the most part, goes unrepresented, unspoken.

This, then, is the stuff out of which much of local, national and world policy is being woven. Is it any wonder that many citizens are confused?

Three questions are in order, and deserve suggested answers:

1. What is the reason for having all these troubles with truth?
2. What should we do about these associational difficulties?
3. Is there a proper place for associational activity as relating to important issues? "And now remains that we find out the cause of this effect; Or, rather say, the cause of this defect, for this effect, defective, comes by cause."

Pointing out causes is a hazardous venture for, as one ancient sage put it, "Even from the beginnings of the world descends a chain of causes." Thus, for the purpose of this critique, it would be folly to attempt more than casual reference to some of our own recent experiences.

First, there doesn't appear to be any widespread, lively recognition of the fact that conscience, reason, knowledge, integrity, fidelity, understanding, judgment and other virtues are the distinctive and exclusive properties of individual persons.

Somehow, there follows from this lack of recognition the notion that wisdom can be derived by pooling the conclusions of a sufficient number of persons, even though no one of them has applied his faculties to the problems in question. With this as a notion the imagination begins to ascribe personal characteristics to a collective-the committee, the group, the association-as though the collective could think, judge, know, or assume responsibility. With this as a notion, there is the inclination to substitute the "decisions of men united in councils" for reason and conscience. With this as a notion, the responsibility for personal thought is relieved and, thus relieved, fails to materialize to its fullest.

A Blind Faith

Second, there is an almost blind faith in the efficacy and rightness of majority decision as though the mere preponderance of opinion were the device for determining what is right. This thinking is consistent with and a part of the "might makes right" doctrine. This thinking, no doubt, is an outgrowth of the American political pattern, lacking, it seems, an observance of the essential distinctions between voluntary and coercive agencies. It is necessary that these distinctions be understood unless the whole associational error is to continue. The following is, at least, a suggested explanation:

Government-organized police force-which according to best American theory should have a monopoly of coercive power, must contain a final authority. Such authority was not planned to be in the person of a monarch, in an oligarchy or even in a set of elected representatives. The ultimate, final authority was designed to derive from and to reside with the people. Erected as safeguards against the despotism that such a democratic arrangement is almost certain to inflict on its members were (1) the Constitution and (2) the legislative, executive and judicial functions so divided and diffused that each might serve as a check on the others. When the concession is made that government is necessary to assure justice and maximum freedom, and when the decision is made that the ultimate authority of that government shall rest with the people, it follows that majority vote is not a matter of choice *but a necessity* whenever this ultimate authority expresses itself. No alternative exists with this situation as a premise. To change from majority vote as a manner of expression would involve changing the premise, changing to a situation in which the ultimate authority rests in one person.

For reasons stated and implied throughout this critique the majority-decision system is considered to be most inexpert. However, it proves to be a virtue rather than a fault as applied to the exceedingly dangerous coercive power, *providing the coercive power is limited to its sphere of policing.* This inexpertness in such a circumstance tends to keep the coercive power from becoming too aggressive.

Conceding the limitation of the coercive power, which was implicit in the American design, the really important matters of life, all of the creative aspects, are outside this coercive sphere and are left to the attentions of men in voluntary effort and free association.

The idea of citizens left free to their home life, their business life, their religious life, with the coercive power limited to protecting citizens in these pursuits presents, roughly, the duality of the American pattern. On the one hand is the really important part of life, the creative part. On the other hand is the minor part, the part having to do with constraint. Constraining and creating call for distinctly different arrangements. Constraint can stop the trains but it is not the force we use to build a railroad.

Out of this pattern has developed a high appreciation for our form of government, particularly as we have compared it with the coercive agencies of the Old World. Here is the point: The majority-decision system, an effect rather than a cause of our form of government, has been erroneously credited as responsible for the superiority of our form of government. It has been thought of as its distinctive characteristic. Therefore, the majority-decision system is regarded as the essence of rightness. Without raising questions as to the distinctions between creating and constraining we have taken a coercive-agency device and attempted its application in free association. Something is not quite right. Perhaps this is one of the causes.

Loss of Reason

Third, we have in this country carried the division-of-labor practice to such a high point and with such good effect in standard-of-living benefits that we seem to have forgotten that the practice has any limitations. Many of us, in respect to our voluntary associational activities, have tried to delegate moral and personal responsibilities to mere abstractions, which is what associations are, without persons. In view of (1) this being an impossibility, (2) our persistent attempts to do it, nonetheless, and (3) the consequent loss of reason and conscience when personal responsibility is not personally assumed, we have succeeded in manufacturing little more than massive quantities of collective declarations and resolutions. These, lacking in both wit and reason, have the power to inflict damage but are generally useless in conferring understanding. So much for causes.

"What should we do about these associational difficulties?" This writer, to be consistent with his own convictions, finds it necessary to drop into first person, singular, to answer this question.

In brief, I do not know what our attitude should be, but only what mine is. *It is to have no part in any association whatever which takes actions implicating me for whom I am not ready and willing to accept personal responsibility.*

Put it this way: If I am opposed, for instance, to spoliation-legal plunder-I am not going to risk being reported in its favor. This is a matter having to do with morals, and moral responsibility is strictly a personal affair. In this, and like areas, I prefer to speak for myself. I do not wish to carry the division-of-labor idea, the delegation of authority, to this untenable extreme.

This determination of mine refers only to voluntary associations and does not include reference to membership in or support of a political party. The latter has to do with my relationship to coercive agencies and these, as I have suggested, are birds of another feather.

One friend who shares these general criticisms objects to the course I have determined on. He objects on the ground that he must remain in associations which persist in misrepresenting him in order to effect his own influence in bettering them. If one accepts this view, how can one keep from "holing up" with any evil to be found, anywhere? If lending one's support to an agency which lies about one's convictions is as evil as lying oneself, and if to stop such evil in others one has to indulge in evil, it seems evident that evil will soon become unanimous. The alternative? Stop doing evil. This at least has the virtue of lessening the evildoers by one.

The question, "Is there a proper place for associational activity as relating to important issues?" is certainly appropriate if the aforementioned criticisms be considered valid.

First, the bulk of activities conducted by many associations are as businesslike, as economical, as appropriate to the division-of-labor process, as is the organization of specialists to bake bread or to make automobiles. It is not this vast number of useful service activities that is in question.

The phase of activities here in dispute has to do with a technic, a method by which reason and conscience such truths as are possessed-are not only robbed of incentive for improvement but are actually turned into fabrications, and then represented as the convictions of persons who hold no such convictions.

It was noted above that not all bodies called committees are true com-mittees-a true committee being an arrangement by which a number of persons bring forth a report consistent with what the majority is willing to state in concert. The true committee is part and parcel of the majority-decision system.

Intellectual Leveling-up

The alternative arrangement, on occasion referred to as a committee, may include the same set of men. The distinction is that the responsibility and the authority for a study are vested not in the collective, the group, but in one person, preferably the one most skilled in the subject at issue. The others serve as consultants. The one person exercises his own judgment as to the suggestions to be incorporated or omitted. The report is his and is presented as his, with such acknowledgments of assistance and concurrence as the facts warrant. In short, the responsibility for the study and the authority to conduct it are reposed where responsibility and authority are capable of being exercised-in a person. This arrangement takes full advantage of the skills and specialism's of all parties concerned. The tendency here is toward an intellectual leveling-up, whereas with the true committee the lowest common denominator opinion results.

On occasion, associations are formed for a particular purpose and sup-ported by those who are like-minded as to that purpose. As long as the associational activities are limited to the stated purpose and as long as the members remain like-minded, the danger of misrepresentation is removed.

It is the multi-purposed association, the one that potentially may take a "position" on a variety of subjects, particularly subjects relating to the rights or the property of others-moral questions-where misrepresentation is not only possible but almost certain.

The remedy here, if a remedy can be put into effect, is for the associa-tion to quit taking "positions" except on such rare occasions as unanimous concurrence is manifest, or except as the exact and precise degree and extent of concurrence is represented.

The alternative step to most associational "positions" is for the members to employ the division-of-labor theory by pooling their resources to supply services to the members-as individuals. Provide headquarters and meeting rooms where they may assemble in free association, exchange ideas, take advantage of the availability and knowledge of others, know of each other's experiences. In addition to this, statisticians, research experts, libraries and a general secretariat and other aids to effective work can be provided. Then, let the individuals speak or write or act as individual persons! Indeed, this is the real, high purpose of voluntary associations.

The practical as well as the ethical advantages of this suggested procedure may not at first be apparent to everyone. Imagine, if you can, Patrick Henry as having said:

I move that this convention go on record as insisting that we prefer death to slavery.

Now, suppose that the convention had adopted that motion. What would have been its force? Certainly almost nothing as compared with Patrick Henry's ringing words:

I know not what course others may take; but as for me, give me liberty or give me death!

No one in this instance concerned himself with what Patrick Henry was trying to do to him or to someone else. One thought only of what Patrick Henry had decided for himself and weighed, more favorably, the merits of emulation. No convention, no association, no "decisions of men united in councils" could have said such a thing in the first place, and second, anything the members might have said in concert could not have equaled this. Third, had the convention been represented in any such sentiments it is likely that misrepresentation would have been involved.

One needs to reflect but a moment on the words of wisdom which have come down to us throughout all history, the words and works that have had the power to live. The words and works around which we have molded much of our lives, and one will recognize that they are the words and works of persons, not collective resolutions, not what men have uttered in concert, not the "decisions of men united in councils."

A Waste of Time

In short, if effectiveness for what's right is the object then the decision-of-men-united-in-council practice could well be abandoned, if for nothing else, on the basis of its impracticality. It is a waste of time in the creative areas, that is, for the advancement of truth. It is a useful and appropriate device only as it relates to the coercive that is to the restrictive, suppressive, destructive functions.

The reasons for the impracticality of this device in the creative areas seem clear. Each of us when seeking perfection, whether of the spirit, of the intellect, or of the body, looks not to our inferiors but to our betters, not to those who self-appoint themselves as our betters, but to those who, in our own humble judgment, are our betters. Experience has shown that such perfection as there is exists in individuals, not in the lowest common-denominator expressions of a collection of individuals. Perfection emerges with the clear expression of personal faiths the truth as it is known, not with the confusing announcement of verbal amalgams-lies.

"... on that day began lies that caused the loss of millions of human beings and which continue their unhappy work to the present day." The evidence, if fully assembled and correctly presented, would, no doubt, convincingly affirm this observation.

How to stop lies? It is simply a matter of personal determination and a resolve to act and speak in strict accordance with one's inner, personal dictate of what is right. And for each of us to see to it that no other man or set of men is given permission to represent us otherwise.

If such truth as we are in possession of were in no manner inhibited, then life on this earth would be at its highest possible best, short of further enlightenment.

– Leonard E. Read

The Law of Love and the Law of Violence (Rudolph Field, N.Y.) p.26

> *"One of the saddest lessons of history is this: If we've been bamboozled long enough, we tend to reject any evidence of the bamboozle. We're no longer interested in finding out the truth. The bamboozle has captured us. It's simply too painful to acknowledge, even to ourselves, that we've been taken. Once you give a charlatan power over you, you almost never get it back."*
>
> … CARL SAGAN, THE DEMON-HAUNTED WORLD: SCIENCE AS A CANDLE IN THE DARK

TAMPERING WITH FREEDOM

I have heard, but never tried to find out for myself, that if one were to place a frog into a pot of water and slowly heat the water, the unwary frog will eventually boil to death when, at any time, it could have saved itself by jumping out of the heating water. Rather than find out for myself, I think I will just save us the trouble of finding a cooperative frog and ask you to take my word for it. Why needlessly kill a frog when the point of bringing it up will be apparent in the short time it will take you to read these few pages?

We comfort ourselves thinking humans are superior animals only to find the fate of the frog happening to people throughout recorded history.

A free people must never take their freedom or their surroundings for granted! Things change! Outside influences will take advantage of us when we let down our guard.

We need only to look at Afghanistan and Iraq for the most recent examples of maniacal activists who took freedom away from their people.

Abuse of basic human freedoms has gone on since people 'grouped up' at the expense of those who didn't ... or wouldn't. THIS merits our attention.

According to James Madison, our fourth President:

"There are more instances of the abridgment of freedom of the people by the gradual and silent encroachment of those in power, than by violent and sudden usurpation."

Today, some of our greatest perils lie within our own borders ... amongst our own citizens as well as the so-called 'foreigners.' America must not continue to be complacent. Truer now than ever before is the phrase, "The price of freedom is *eternal vigilance*". After some research to credit the original author, the earliest version seems to be:

"It is the common fate of the indolent to see their rights become a prey to the active. The condition upon which God hath given liberty to man is eternal vigilance; which condition if he break, servitude is at once the consequence of his crime and the punishment of his guilt."
— John Philpot Curran*

*Speech upon the Right of Election, 1790 (Speeches. Dublin, 1808)

That quote is worthy of several readings to let it sink in.

Consider this from Benjamin Franklin:

"A nation of well informed men who have been taught to know and prize the rights which God has given them cannot be enslaved. It is in the region of ignorance that tyranny begins."

Today, our beloved Constitution is under attack by activists as out-of-date and no longer responsive to the needs of the people. The activists attack the Ten Amendments seeking to gut it on several fronts. Think about it. Some people want to abolish or alter the constitutional protection of the rights of individuals ... the very rights that protect each American from governmental abuse of power.

The recent 2000 presidential election exposed a danger to our country. It confirmed what many take for granted - the apparent 'security' of our American way of life. In the 2000 presidential election, our Constitution worked exactly as our brilliant Founding Fathers intended. Realizing that politics is an integral part of every society, they designed and integrated a system of government that included the judiciary. Republicans and Democrats bemoaned the apparent politically motivated decisions of the Florida Supreme Court and the United States Supreme Court. So what! The system worked its way through to a logical and constitutional political result. The system was designed that way over 200 years ago and should survive the attempts of those who would change it for selfish political ends.

Whenever citizens ignore the work of the designers of our society, bureaucrats, politicians and political activists will try to tamper with the magnificent work of our Founding Fathers and ... *they will screw it up!* Per Mr. Curran, our rights *are* more than ever, becoming prey to the active.

Consider this knee jerk reaction from a recent national election: Then First Lady Hillary Clinton, the defeated Senator Gore and others advocated elimination of the 'outmoded' Electoral College and replacing it with a national popular vote.

Common sense prevailed when the Founding Fathers created the Electoral College to avoid what happened a hundred or so years earlier in Poland - a civil war. Yes, what amounted to a civil war resulted from a close popular vote in a national election. Could violence have happened in the USA in 2000? We were ever so close, but for the foreseen danger envisioned over 225 years ago.

Mobs of angry people in Florida in both political camps exchanged heated conversations and the situation had the potential to result in violent confrontation. The electoral votes were a state issue because of the electoral process designed over two hundred years ago. Responsible leaders pleaded to let the system take its course to an acceptable result. It did! Yet, the short sighted say the Electoral College didn't work — was it because they drew the short straw this time?

Decentralizing the risk and limiting potential violence to one or two states may have saved the country. Understanding the pros and cons about the Electoral College is another example of the wisdom of knowing both sides of an issue.

The Seventeenth Amendment is another example of not leaving well enough alone. In 1913, the Seventeenth Amendment was ratified. It changed selection of US Senators to a direct, popular vote of the citizens within the state. This opened the doors of the United States Senate to corrupt politicians.

Previously, the Constitution had provided for the various states to *appoint* Senators. The reasoning was that responsible leaders had already been elected by the citizens and were best suited to select the most qualified. Respected prominent citizens and career politicians were selected by *their elected peers* to become America's future statesmen.

The legacy of the tampering of 1913: In recent history we had a Senator from New Jersey who was so wealthy he poured 65 MILLION dollars into a campaign for a job paying what amounts to pocket change...for him. (Update inserted: That senator became a governor then made it to private industry, M.F. Global, and now about a billion dollars of invest or money is missing. Makes one wonder where the 65 million came from?)

A newly rich stock market dot.com millionaire 'bought' a senate seat from the State of Washington only to praise Osama Bin Laden for building schools and roads for the people of Afghanistan....hmmm...do terrorists need roads to move troops and schools to brainwash their countrymen?

We now have a disgraced former Governor of Illinois sitting in prison for attempting to sell a seat in the U.S. Senate. Wouldn't it have been better to do as the Founding Fathers specified by letting the State Legislature appointing a worthy and respected politician, businessperson or someone of stature in the community rather than auctioning the seat off to the highest bidder?

Sadly, the once highly respected US Senate is becoming the exclusive club of choice for the rich and famous. How do the rich and famous manage to win without prior notable public service? They buy advertising, public relations and marketing experts. They do it by going directly to the generally uninformed masses with massive advertising especially television. Candidates are 'sold' to voters with clever slogans – yes sold, like soap, cereal and fast food. The Founding Fathers couldn't have envisioned *that* in a day when a good public service reputation counted.

Tampering with the shortest (4,400 words) and longest surviving Constitution in the world can come to no good. By 'dumbing down' our 'statesmen' America is at risk.. Practical political experience and prior public service is vital and on the job training is dangerous. Voters should consider the depth of a candidate's qualifications and choose not based on the depth of the bankroll. In every instance, one should try to understand the source of the 'bankroll' and why the money is available. Truth is: There is always a payoff — one's instinct should be trusted! As Ronald Reagan said, "Trust, but verify."

Politicians talk about campaign finance reform. Do you believe for a moment that they will ever look to the 17th Amendment as part of or most of the problem?

Today, people are discouraged and disappointed in their government. I find them to be angry. Many have thrown their hands up in despair. Some have sworn off politics, voting and government for good - *to their own peril*. That plays into the hands of the activists by giving *them* your forfeited vote. We *must become involved* as strong and informed individual citizens … and never concede *our* rights!

If you managed to read to this point, we are still on the "same page". This is where I must convince you of the importance of the mission I formally committed to on January 15, 2001 regarding income taxation. Initially, I felt a need to alert people, but now I prefer to make available information on both sides about the wisdom of the 16th Amendment which authorized the income tax. This by the same democrat led Congress who started the income tax mess in 1909 and was, allegedly, ratified by the states.

Each citizen needs to consider the impact of the income tax system. Personally, I believe the most dangerous internal threat, apart from terrorism, to the personal security of all American citizens is the income tax. I also believe it robs us of personal freedoms, the right to complete invasion of privacy by government by its inquisitional nature and I believe it destroys more families than drinking and illegal drugs. The income tax is a form of government slavery.

Hey, we are a 'free country' – right? Yes, we have been taught that but consider this question: What is government? This description by George Washington, our first President pretty much defines the danger of government:

"Government is not reason it is not eloquence it is force! Like fire, it is a dangerous servant, and a fearful master."

Now you say, Rod, government domination and enslavement of its citizens. C'mon now - isn't that a bit scary... a real stretch? Well, in 1891, Leo Tolstoy, the author of War and Peace said,

"The essence of all slavery consists in taking the produce of another's labor by force. It is immaterial whether this force is founded on ownership of the slave or ownership of the money that he must get to live on."

See? It doesn't matter if you own the slave or control the slave's money – *it is still slavery*. When a government confiscates the product of your labor, *by force*, you are enslaved in direct proportion to the percentage taken. Long term, overall taxation has never gone down, only up. Is there an end in sight? What is the true price paid? What is the true price paid now and in the future?

The IRS fights an ongoing battle with 25 million American families and sends out 100 million notices every year claiming taxpayers have filed incorrect forms and that more money is owed. Notices are sent because the IRS knows its fear machine can be used to intimidate those not able to afford high priced legal and accounting services.

Every year the IRS outright lies to citizens 60% to 90% of the time according to IRS consultants. They wrongfully impose additional taxes, penalties and interest, garnish paychecks, and seize homes and businesses, subject citizens to demeaning audits, demand unreasonable, productivity killing paperwork and worst of all, their high pressure tactics results in the destruction of jobs and families.

Small businesses have IRS paperwork costs of $4 for every $1 dollar paid in taxes. This, plus the loss of productivity is a terrible economic burden. Why does that make sense? How much greater would personal and business productivity be without all that hassle? Wouldn't it make sense to eliminate the $4 in paperwork, send that amount (four times the revenue that government gets now) to the Treasury Department and keep the extra dollar for yourself? Would **YOU** be better off with a different tax system? The government would.

Today, the IRS is running on the same set of tracks that gave the world the KGB, the Gestapo and other government run police state organizations. In my personal opinion, the efforts of some 100,000 IRS employees should use their collective and considerable skills against enemies of the United States – not against the American people.

The IRS is armed with a huge database of information on nearly every man, woman and child in America. They can 'get to' any one, at any place and at any time. With ever increasing power, can any reasonable person think the IRS will ever be truly "kinder and gentler?"

Thomas Jefferson wrote,

"The natural progress of things is for liberty to yield and government to gain ground. This is so because those who gain positions of power tend always to extend the bounds of it. Power must always be constrained or limited else it will increase to the level that it will be despotic."

The only way to avert year after year domestic economic terrorism is to derail the IRS fear machine. To do that, we need to repeal the Sixteenth Amendment (1913) (income tax) **and/or** eliminate the income tax *irrevocably*. There is a better way. Americans deserve a better system.

Government needs money to preserve, protect and defend its citizens. It must *promote* the general welfare of its citizens – not *supply* it. America simply needs a fairer, less intrusive and less costly tax system. Computing technology is better used for collecting taxes than aiding and abetting in collecting the hearts, souls and assets of America's working citizens. Armed with a staff of 40,000 employees, I believe 535 Members of Congress are up to the task of doing the right thing and replacing the income tax whilst moving the zealous IRS fear machine to homeland security missions and, even then, Congress must insure that abuses by the combined agencies are tightly monitored.

American's must unite to take the fear out of government. Americans must not tolerate the fearsome income tax. Before any new tax system is put in place, the 16th Amendment should be repealed, lest we unwittingly permit Congress to add a new layer of taxation. To accomplish this difficult goal, two-thirds of the House and Senate and three-quarters of the states must vote to repeal. In the alternative, a replacement tax system should be implemented with a proviso that an income tax may not be re-instituted without repeal of any replacement tax system.

Repealing an Amendment to the Constitution is difficult, but it *has* been done. Prohibition went in 1919 and came back out in 1933. America would no longer tolerate Prohibition and its related problems. Now, I believe American citizens face a more dangerous problem and must demand to be heard again. The impossible just takes a little longer.

It is often said that if we don't pay attention to the lessons of history, history will repeat itself. Obviously, our Founding Fathers knew their history. Once again:

"Government is not reason it is not eloquence it is force! Like fire, it is a dangerous servant, and a fearful master." - George Washington

Try never to forget that quotation! Washington and his compatriots knew *their* history of the world; since the colonies had little of their own, save for a new world status and subservience to the British Empire.

In 1776, Thomas Jefferson wrote these words into the Declaration of Independence

"... Whenever any form of government becomes destructive...it is the right of the people to alter or abolish it..."

Jefferson also wrote:

"No free man shall ever be debarred the use of arms. The strongest reason for people to retain their right to keep and bear arms is as a last resort to protect themselves against tyranny in government."

That last statement is a bit off the subject and the N.R.A. seems to have that battle in hand. I just mention it here as another example of how those without a sense of history can trivialize the wisdom of our Founding Fathers. Those misguided souls call for all kinds of 'gun control' laws which unwittingly sets the stage for total government domination and enslavement of citizens.

In the context of weaponry and government, consider these words from Joseph Stalin:

"Ideas are more powerful than guns. We would not let our enemies have guns, why should we let them have ideas."

As one ponders the 'gun issue', more 'advice' from Stalin is worth mentioning:

"It is enough that the people know there was an election. The people who cast the votes decide nothing. The people who count the votes decide everything."

Again, this reflects the thinking of the power-seekers among us. What could occur should we place our entire trust in bureaucrats and politicians WITHOUT a last ditch resource to protect our lives and liberty? Care to guess?

We must never forget there are those who seek power and control over our lives. Our founders gave us the right to vote and therein lay our protection ... but we must be wise in how we vote.

Responsible voting to me means voting with a view toward the common good of the individual. Too many people are group-driven meaning they vote according to the agenda of an organization such as a union, political party and so on. This, to me, is a threat to liberty. When voting, one should ask, "Is this vote a vote for my personal interests at the expense of others?"

I like what George Bernard Shaw said,

"A government which robs Peter to pay Paul can always depend on the support of Paul."

After all, the Paul's *do* have their ***rights***. Then, so do those who are the most productive members of our society and don't wish to be slaves to Paul.

Am I wrong? Can anyone, Republican or Democrat argue this point? Well, I am willing to bet that some pseudo-intellectual type will take issue with Shaw's common sense and come up with a goofy theory about how Shaw's comment is outmoded thinking.

Some people are educated beyond the level of their intelligence. Don't let their perverted ideas about things that impact your liberties take precedence over the wisdom of the founders of our great nation.

The best 'security' one can have in life is the security one builds for himself or herself. Many people seek security, but security demands definition. For those who say security is their priority, I usually advise them to rob a bank. They will get caught and they will go to jail for a long time. What better security is there than food, clothing, shelter and the assurance that it cannot be taken away any time soon?

As always, be careful what you wish for, you may just get it!

– Rod Miller 2002 with a few 2012 updates inserted.

May be reprinted with the following attachment: ©The Spirit of Freedom Foundation

> "The essence of all slavery consists in taking the produce of another's labor by force. It is immaterial whether this force is founded on ownership of the slave or ownership of the money that he must get to live on."
>
> … LEO TOLSTOY

GOVERNMENT AS SLAVE OWNER

The Declaration of Independence proclaimed that "all men … are endowed by their Creator with certain inalienable rights." This assertion captured the idealism and the principles of this nation's Founding Fathers.

Unfortunately, the notion of the citizen's inviolable right to liberty is vanishing from the American political landscape. Attorney General Janet Reno, in a 1995 speech vindicating federal actions at Waco, informed a group of federal law enforcement officers: "You are part of a government that has given its people more freedom … than any other government in the history of the world."

Contemporary politicians and political scientists have greatly improved on Thomas Jefferson. Progressive thinking about government is exemplified in a new book titled The Cost of Rights: Why Liberty Depends on Taxation (Norton, 1999), by Princeton University professor Stephen Holmes and University of Chicago law professor Cass Sunstein.

Holmes and Sunstein perform dazzling intellectual gymnastics that leave common sense in the dust. They begin by asserting that "the individual rights of Americans, including the right to private property, are generally funded by taxes, not by fees. This all-important funding formula signals that, under American law, individual rights are public not private goods." Thus, it is completely up to the current government what rights-if any-today's citizens will have.

The American Revolution was fought in large part because colonists believed the British government was violating their preexisting rights. However, Holmes and Sunstein reveal that "rights are rooted in the most shifting of all political soils, that of the annual budgetary process, a process thick with ad hoc political compromises." All rights are mysteriously created somewhere in the congressional appropriation process-somewhere between the first draft of a legislative bill on an intern's laptop and the notes a lobbyist slips to a congressman while wheeling and dealing on the final version.

Holmes and Sunstein spare no effort to stomp out any notion of inviolable rights. They say, "It is more realistic and more productive to define rights as ... selective investments of scarce collective resources, made to achieve common aims and to resolve what are generally perceived to be urgent common problems." The authors also define rights as "welfare-enhancing investments, extracted by society for society's purposes" and assert that "all legal rights are, or aspire to be, welfare rights."

Thus when the Founding Fathers proclaimed in the Bill of Rights that "Congress shall make no law ... abridging the freedom of speech, or of the press" it was no different from contemporary congressmen's voting for food stamps.

Freedom through Intervention

Holmes and Sunstein work overtime to attribute every freedom to government intervention, asserting that "Religious liberty is certainly no more costless than other legal rights. American citizens are more or less free to worship or not, as they wish, but their freedom in this respect makes a claim upon the public, even when it is not subsidized out of public budgets (through, for example, police and fire protection of churches and other religious institutions)." If a single drop of government money could conceivably be involved in some activity, the entire activity becomes the equivalent of a government handout. And regardless of how much in taxes a person pays, if he receives any benefit at all from any government activity, he becomes the moral equivalent of a public-housing resident who never worked a day in his life.

In perhaps the book's most creative passage, Holmes and Sunstein reveal that "Our freedom from government interference is no less budget-dependent than our entitlement to public assistance. Both freedoms must be interpreted. Both are implemented by public officials who, drawing on the public purse, have a good deal of discretion in construing and protecting them." The fact that you can see the words on this page clearly is only because some police supervisor deterred a traffic cop from whacking you in the head with his billy club this morning. The Bill of Rights was created as a bulwark to defend citizens against government. Yet because government lawyers must occasionally interpret its clauses (usually to subvert plain meaning), any citizen not boar hogged by government officials miraculously becomes a government dependent.

Holmes and Sunstein reveal that "rights depend in practice on the going rate of taxation." Thus the higher the tax rates, the more rights people have. Unless citizens live under the heel of the tax collector, they cannot hope to have any freedom. The Internal Revenue Service is never mentioned in the book. Instead, taxation is portrayed practically as an abstraction, as something that just happens and automatically fills up government coffers with rights fodder.

"A tax deduction is a form of public subsidy," write Holmes and Sunstein. But to believe this is to assume that politicians are entitled to 100 percent of everyone's income. If politicians set the tax rate at 99 percent, and allow people a tax deduction for food and clothing, then everyone's budget supposedly becomes a government handout.

The so-called tax burden is an illusion because whatever title anyone has to own something came originally from government. In an earlier book, Sunstein stressed that "a system of private property is a construct of the state" and "governmental rules are implicated in, indeed constitute, the distribution of wealth and entitlement in the first instance." Thus government can presumably revoke the rights to any property without violating the rights of the purported owner. This presumes that government is the equivalent of some pagan Earth Mother from whom all things come-and who thus has a right to take all things back.

The only way to justify treating tax burdens as morally irrelevant is to assume that government owns all the labor of all the citizens in society. Taxes are not an imposition but merely government reclaiming its rightful property. But did the government bequeath the sweat of the brow of the carpenter who built a house that he sold, or the muscle by which a laborer dug a ditch, or the idea that the software writer used to revolutionize computer use around the world, or the courage of a businessman who staked his life savings on a new product that made life easier for millions? An edifice of freedom cannot be built on a foundation of slave ethics.

Holmes and Sunstein argue in effect that because politicians help set the rules for economic markets, they somehow become entitled to what anyone produces. This makes as much sense as saying that federal patent clerks deserve all the rewards for new inventions, since they approve and register new patents, or that a bank security guard is entitled to carry home armfuls of money from the vaults he guards.

Citizens at Fault

Every failure of government is somehow the citizens' fault. Sunstein notes that "The Fourth Amendment right [against unreasonable government searches and seizures] cannot be absolute unless the public is willing to invest the enormous amounts necessary to ensure that it is seldom violated in practice. The fact that the Fourth Amendment is violated so regularly shows that the public is not willing to make that investment." Thus the only reason that police routinely carry out unconstitutional searches is that taxes are not high enough.

The one part of the Bill of Rights that Holmes and Sunstein strictly avoid mentioning is the Second Amendment, which guarantees citizens the right to keep and bear arms. The Founding Fathers saw widespread private gun ownership as a necessary check against the threat of tyranny. Even Harvard law professor and "progressive" icon Laurence Tribe recently admitted that "It becomes impossible to deny that some right to bear arms is among the rights of American citizens." Presumably the authors believe that people must pay taxes so that government can confiscate everyone's guns.

Holmes and Sunstein see government as the alpha and omega of all rights, all liberties, all existence: They cannot conceive of anything happening that was not first ordained by politicians and inflicted by bureaucrats. They declare that "To take the cost of rights into account is therefore to think something like a government procurement officer, asking how to allocate limited resources intelligently while keeping a wide array of public goods in mind." Neither Sunstein nor Holmes has spent time around the General Services Administration headquarters, where real procurement officers waste billions every day.

The authors never attempt to explain where or how government got all the rights. Supposedly, government officials have them because government spends the money to protect them. But the money government spends was first earned by private citizens. How can citizens acquire rights only by government's taking away much of their paychecks in order to protect the remainder of their income and their other rights? If rights are the result of the government budget, then the rights must originate with the person who produced the money, not with the government agents who seized it. The adulation of government turns into a tautology: In the final realm, government is the source of all rights merely because it has the power to fleece and subjugate its citizens.

Portraying all rights as dispensations of government is a scam to convey absolute power to government officials. Since rights are solely the creation of government, any limitation on government power supposedly becomes a threat to rights.

Americans endorsed the creation of the federal government over 200 years ago so that it could fulfill a handful of narrowly prescribed functions. Government was intended to be a hired clerk, not a divine master. Each person has a natural right not to be made a government pawn, a right to sovereignty over his own body, his own life, and his own peaceful actions. As Etienne de la Boèttie, a sixteenth-century French thinker, observed, "It is fruitless to argue whether or not liberty is natural, since none can be held in slavery without being wronged."

Americans must choose between "government-issue liberty" and "self-reliant liberty." The choice is between a concept of freedom based on government handouts and a concept of freedom based on restraint of government, between a liberty in which people are perpetually treated as children needing to be restrained and a liberty in which they are allowed to experiment, take chances, and pay for their own bloody noses. It is a choice between a freedom in which each person can make his own mistakes or a freedom in which each person becomes another statistic in the government's mistakes. The choice between the two freedoms comes down to a question of whether people will benefit more from being left alone to build their own lives or from somebody's confiscating much of their building material and imposing the structure he thinks best. A good definition of liberty must provide a barricade that 10,000 enforcement agents can't breach.

– James Bovard

At the time of the original publication, James Bovard is the author of Freedom in Chains: The Rise of the State & the Demise of the Citizen (St. Martin's Press, 1999).

Reprinted with permission from The Freeman, a publication of The Foundation for Economic Education, Inc., February 2000, Vol. 50, No. 2.

> *"All compromise is based on give and take, but there can be no give and take on fundamentals. Any compromise on mere fundamentals is a surrender. For it is all give and no take."*
>
> ... MAHATMA GANDHI

THE PENALTY OF SURRENDER

THESE remarks, hardly more than a personal confession of faith, have their origin in an attitude or behavior commonly referred to as "compromising." The compromising attitude is exalted by many and deplored by only a few.

As an example of the way this attitude is exalted, a certain business leader, perhaps the most publicized one in the country, once severely lectured me on my unswerving and uncompromising behaviors. He charged that I saw things only in blacks and whites. He said that practical life was lived in shades of grays, actually in the shadows of these two extremes. He suggested that I had a nice chance of "going far" in the world if only I would become more pliable to the thoughts and actions of my fellows.

This criticism by so popular a person left me somewhat speechless. While it is true that I felt no sense of guilt whatever, nor even any unfaithfulness to those who thought differently than I, nonetheless, I found myself unable to do more than stammer in my own defense. Did you ever experience a feeling of rightness in the face of criticism, but were unable to explain your feeling. If so, you now know how I felt on that occasion five years ago.

Thus I was happy to accept this invitation to talk about "The Futility of Compromise." Here was an opportunity for me to think this thing through, to give expression to something that had too long remained in the vague area of feeling. Here was the chance to say what I mean to explain to myself-and not, as you shall see, to impose my ideas on any other person.

Compromise, like many other words, has different meanings for different persons. After some reflection I concluded that it was a confusion in the meaning of words that was largely responsible for so much misunderstanding; that maybe it wasn't compromise after all which deserved condemnation.

Physical Compromise Is *Possible*

I want to use the term in this definition by Webster, one of several, "The result or embodiment of concession or adjustment." I want to show that compromise is potentially good when applied in a physical sense and that it has no application whatever in a moral sense.

For example, you and your wife are spending what is hoped will be a happy evening at home. She chooses to listen to the radio and you elect to figure out what Toynbee is driving at in his *Study of History.* The scene appears peaceful as you sit side by side near this beautiful piece of furniture. But to you the furniture is making a lot of distracting noise.

Here are all the possibilities for turning a cheerful evening into one of disharmony. But compromise can come to your aid. Your wife can decrease the noise of the radio to the point where she can still hear it, and you can move to some remote corner where you can comprehend Toynbee just as well as anywhere else. Harmony can thus be preserved by compromise.

Compromise in this sense is an adjustment of physical situations. It is the process by which conflicts are reduced to the point most satisfactory to all parties concerned. When thought of in this way, compromise is the great harmonizer, the attitude that makes living together-social life-a pleasure.

Indeed, the market place, where tens of millions of transactions go on daily, is one vast area of compromise. Buyers aim at low prices. Sellers aim at high prices. In a free market there is an adjustment of these diverse desires. Compromise establishes the price at which the mutual satisfaction of buyer and seller is at its highest level.

It is in this physical realm that most of our daily life is lived. In this realm compromise is good and it is practical. It begets harmony and peace.

Moral Compromise Is Impossible

How easy it would seem then, finding compromise so useful in such a vast segment of life, to conclude un-thoughtfully that it has an equal place, a comparable value, in that phase of life which consciously occupies our thoughts so little: moral life.

But this is precisely the point where I believe many of us are the victims of a confusion of terms. What is compromise in physical affairs, that is, in an adjustment of physical positions, is something entirely different when applied to principles and morality.

For example, let us make the reckless assumption that most of us are committed to the Biblical injunction, "Thou shalt not steal." This is a moral principle. The point I want to make-my major point-is that this *as a principle* defies compromising. You either take someone else's property without his consent, or you do not. If you steal just a teensy weensy bit you do not compromise the principle. You abandon it. You surrender your principle.

By taking only a *little* of someone else's property without his consent, as distinguished from taking a *lot* of someone else's property without his consent, you do compromise in the physical sense. You compromise the physical amount you steal. But the moral principle, whatever the amount of the theft may be, is surrendered and utterly abandoned.

If all the rest of mankind are in favor of passing a law that would take the property, honestly acquired, of only one person *without due compensation,* even though the purpose be allegedly for the so-called social good, you cannot adjust yourself both to the moral principle, "Thou shalt not steal," and to the demand of the millions. Principle does not lend itself to bending or to compromising. It stands impregnable. I must either abide by it, or in all fairness I must on this point regard myself, not as a rational, reasonable person, but rather as an unprincipled person.

What Are Moral Principles?

The question immediately arises as to what constitutes principle. Here again is a term with many meanings. I cannot derive the exact satisfaction I want from reading the several definitions; therefore, it seems necessary to define what I mean.

The Ten Commandments are principles, moral principles. They were principles at least to the ones who wrote them, and they have been adopted and held as principles by countless millions. They receive their validity as principles through the deductions of the wiser among us and through centuries of observations and experience. Actually, they are principles only insofar as they are revealed truth to particular persons.

What may be a principle to one is not necessarily a principle to another. It is a matter of revealed truth, that is, revelation, "the disclosing or discovering ... of what was before unknown ...."

To me, "Thou shalt not steal" is a principle not because some sage of antiquity said so but because, in my own experience, it has been revealed as a principle which must be adhered to if we are not to perish from the face of the earth.

To the ones who have not been graced with this revelation; to the ones who hold that they should gratify their personal charitable feelings, not with their own goods, but by using the police force to take goods from others; to those who would indulge in legal thievery and honestly think the practice right and honorable-to those, I say, "Thou shalt not steal" is no principle at all. It is only the principle of someone else.

A principle, then, is what one holds to be a fact of life, of nature, or, as some of us would put it, of God. If this is correct, it follows that a principle is a matter of personal individual judgment. Judgment is fallible. Therefore, there are wrong principles as well as right principles. Aristotle said there were a million ways to be wrong, only one way to be right. That suggests the measure of fallibility among us.

Moral Principles Require Understanding

Now then, if principle is a matter of personal judgment, and judgment is conceded to be fallible, on what is right principle dependent?

The discovery and adoption of right principle are dependent on the evolution of judgment through logic, reason, observation and honesty. When judgments deteriorate we have what history refers to as the "Dark Ages." When judgments evolve or improve, reference is made to "The Renaissance." The question that grows out of this reasoning is how does judgment evolve? My answer is, by revelation.

For instance, I am convinced that no person is capable of rising above his best judgment. To live in strict accordance with one's best judgment is to live as perfectly as one can, as humble or as mediocre as that may be. The one hope for personal betterment lies in raising the level of one's judgment; judgment is a limiting factor.

If the evolution of judgment rests on revelation how is revelation to be achieved? I can think of no answer superior to that suggested by Goethe:

Nature understands no jesting; she is always true, always serious, and always severe; she is always right, and the errors and faults are always those of man. The man incapable of appreciating her she despises; and only to the apt, the pure, and the true, does she resign herself, and reveal her secrets.

The sole way to revelation, to ultimate truth, to nature, as Goethe puts it, or to God, as I put it, lies through one's own person. It is my faith that the individual is God's manifestation so far as any given individual is concerned. My way to God is through my own person. He will reveal Himself to me; I will be His manifestation, only to the extent that I am "apt, pure and true."

Understanding Requires Effort

But the revelation of truth and of principles does not come automatically, without effort, like "manna from Heaven." Revelation is the product of a diligent application of an individual's mental resources. Truth must be sought, and its revelation is most likely in an active mind.

It is rather easy to observe that to some, very little, if anything is ever revealed. To others there come revelations far beyond anything I now possess or have any right seriously to expect. Anyway, with this as a faith, based, as it is, on such revelation as is mine, God is as intimate to me as my own person. He exists for each of us only insofar as we achieve our own conception of His likeness.

God and Individual Liberty Are One

This is why I believe, so fervently, in the sanctity and dignity of the individual. This is why I subscribe to the philosophy that each person has inalienable rights to life, liberty and the pursuit of happiness. For me to deny this philosophy by violating the life, liberty or property of another, by inflicting my ways on other persons, is for me to assert myself as a god over God, to interfere with another person's relationship with God. For me to use compulsion in any manner whatsoever to cast others in my image is for me to rebuke God in his several manifestations.

If one accepts the individual in this light, a rule of conduct emerges with crystal clarity: *reflect in word and indeed, always and accurately, that which one's best judgment dictates.* This is you in such godliness as you possess. To do less, to deviate one iota, is to sin against yourself, that is, against your Maker as He has manifested Himself in you. To do less is not to compromise. To do less is to surrender!

Certainly, there is nothing new about the efficacy of accurately reflecting one's best judgment. This principle of conduct has been known throughout the ages. Now and then it has been expressed beautifully and simply. Shakespeare enunciated this principle when he had Polonius say these words:

This above all: To thine own self be true,
And it must follow, as the night the day,
Thou canst not then be false to any man.

Edmond Rostand meant nothing different when he wrote this line for Cyrano:

Never to make a line I have not heard in my own heart;

American folklore counseled intellectual integrity with: *Honesty is the best policy.*

The Price of Untruth

The Bible announces the penalty of surrender; what it means to abandon principle. It says:

The wages of sin is death.

Whether the wages of sin be mere physical death or the death of man's spirit-his character, his integrity, his self respect-one needs to make no further inquiry to verify this Biblical pronouncement. Abundant testimony has been provided all of us in our lifetime. Nor is the end in sight. All the world is filled with examples of warped judgments and principles abandoned: men ruling over man; the glamour of popularity rather than the strictness of judgment directing policy; expediency substituting for such truth as is known; businessmen employing experts to help them *seem* right, often at the expense of rightness itself; labor leaders justifying any action that gratifies their lust for power; political leaders asserting that the end justifies the means; clergymen preaching expropriation of property without consent in the name of the "common good"; teachers advocating collectivism and denying the sanctity and the dignity of the individual; politicians building platforms from public-opinion polls; farmers and miners joining other plunderbundists in demands for other people's property; arrogance replacing humility; in short, we are sinking into a new dark age, an age darkened by persons who have abandoned intellectual integrity; who through ignorance or design, have adopted bad ideas and principles.

If we were suddenly to become aware of foreign vandals invading our shores, vandals that would kill our children, rape our women and pilfer our industry, every last man of us would rise in arms that we might sweep them from our land.

Yes, these bad ideas, these ideas based on the abandonment of absolute integrity, are the most depraved and dangerous vandals known to man. Is the Bible right that "the wages of sin is death"? I give you the last two wars, wars born of unreason and lies. And the present so-called peace! I give you the Russia of 1929-1932 where millions died of starvation and, in other years, where other millions died in this and other ways. I give you almost any place in the world today.

Is Honesty Dangerous?

Perhaps the reason that so many fears stating accurately what they believe is that they are not aware that it is safe to do so.

Does it take courage to be honest, that is, does one have to be brave to state accurately one's highest opinion? Indeed, not. A part of revealed truth is: *It is not dangerous to be honest.* One who possesses this revelation is to that extent intelligent. Being honest, not surrendering principle rests only upon intelligence, not at all upon courage. Relying, erroneously, on courage, many persons become blusterous with their opinions; they get cantankerous when they are honest. But, in this case, the villain is their cantankerousness, not their honesty.

Finally, some may contend that-due to the great variety of judgments-differences and antagonisms would still remain even if everyone were a model of intellectual integrity. This is true. But differences lend themselves to a change toward the truth in an atmosphere of honesty. Under these circumstances they can be endured. For after all, life, in a physical sense, is-and for ages to come, will be-a compromise. But if principle is abandoned, even compromise will not be possible. Nothing but chaosl.

Honesty-each person true to himself at his best-is the condition from which revelation springs; from which knowledge expands; from which intelligence grows; and from which judgments improve.

Honesty and intelligence are godlike and are, therefore, primary virtues. Anyone is capable of being true to himself. That is the one equality we were all born with. Its abandonment is the greatest sin of all.

If there be no falseness there will then be as much intelligence as we are capable of. How nearer God can we get?

– Leonard E. Read

> *"The poor suffer the worst when their very poverty is both perpetuated by the welfare state and deepened by the hidden transfers from the powerless to the powerful caused by protectionism, licensing, and other restrictions on labor market freedom that the powerful and educated create at the expense of the voiceless and disempowered."*
>
> ... PAGE 8, THE TRAGEDY OF THE WELFARE STATE, TOM PALMER.

MORALS AND THE WELFARE STATE

To many persons, the Welfare State has become a symbol of morality and righteousness. This makes those who favor the Welfare State appear to be the true architects of a better world; those who oppose it, immoral rascals who might be expected to rob banks, or to do most anything in defiance of ethical conduct. But is this so? Is the banner of morality, when applied to the concept of the Welfare State, one that is true or false?

Now what is the test of morality or immorality to be applied to the Welfare State idea? I should like to pose five fundamental ethical concepts, as postulates, by which to test it. They are the ethical precepts found in the true Christian religion-true to its original foundations; and they are likewise found in other religious faiths, wherever and under whatever name these other religious concepts assist persons to perceive and practice the moral truths of human conduct.*

*A brief statement on the mechanisms of the Welfare State idea is appended to this discussion.

Moral Postulate No.1

ECONOMICS AND MORALS ARE BOTH PARTS OF ONE INSEPARABLE BODY OF TRUTH. THEY MUST, THEREFORE, BE IN HARMONY WITH ONE ANOTHER.

What is right morally must also be right economically, and vice versa. Since morals are a guide to betterment and to self-protection, economic policies that violate Moral Truth, will, with certainty, cause degeneration and self-destruction.

This postulate may seem simple and self-evident. Yet many economists and others of my acquaintance, including one who was a most capable and admired teacher, presume to draw some kind of an impassable line of distinction between morals and economics. Such persons fail to test their economic concepts against their moral precepts. Some even scorn the moral base for testing economic concepts, as though it would somehow pollute their economic purity.

An unusually capable minister recently said that only a short time before, for the first time, he had come to realize the close connection and inter-harmony that exist between morals and economics. He had always tried to reserve one compartment for his religious thought and another separate one for his economic thought. "Fortunately," he said, in essence, "my economic thinking happened to be in harmony with my religious beliefs; but it frightens me now to realize the risk I was taking in ignoring the harmony that must exist between the two."

This viewpoint-that there is no necessary connection between morals and economics-is all too prevalent. It explains, I believe, why immoral economic acts are tolerated, if not actively promoted, by persons of high repute who otherwise may be considered to be persons of high moral standards.

Moral Postulate No.2

THERE IS A FORCE IN THE UNIVERSE WHICH NO MORTAL CAN ALTER.

Neither you nor I nor any earthly potentate with all his laws and edicts can alter this rule of the universe, no matter how great one's popularity in his position of power. Some call this force God. Others call it Natural Law. Still others call it the Supernatural. But no matter how one may wish to name it, there is a force which rules without surrender to any mortal man or group of men a force that is oblivious to anyone who presumes to elevate himself and his wishes above its rule.

This concept is the basis for all relationships of cause and consequence-all science-whether it is something already discovered or something yet to be discovered. Its scope includes phenomena such as those of physics and chemistry; it also includes those of human conduct. The so-called Law of Gravity is one expression of Natural Law. Scientific discovery means the unveiling to human perception of something that has always existed. If it had not existed prior to the discovery-even though we were ignorant of it-it could not have been there to be discovered. That is the meaning of the concept of Natural Law.

This view-there exists a Natural Law which rules over the affairs of human conduct-will be challenged by some who point out that man possesses the capacity for choice; that man's activity reflects a quality lacking in the chemistry of a stone and in the physical principle of the lever. But this trait of man-this capacity for choice-does not release him from the rule of cause and effect, which he can neither veto nor alter. What the capacity for choice means, instead, is that he is thereby enabled, by his own choice, to act either wisely or unwisely-that is, in either accord or discord with the truths of Natural Law. But once he has made his choice, the inviolate rule of cause and consequence takes over with an iron hand of justice, and renders unto the doer either a prize or a penalty, as the consequence of his choice.

It is important, at this point, to note that morality presumes the existence of choice. One cannot be truly moral except as there exist the option of being immoral and except as he selects the moral rather than the immoral option. In the admirable words of Thomas Davidson, "That which is not free is not responsible, and that which is not responsible is *not moral." This means that free choice is a prerequisite of morality.*

If I surrender my freedom of choice to a ruler-by vote or otherwise-I am still subject to the superior rule of Natural Law or Moral Law. Although I am subservient to the ruler who orders me to violate Truth, I must still pay the penalty for the evil or foolish acts in which I engage at his command.

Under this postulate-that there is a force in the universe which no mortal can alter-ignorance of Moral Law is no excuse to those who violate it, because Moral Law rules over the consequences of ignorance the same as over the consequences of wisdom. This is true whether the ignorance is accompanied by good intentions or not; whether it is carried out under the name of some religion or the Welfare State or whatnot.

What, then, is the content of a basic moral code? What are the rules which, if followed, will better the condition of men?

Moral Postulate No.3

THE GOLDEN RULE AND THE DECALOGUE**, AND THEIR NEAR EQUIVALENTS IN OTHER GREAT RELIGIONS, PROVIDE THE BASIC MORAL CODES FOR MAN'S CONDUCT.

The Golden Rule and the Decalogue are basic moral guides having priority over all other considerations. It is these which have guided the conduct of man in all progressive civilizations. With their violation has come the downfall of individuals, and therefore of civilizations.

Some may prefer as a moral code something like: "Do as God would have us do "or" Do as Jesus would have done." But such as these, alone, are not adequate guides to conduct unless they are explained further, or unless they serve as symbolic of a deeper specific meaning. What *would* God have us do? What *would* Jesus have done? Only by adding some guides such as the Golden Rule and the Ten Commandments can we know the answers to these questions.

The Golden Rule-the rule of refraining from imposing on others what I would not have them impose on me means that moral conduct for one is moral conduct for another; that there is not one set of moral guides for Jones and another for Smith; that the concept of equality under Moral Law is a part of morality itself. This alone is held by many to be an adequate moral code. But in spite of its importance as part of the moral code of conduct in this respect, the Golden Rule is not, it seems to me, sufficient unto itself. It is no more sufficient than the mere admonition, "Do good" which leaves undefined what is good and what is evil. The murderer, who at the time of the crime felt justified in committing it, can quote the Golden Rule in self-defense: "If I had done what that so-and-so did, and had acted as he acted, I would consider it fair and proper for someone to murder me." And likewise the thief may argue that if he were like the one he has robbed, or if he were a bank harboring all those "ill-gotten gains," he would consider himself the proper object of robbery. Some claim that justification for the Welfare State, too, is to be found in the Golden Rule. So, in addition to the Golden Rule, further rules are needed as guides for moral conduct.

The Decalogue embodies the needed guides on which the Golden Rule can function. But within the Ten Commandments, the two with which we shall be especially concerned herein are: (1) Thou shalt not steal. (2) Thou shalt not covet.

The Decalogue serves as a guide to moral conduct which, if violated, brings upon the violator a commensurate penalty. There may be other guides to moral conduct which one might wish to add to the Golden Rule and the Decalogue, as supplements or substitutes. But they serve as the basis on which others are built. Their essence, in one form or another, seems to run through all great religions. That, I believe, is not a happenstance, because if we embrace them as a guide to our conduct, it will be both morally and economically sound.

This third postulate embodies what are judged to be the *principles* which should guide individual conduct as infallibly as the compass should guide the mariner. "Being practical" is a common popular guide to conduct; principles are scorned, if not forgotten. Those who scorn principles assert that it is foolish to concern ourselves with them; that it is hopeless to expect their complete adoption by everyone. But does this fact make a principle worth less? Are we to conclude that the moral code against murder is worthless because of its occasional violation? Or that the compass is worthless because not everyone pursues to the ultimate the direction which it indicates? Or that the Law of Gravity is made impractical or inoperative by someone walking off a cliff and meeting death because of his ignorance of this principle? No. A principle remains a principle in spite of its being ignored or violated -or even unknown. A principle, like a compass, gives one a better sense of direction, if he is wise enough to know and to follow its guidance.

Moral Postulate No.4

MORAL PRINCIPLES ARE NOT SUBJECT TO COMPROMISE.

The Golden Rule and the Decalogue, as representing moral principles, are precise and strict. They are not a code of convenience. A principle can be broken, but it cannot be bent.

If the Golden Rule and the Decalogue were to be accepted as a code of convenience, to be laid aside or modified whenever "necessity seems to justify it" (whenever, that is, one desires to act in violation of them), they would not then be serving as moral guides. A moral guide which is to be followed only when one would so conduct himself anyhow, in its absence, has no effect on his conduct, and is not a guide to him at all.

The unbending rule of a moral principle can be illustrated by some simple applications. According to one Commandment, it is wholly wrong to steal all your neighbor's cow; it is also wholly wrong to steal half your neighbor's cow, not half wrong to steal half your neighbor's cow. Robbing a bank is wrong in principle, whether the thief makes off with a million dollars or a hundred dollars or one cent. A person can rob a bank of half its money, but in the sense of moral principle there is no way to half rob a bank; you either rob it or you do not rob it.

In like manner, the Law of Gravity is precise and indivisible. One either acts in harmony with this law or he does not. There is no sense in saying that one has only half observed the Law of Gravity if he falls off a cliff only half as high as another cliff off which he might have fallen.

Moral laws are strict. They rule without flexibility. They know not the language of man; they are not conversant with him in the sense of compassion. They employ no man-made devices like the suspended sentence-"Guilty" or "Not guilty" is the verdict of judgment by a moral principle.

As moral guides, the Golden Rule and the Decalogue are not evil and dangerous things, like a painkilling drug, to be taken in cautious moderation, if at all. Presuming them to be the basic guides of what is right and good for civilized man, one cannot overindulge in them. Good need not be practiced in moderation.

Moral Postulate No.5

GOOD ENDS CANNOT BE ATTAINED BY EVIL MEANS.

As stated in the second postulate, there is a force controlling cause and consequence which no mortal can alter, in spite of any position of influence or power which he may hold. Cause and consequence are linked inseparably.

An evil begets an evil consequence; a good, a good consequence. Good intentions cannot alter this relationship. Nor can ignorance of the consequence change its form. Nor can words. For one to say, after committing an evil act, "I'm sorry, I made a mistake," changes not one iota the consequence of the act; repentance, at best, can serve only to prevent repetition of the evil act, and perhaps assure the repenter a more preferred place in a Hereafter. But repentance *alone* does not bring back to life a murdered person, nor return the loot to the one who was robbed. Nor does it, I believe, fully obliterate the scars of evil on the doer himself.

Nor does saying, "He told me to do it," change the consequence of an evil act into a good one. For an evildoer to assert, "But it was the law of my government, the decree of my ruler," fails to dethrone God or to frustrate the rule of Natural Law.

A Vicious Concept

The belief that good ends are attainable through evil means is one of the most vicious concepts of the ages. The political blueprint, *The Prince,* written around the year 1500 by Machiavelli, outlined this notorious doctrine. And for the past century it has been part and parcel of the kit of tools used by the Marxian communist-socialists to mislead people. Its use probably is as old as the conflict between temptation and conscience, because it affords a seemingly rational and pleasant detour around the inconveniences of one's conscience.

We know how power-hungry persons have gained political control over others by claiming that they somehow possess a special dispensation from God to do good through the exercise of means which our moral code identifies as evil. Thus arises a multiple standard of morals. It is the device by which immoral persons attempt to discredit the Golden Rule and the Decalogue, and make them inoperative.

Yet if one will stop to ponder the question just a little, he must surely see the unimpeachable logic of this postulate: Good ends cannot be attained by evil means. This is because the end pre-exists in the means, just as in the biological field we know that the seed of continued likeness pre-exists in the parent. Likewise in the moral realm, there is a similar moral reproduction wherein like begets like. This precludes the possibility of evil means leading to good ends. Good begets good; evil, evil. Immoral means cannot beget a good end, any more than snakes can beget roses.

The concept of the Welfare State can now be tested against the background of these five postulates:

1. *Harmony exists between moral principles and wise economic practices.*
2. *There is a Universal Law of Cause and Effect, even in the areas of morals and economics.*
3. *A basic moral code exists in the form of the Golden Rule and the Decalogue.*
4. *These moral guides are of an uncompromising nature.*
5. *Good ends are attainable only through good means.*

Moral Right to Private Property

Not all the Decalogue, as has been said, is directly relevant to the issue of the Welfare State. Its program is an economic one, and the only parts of the moral code which are directly and specifically relevant are these: (1) Thou shalt not steal. (2) Thou shalt not covet.

Steal what? Covet what? Private property, of course. What else could I steal from you, or covet of what is yours? I cannot steal from you or covet what you do not own as private property. As Dr. D. Elton Trueblood has aptly said: "Stealing is evil because ownership is good." Thus we find that the individual's right to private property is an unstated assumption which underlies the Decalogue. Otherwise these two admonitions would be empty of either purpose or meaning.

The right to have and to hold private property is not to be confused with the recovery of stolen property. If someone steals your car, it is still—by this moral right your car rather than his; and for you to repossess it is merely to bring its presence back into harmony with its ownership. The same reasoning applies to the recovery of equivalent value if the stolen item itself is no longer returnable; and it applies to the recompense for damage done to one's own property by trespass or other willful destruction of private property. These means of protecting the possession of private property, and its use, are part of the mechanisms used to protect the moral right to private property.

To Aspire Is Not To Covet

Another point of possible confusion has to do with coveting the private property of another. There is nothing morally wrong in the admiration of something that is the property of another. Such admiration may be a stimulus to work for the means with which to buy it, or one like it. The moral consideration embodied in this Commandment has to do with thoughts and acts leading to the violation of the other Commandment, though still short of actual theft.

The moral right to private property, therefore, is consistent with the moral codes of all the great religious beliefs. It is likely that a concept of this type was in the mind of David Hume, the moral philosopher, who believed that the right to own private property is the basis for the modern concept of justice in morals.

Nor is it surprising to discover that two of history's leading exponents of the Welfare State concept found it necessary to denounce this moral code completely. Marx said: "Religion is the opium of the people." And Lenin said: "Any religious idea, any idea of a 'good God' ... is an abominably nasty thing." Of course they would have to say these things about religious beliefs. This is because the moral code of these great religions, as we have seen, strikes at the very heart of their immoral economic scheme. Not only does their Welfare State scheme deny the moral right to private property, but it also denies other under lying bases of the moral code, as we shall see.

Moral Right to Work and To Have

Stealing and coveting are condemned in the Decalogue as violations of the basic moral code. It follows, then, that the concepts of stealing and coveting presume the right to private property, which then automatically becomes an implied part of the basic moral code. But where does private property come from?

Private property comes from what one has saved out of what he has produced, or has earned as a productive employee of another person. One may also, of course, obtain private property through gifts and inheritances; but in the absence of theft, precluded by this moral code, gifts come from those who have produced or earned what is given. So the right of private property, and also the right to have whatever one has produced or earned, underlies the admonitions in the Decalogue about stealing and coveting. Nobody has the moral right to take by force from the producer anything he has produced or earned, for any purpose whatsoever-even for a good purpose, as he thinks of it.

If one is free to have what he has produced and earned, it then follows that he also has the moral right to be free to choose his work. He should be free to choose his work, that is, so long as he does not violate the moral code in doing so by using in his productive efforts the property of another person through theft or trespass. Otherwise he is free to work as he will, at what he will, and to change his work when he will. Nobody has the moral right to force him to work when he does not choose to do so, or to force him to remain idle when he wishes to work, or to force him to work at a certain job when he wishes to work at some other available job. The belief of the master that his judgment is superior to that of the slave or vassal, and that control is "for his own good," is not a moral justification for the idea of the Welfare State.

Intuitive Morality

We are told that some misdoings occurred in a Garden of Eden, which signify the evil in man. And I would concede that no mortal man is totally wise and good. But it is my belief that people generally, up and down the road, are intuitively and predominantly moral. By this I mean that if persons are confronted with a clear and simple decision involving basic morals, most of us will conduct ourselves morally. Most everyone, without being a learned scholar of moral philosophy, seems to have a sort of innate sense of what is right, and tends to do what is moral *unless and until he becomes confused by circumstances which obscure the moral issue that is involved.*

Immorality Is News

The content of many magazines and newspapers with widespread circulations would seem to contradict my belief that most people are moral most of the time. They headline impressive and unusual events on the seamy side of life, which might lead one to believe that these events are characteristic of everyday human affairs. It is to be noted, however, that their content is in sharp contrast to the local, home-town daily or weekly with its emphasis on the folksy reports of the comings and goings of friends. Why the difference? Those with large circulations find that the common denominator of news interest in their audience is events on the rare, seamy side of life; widely scattered millions are not interested in knowing that in Centerville, Sally attended Susie's birthday party last Tuesday.

It is the rarity of evil conduct that makes it impressive news for millions. Papers report the events of yesterday's murder, theft, or assault, together with the name, address, age, marital status, religious affiliation, and other descriptive features of the guilty party because these are the events of the day that are unusual enough to be news worthy. What would be the demand for a newspaper which published all the names and identifications of all the persons who yesterday failed to murder, steal, or assault? If it were as rare for persons to act morally as it is now rare for them to act immorally, the then rare in stances of moral conduct would presumably become the news of the day. So we may conclude that evil is news because it is so rare; that being moral is not news because it is so prevalent.

But does not this still prove the dominance of evil in persons? Or, since magazines and newspapers print what finds a ready readership in the market, does not that prove the evilness of those who read of evil? I believe not. It is more like the millions who attend zoos, and view with fascination the monkeys and the snakes; these spectators are not themselves monkeys or snakes, nor do they want to be; they are merely expressing an interest in the unusual, without envy. Do not most of us read of a bank robbery or a fire without wishing to be robbers or arsonists?

What else dominates the newspaper space, and gives us our dominant impressions about the quality of persons outside our circle of immediate personal acquaintance? It is mostly about the problems of political power; about those who have power or are grasping for power, diluted with a little about those who are fighting against power. Lord Acton said: "Power tends to corrupt, and absolute power corrupts absolutely." This dictum seems to be true, as history has proved and is proving over and over again. So we can then translate it into a description of much of the news of the day: News is heavily loaded with items about persons who, as Lord Acton said, are either corrupt or are in the process of becoming more corrupt.

If one is not careful in exposing himself to the daily news-if he fails to keep his balance and forgets how it contrasts with all those persons who comprise his family, his neighbors, his business associates, and his friends-he is likely to conclude falsely that people are predominantly immoral. This poses a serious problem for historians and historical novelists to the extent that their source of information is the news of a former day-especially if they do not interpret it with caution.

To Steal or Not To Steal

As a means of specifically verifying my impression about the basic, intuitive morality of persons, I would pose this test of three questions:

1. Would you steal your neighbor's cow to provide for your present needs? Would you steal it for any need reasonably within your expectation or comprehension? It should be remembered that, instead of stealing his cow, you may explore with your neighbor the possible solution to your case of need; you might arrange to do some sort of work for him, or to borrow from him for later repayment, or perhaps even plead with him for an outright gift.

2. Would you steal your neighbor's cow to provide for a known case of another neighbor's need?

3. Would you try to induce a third party to do the stealing of the cow, to be given to this needy neighbor? And do you believe that you would likely succeed in inducing him to engage in the theft?

I believe that the almost universal answer to all these questions would be: "No." Yet the facts of the case are that all of us are participating in theft every day. How? By supporting the actions of the collective agent which does the stealing as part of the Welfare State program, already far advanced in the United States. By this device, Peter is robbed to "benefit" Paul, with the acquiescence if not the active support of all of us as taxpayers and citizens. We not only participate in the stealing-and share in the division of the loot-but as its victims we also meekly submit to the thievery.

A Confusing Process

Isn't it a strange thing that if you select any three fundamentally moral persons and combine them into a collective for the doing of good, they are liable at once to become three immoral persons in their collective activities? The moral principles with which they seem to be intuitively endowed are somehow lost in the confusing processes of the collective. None of the three would steal the cow from one of his fellow members as an individual, but collectively they all steal cows from each other. The reason is, I believe, that the Welfare State-a confusing collective device which is believed by many to be moral and righteous-has been falsely labeled. This false label has caused the belief that the Welfare State can do no wrong, that it cannot commit immoral acts, especially if those acts are approved or tolerated by more than half of the people, "democratically."

This sidetracking of moral conduct is like the belief of an earlier day: The king can do no wrong. In its place we have now substituted this belief: The majority can do no wrong. It is as though one were to assert that a sheep which has been killed by a pack of wolves is not really dead, provided that more than half of the wolves have participated in the killing. All these excuses for immoral conduct are, of course, nonsense. They are nonsense when tested against the basic moral code of the five postulates. Thievery is thievery, whether done by one person alone or by many in a pack-or by one who has been selected by the members of the pack as their agent.

"Thou Shalt Not Steal, Except . . ."

It seems that wherever the 'Welfare State is involved, the moral precept, "Thou shalt not steal," becomes altered to say: "Thou shalt not steal, except for what thou deemest to be a worthy cause, where thou thinkest that thou canst use the loot for a better purpose than wouldst the victim of the theft."

And the precept about covetousness, under the administration of the Welfare State, seems to become: "Thou shalt not covet, except what thou wouldst have from thy neighbor who owns it."

Both of these alterations of the Decalogue result in complete abrogation of the two moral admonitions-theft and covetousness-which deal directly with economic matters. Not even the motto, "In God we trust," stamped by the government on money taken by force in violation of the Decalogue to pay for the various programs of the Welfare State, can transform this immoral act into a moral one.

In A *Hurry to* Do *Good*

Herein lies the principal moral and economic danger facing us in these critical times: Many of us, albeit with good intentions but in a hurry to do good because of the urgency of the occasion; have become victims of moral schizophrenia. While we are good and righteous persons in our individual conduct in our home community and in our basic moral code, we have become thieves and coveters in the collective activities of the Welfare State in which we participate and which many of us extol.

Typical of our times is what usually happens when there is a major catastrophe, destroying private property or injuring many persons. The news circulates, and generates widespread sympathy for the victims. So what is done about it? Through the mechanisms of the collective, the good intentions take the form of reaching into the other fellow's pocket for the money with which to make a gift. The Decalogue says, in effect: "Reach into your *own* pocket-not into your neighbor's pocket-to finance your acts of compassion; good cannot be done with the loot that comes from theft." The pickpocket, in other words, is a thief even though he puts the proceeds in the collection box on Sunday, or uses it to buy bread for the poor. Being an involuntary Good Samaritan is a contradiction in terms.

When thievery is resorted to for the means with which to do good, compassion is killed. Those who would do good with the loot then lose their capacity for self-reliance, the same as a thief's self-reliance atrophies rapidly when he subsists on food that is stolen. And those who are repeatedly robbed of their property simultaneously lose their capacity for compassion. The chronic victims of robbery are under great temptation to join the gang and share in the loot. They come to feel that the voluntary way of life will no longer suffice for needs; that to subsist, they must rob and be robbed. They abhor violence, of course, but approve of robbing by "peaceful means." It is this peculiar immoral distinction which many try to draw between the Welfare State of Russia and that of Britain: The Russian brand of violence, they believe, is bad; that of Britain, good. This version of an altered Commandment would be: "Thou shalt not steal, except from non-resisting victims."

Under the Welfare State, this process of theft has spread from its use in alleviating catastrophe, to anticipating catastrophe, to conjuring up catastrophe, to the "need" for luxuries for those who have them not. The acceptance of the practice of thus violating the Decalogue has become so widespread that if the Sermon on the Mount were to appear in our day in the form of an address or publication, it would most likely be scorned as "reactionary, and not objective on the realistic problems of the day." Forgotten, it seems, by many who so much admire Christ, is the fact that he did not resort to theft in acquiring the means of his material benefactions. Nor did he advocate theft for any purpose-even for those uses most dear to his beliefs.

Progress of Moral Decay

Violation of the two economic Commandments-theft and covetousness-under the program of the Welfare State, will spread to the other Commandments; it will destroy faith in, and observance of, our entire basic moral code. We have seen this happen in many countries. It seems to have been happening here. We note how immorality, as tested by the two economic Commandments, has been spreading in high places. Moral decay has already spread to such an extent that violations of all other parts of the Decalogue, and of the Golden Rule, have become accepted as commonplace-even proper and worthy of emulation.

And what about the effectiveness of a crime investigation conducted under a Welfare State government? We may question the presumed capability of such a government-as distinct from certain investigators who are admittedly moral individuals-to judge these moral issues. We may also question the wisdom of bothering to investigate the picayune amounts of private gambling, willingly engaged in by the participants with their own money, when untold billions are being taken from the people repeatedly by the investigating agent to finance its own immoral program. This is a certain loss, not even a gamble.

Once a right to collective looting has been substituted for the right of each person to have whatever he has produced, it is not at all surprising to find the official dispensers deciding that it is right for them to loot the loot for a "worthy" purpose, of course. Then we have the loot used by the insiders to buy votes so that they may stay in power; we have political pork barrels and lobbying for the contents; we have political patronage for political loyalty-even for loyalty to immoral conduct; we have deep freezers and mink coats given to political or personal favorites, and bribes for the opportunity to do privileged business with those who hold and dispense the loot. Why not? If it is right to loot, it is also right to loot the loot. If the latter is wrong, so also is the former.

If we are to accept Lord Acton's axiom about the corrupting effect of power-and also the reasoning of Professor Hayek in his book, *The Road to Serfdom,* about why the worst get to the top in a Welfare State-then corruption and low moral standards in high political places should not be surprising. But when the citizens come more and more to laugh and joke about it, rather than to remove the crown of power and dismantle the throne, a nation is well on its way to moral rot, reminiscent of the fall of the Roman Empire and others.

Nor should we be surprised that there is some juvenile delinquency where adult delinquency is so rampant, and where the absence of any basic moral code among adults precludes even the possibility of their effectively teaching a moral code that will prevent delinquency in the young. If, as adults, we practice collective thievery through the Welfare State, and advocate it as right and good, how can we question the logic of the youths who likewise form gangs and rob the candy store? If demonstration is the best teacher, we adults must start with the practice of morality ourselves, rather than hiring some presumed specialist to study the causes of similar conduct among the youngsters; their conduct is the symptom, not the disease.

Thievery and covetousness will persist and grow, and the basic morals of ourselves, our children, and our children's children will continue to deteriorate unless we destroy the virus of immorality that is embedded in the concept of the Welfare State; unless we come to understand how the moral code of individual conduct must apply also to collective conduct, because the collective is composed solely of individuals. Moral individual conduct cannot persist in the face of collective immorality under the Welfare State program. One side or the other of the double standard of morals will have to be surrendered.

APPENDIX

The Welfare State Idea

The concept of the Welfare State appears in our everyday life in the form of a long list of labels and programs such as: Social Security; parity or fair prices; reasonable profits; the living wage; the TVA, MVA, CVA; federal aid to states, to education, to bankrupt corporations; and so on. But all these names and details of the Welfare State program tend only to obscure its essential nature. They are well-sounding labels for a laudable objective-the relief of distressing need, prevention of starvation, and the like. But how best is starvation and distress to be prevented? It is well, too, that prices, profits, and wages be fair and equitable. But what is to be the test of fairness and equity? Laudable objectives alone do not assure the success of any program; a fair appraisal of the program must include an analysis of the means of its attainment.

The Welfare State is a name that has been substituted as a more acceptable one for communism-socialism wherever, as in the United States, these names are in general disrepute.

The Welfare State plan, viewed in full bloom of completeness, is one where the state prohibits the individual from having any right of choice in the conditions and place of his work; it takes ownership of the product of his labor; it prohibits private property. All these are done ostensibly to help those whose rights have been taken over by the Welfare State.*

But these characteristics of controlled employment and confiscation of income are not those used in promotion of the idea of the Welfare State. What are usually advertised, instead, are the "benefits" of the Welfare State-the grants of food and housing and whatnot-which the state "gives" to the people. But all these "benefits" are merely the other side of the forfeited rights to choose one's own occupation and to keep whatever one is able to produce. In the same sense that the Welfare State grants benefits, the slave-master grants to his slaves certain allotments of food and other economic goods. In fact, slavery might be described as just another form of Welfare State, because of its likeness in restrictions and "benefits."

Yet the state, as such, produces nothing with which to supply these "benefits." Persons produce everything which the Welfare State takes, before it gives some back as "benefits"; but in the process, the bureaucracy takes its cut. Only by thus confiscating what persons have produced can the Welfare State "satisfy the needs of the people." So, the necessary and essential idea of the Welfare State is to control the economic actions of the vassals of the state, to take from producers what they produce, and to prevent their ever being able to attain economic independence from the state and from their fellow men through ownership of property.

To whatever extent an individual is still allowed freedom in any of these respects while living under a government like the present one in the United States, then to that extent the development of the program of the Welfare State is as yet not fully completed. Or perhaps it is an instance of a temporary grant of freedom by the Welfare State such as when a master allows his slave a day off from work to spend as he likes; but the person who is permitted some freedom by the Welfare State is still a vassal of that state just as a slave is still a slave on his day off from work.

– *F. A. Harper*

°The concepts of the Welfare State, in more detail but still in condensed form, are revealed in *The Communist Idea* series (following chapter).

** The Decalogue is the Ten Commandments

> "*Communism and fascism or Nazism, although poles apart in their intellectual content are similar in this, that both have emotional appeal to the type of personality that takes pleasure in being submerged in a mass movement and submitting to superior authority.*"
>
> ... JAMES A. C. BROWN

THE COMMUNIST IDEA

PART I

We were warned of the general procedure and the specific measures for a successful communist or socialist revolution by Karl Marx, the "father" of communism, in 1848:

"We have seen ... that the first step in the revolution by the working class is to raise the proletariat to the position of the ruling class; to win the battle of democracy. The proletariat will use its political supremacy to wrest, by degrees, all capital from the bourgeoisie; to centralize all instruments of production in the hands of the State. . . .

These measures will, of course, be different in different countries. Nevertheless in the most advanced countries the following will be pretty generally applicable:

1. Abolition of property in land and application of all rents of land to public purposes.
2. A heavy progressive or graduated income tax.
3. Abolition of all right of inheritance.
4. Confiscation of the property of all emigrants and rebels.
5. Centralization of credit in the hands of the State, by means of a national bank with State capital and an exclusive monopoly.
6. Centralization of the means of communication and transport in the hands of the State.
7. Extension of factories and instruments of production owned by the State; the bringing into cultivation of waste lands, and the improvement of the soil generally in accordance with a common plan.
8. Equal liability of all to labor. Establishment of industrial armies, especially for agriculture.
9. Combination of agriculture with manufacturing industries: gradual abolition of the distinction between town and country, by a more equable distribution of the population over the country.
10. Free education for all children in public schools. Abolition of children's factory labor in its present form. Combination of education with industrial production, etc.

PART II

Earl Browder, former leader of the Communist party in America, discusses the American trend toward communism in a recent pamphlet:

"State capitalism leaped forward to a new high point in America in the decade 1939-1949 .... State capitalism, in substance if not in formal aspects, has progressed farther in America than in Great Britain under the Labor Government, despite its nationalization of certain industries, which is a formal stage not yet reached in America; the actual, substantial concentration of the guiding reins of national economy in governmental hands is probably on a higher level in the U. S. A."

In appraising a list of 22 specific items of American governmental policy, Mr. Browder states:

"They have the single feature in common that ... they express *the growth of state capitalism....* [This is] an essential feature of the confirmation of the Marxist theory.... It represents the maturing of the objective (material) prerequisites for socialism, the basic factor which makes socialism inevitable...

1. Government deficit financing.
2. Manipulation of bank reserves requirements.
3. Insurance of bank deposits.
4. Guarantee of mortgages.
5. Control of bank credits.
6. Tinkering with the currency system.
7. Regulation of installment buying.
8. Price controls.
9. Price support for farm products.
10. Agricultural credits.
11. R.F.C. loans to business corporations.
12. Social security systems for workers.
13. Various benefits for veterans.
14. Government housing.
15. Public works to provide employment.
16. Many projects for conservation of natural resources.
17. Juggling of the tax structure.
18. New tariff regulations.
19. Government-organized foreign loans.
20. The Employment Act.
21. The President's economic committee.
22. Last but by no means least, stimulated war armaments production on a large scale."

PART III

SOCIALISM has been defined as *governmental ownership* or *control of the means of production.*

And communism, in this and most other respects, is the same thing as socialism. Marx was a Socialist by his own definition. Russia, after the communist revolution, became the U.S.S.R. -the Union of Soviet *Socialist* Republics.

Invasion of the United States by communism, as thus defined, is evidenced in different ways. Among them are the following:

GOVERNMENT OWNERSHIP IN U.S.A. PER CENT OF TOTAL WEALTH	COVERNMENT CONTROL IN U.S.A.
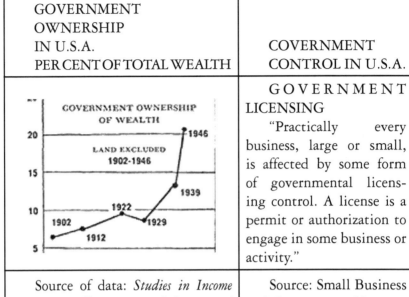	GOVERNMENT LICENSING "Practically every business, large or small, is affected by some form of governmental licensing control. A license is a permit or authorization to engage in some business or activity."
Source of data: *Studies in Income* Source: *Small Business and Govern and Wealth,* Vol. XII, p. 535; National Bureau of Economic **Research**, 1950 *Statistical Research by* F. A. *Harper.*	Source: Small Business and Government Licenses, U.S. Department of Commerce, Pg. 1: Government Printing Office, 1950.

ANALYSIS

Since the above chart illustrates dates of 1946 and 1950, what possibly could have happened in the ensuing sixty and more years that to convince any reasonable person to conclude the trend has not continued?

As this is written, one of the once great American corporations is largely owned by a significant non-business, unprofitable entity ... the United States Government. General Motors is now widely known as Government Motors. And there are more businesses controlled by government either by circumstances related to keeping those companies from going 'belly up' or questionable government 'investment' of grants and loans. Sponsoring new businesses possessed of socially acceptable missions rather than by the tried and true pursuit of the profit motive and lead to little good.

Is it a surprise that bureaucrats are notoriously inept at running businesses when everything government runs results in failure when compared to private business? One has only to look at the postal service about which it is claimed not to be government owned. The United States Postal Service (USPS), also known as the Post Office and U.S. Mail, is an independent agency of the United States government responsible for providing postal service in the United States. The USPS has not directly received taxpayer-dollars since the early 1980s and it incurred a record net loss of $15.9 billion for fiscal year 2012, compared to a net loss of $5.1 billion loss in fiscal year 2011. Seventy percent (70%) of this loss are Congressionally-mandated prefunded health retiree benefits. The USPS has been unable to fund this obligation from operations and has used all of its retained earnings and drawn down from its $15 billion borrowing authority from the U.S. Treasury. So you see, eventually the taxpayers will get stuck for the losses. My question: How can the USPS be an 'independent agency' when its benefits are subject to Congressional mandates and its survival depends on the U.S. Treasury. Enter FedEx and UPS for a free enterprise rescue? If only it could be?

Public Ownership and Common Ownership in Perspective

'The acknowledged aim of socialism is to take the means of production out of the hands of the capitalist class and place them into the hands of the workers. This aim is sometimes spoken of as public ownership, sometimes as common ownership of the production apparatus. There is, however, a marked and fundamental difference.

Public ownership is the ownership, i.e. the right of disposal, by a public body representing society, by government, state power or some other political body. The persons forming this body, the politicians, officials, leaders, secretaries, managers, are the direct masters of the production apparatus; they direct and regulate the process of production; they command the workers. Common ownership is the right of disposal by the workers themselves; the working class itself — taken in the widest sense of all that partake in really productive work, including employees, farmers, scientists — is direct master of the production apparatus, managing, directing, and regulating the process of production which is, indeed, their common work.

Under public ownership the workers are not masters of their work; they may be better treated and their wages may be higher than under private ownership; but they are still exploited. Exploitation does not mean simply that the workers do not receive the full produce of their labor; a

305

considerable part must always be spent on the production apparatus and for unproductive though necessary departments of society. Exploitation consists in that others, forming another class, dispose of the produce and its distribution; that they decide what part shall be assigned to the workers as wages, what part they retain for themselves and for other purposes. Under public ownership this belongs to the regulation of the process of production, which is the function of the bureaucracy. Thus in Russia bureaucracy as the ruling class is master of production and produce, and the Russian workers are an exploited class.'

... *Source: Western Socialist, November 1947*

> *"All initiation of force is a violation of someone else's rights, whether initiated by an individual or the state, for the benefit of an individual or group of individuals, even if it's supposed to be for the benefit of another individual or group of individuals."*
>
> ... CONGRESSMAN RON PAUL

FOR A MORAL REVOLUTION

So consistent is the record of history, that I dare say it could be stated as a natural law of societal behavior that: "The measure of morality in public office will be in inverse ratio to the amount of state interventionism which may exist."

There is nothing new in state interventionism. It is as old and reactionary as societal organization itself. Always, when it permeates the body politic, it kills the nation.

This assertion repeatedly is confirmed by history. The Hammurabi Code, promulgated earlier than 2000 *B.C.*, by imposing controls over wages, prices, production, consumption, and all the rest of the economy, wrecked Babylonia. Governmental extravagance and a bloated bureaucracy killed individual initiative and led to the fall of ancient Greece. A planned economy of state maintenance for the slothful -plus excessive taxation -brought the collapse of the later Roman Empire and the regression of a civilized society into the Dark Ages. The welfare state of the Incas became so debilitated as to become easy prey for Pizarro and his "Conquistadores." In its turn, the great Spanish Empire broke when the throne so regimented every activity that no one could earn a living except by being a public employee, a priest, or a sailor. For the same reasons the British Empire is now dissolving before our eyes.

You are all too sadly acquainted with how low the ethical standards of a few public servants have sunk. Equally bad and even worse occurrences have been uncovered in many of our state and municipal governments.

Almost everywhere politicians and "do-gooders," by camouflaging ill-considered or bad enactments as welfare or defense measures, are enticing their peoples down the path of dalliance into systems of state interventionism. They are leading them to eventual destruction. They are concentrating power in Washington under a bureaucracy already expanded beyond manageable dimensions and which increasingly resorts to uncontrolled extravagance and extravagant controls. They are murdering the nation. Can there be greater treason?

Too many laws create confusion, unwise law corruption. Together they nurture absolutism and criminality.

There are, for example, many enterprises which could not operate profitably were they to obey, to the letter, a complexity of laws and regulations, which sometimes almost seem to have been enacted with malice aforethought. As a result, these businessmen are easy prey for gangsters and crooked officials, both high and low, who exact tribute for what they call "protection." In these cases the quickest prophylactic would be to do away with the unwise laws and regulations.

Jefferson once remarked that a revolution every so often is a good thing. This country desperately a moral revolution right now I pray that it comes soon, before it is too late. I pray that it will be brought on by an outraged public opinion, resulting from each individual reassuming his personal responsibilities and then joining with others to make their voices heard. I pray that it will re-implant the Decalogue and the Golden Rule as the ethical code of the American people. I pray that under its impact the love and old-fashioned discipline exercised within the families of this nation will again be exerted against immorality and crime, corruption and venality.

Such a revolution will return the United States to morality and straight thinking, and thereby resolve the crisis which now confronts us.

Then, we may hope the rest of the world may emulate the salutary results obtained here.

– Spruille Braden (1952 or about a hundred years after Bastiat

> *"America was founded on the principle of inalienable rights not dictated duties. The Declaration of Independence states that every human being has a right to life, liberty and the pursuit of happiness. It does not state that he is born a slave to the needs of others."*
>
> ...ALEX EPSTEIN

INDIVIDUALISM VS. COLLECTIVISM (LIVING FREE VS. FREE LIVING)

We must assume that anyone who happens upon this book will have pre-conceived ideas about matters political in which case our attempts to delineate individual freedom and collectivism will probably fall on deaf ears. Every chapter deserves a book of its own and what you have read thus far is a topic highlight or overview of the subject matter. For many, what follows can be confusing because we are attempting to provoke THINKING and that is precisely why conflicting thoughts are included. So let us ask for an open mind as we move forward. It is too early to choose sides.

Per Wikipedia, "A **comprehensive world view** (or **worldview**) is the fundamental cognitive orientation of an individual or society encompassing the entirety of the individual or society's knowledge and **point-of-view**, including natural philosophy; fundamental, existential, and normative postulates; or themes, values, emotions, and ethics. Additionally, it refers to *the framework of ideas and beliefs through which an individual, group or culture interprets the world and interacts with it.*"

History shows living can go on under collectivism however the quality of life depends on the degree of freedom its leaders choose to tolerate ... if at all. Socialism is the yellow brick road that leads to communism, so let us cut to the chase and identify ourselves with Individual Freedom or Communism (collectivism).

Our purpose now is to see if we can help you clarify your own personal worldview. Would you like to live your life as a free person or would you prefer to live in a full-blown collectivist society as some people openly admit today? THAT is the ultimate question ... and it is a fair question in light of the America we now live in.

A mother-to-be cannot be classified as partially pregnant ... right? Like pregnancy, socialism takes root, advances in stages and ultimately gives birth to an ism that if left unattended becomes communism.

So let us now eliminate the political gestation period. For the purposes of argument, let us *ASSUME* that here and now, there is no middle ground and that we must choose up sides and start a new society at the extremes. No in between here ... we are "pretending" to be one or the other and must identify ourselves as INDIVIDUALS or COMMUNISTS. No other designation is acceptable here. Republican is not. Democrat is not. Political parties are not and that includes Constitutionalists, Libertarians, Greens, Conservatives, Liberals, Progressives, Whigs, Socialist Workers et al are excluded. Forget for a moment that your family always voted for a certain party, forget your loyalty to your company or union and forget about anything related to politics or religion. Ask yourself this question: Which quote seems right to me?

The secret here is to abandon any pre-conceived thoughts or ideas as to how you view yourself now. This exercise calls for a completely open and honest mind. Assuming you have read everything written up to this point, it is possible you have already made up your mind, but *let it all go for now*.

The following quotations from prominent advocates of communism and anti-communists present both extremes of freedom versus power.

Take in the following quotations, pro and con, and decide where your heart and mind leads you if you had to choose one system to best fit the life you want to lead:

"Don't go around saying the world owes you a living; the world owes you nothing; it was here first." – Mark Twain

"You can talk about capitalism and communism and all that sort of thing, but the important thing is the struggle everybody is engaged in to get better living conditions, and they are not interested too much in government." – **Bernard Baruch**

*"Communism is inequality, but not as property is. Property is exploitation of the weak by the strong. Communism is exploitation of the strong by the weak." –**Pierre-Joseph Proudhon***

"The theory of Communism may be summed up in one sentence: Abolish all private property." – **Karl Marx**

*"Communism doesn't work because people like to own stuff." – **Frank Zappa***

"Democracy is the road to socialism." – **Karl Marx**

*"The goal of socialism is communism." – **Vladimir Lenin***

"Communism is not love. Communism is a hammer which we use to crush the enemy." – **Mao Tse Tung**

*"I am for socialism, disarmament, and, ultimately, for abolishing the state itself... I seek the social ownership of property, the abolition of the propertied class, and the sole control of those who produce wealth. Communism is the goal." – **Roger Nash Baldwin***

"The communism of Marx seeks a strong state centralization, and where this exists, there the parasitic Jewish nation - which speculates upon the labor of people - will always find the means for its existence." – **Mikhail Bakunin**

*"Let's not talk about Communism. Communism was just an idea, just pie in the sky." – **Boris Yeltsin***

"Even now we feel that Stalin was devoted to Communism, he was a Marxist, this cannot and should not be denied." – **Nikita Khrushchev**

*"I grew up under Communism so we could only learn Russian, and then when Communism fell in 1989 we could learn a few more things and have the freedom to travel and the freedom of speech - and the freedom of dreaming, really." – **Petra Nemcova***

"Socialism only works in two places: Heaven where they don't need it, and hell where they already have it." –**Ronald Reagan**

"Communism is like Prohibition, it's a good idea but it won't work" – **Will Rogers**

"Communism is the graveyard of ambition" – **Daniel R. Bou Diab**

"Justice is always naive and self-confident; believing that it will immediately win once recognized. That is the reason why the forces of Justice are so poorly organized. On the other hand, the Evil is cynic, sly and fantastically organized. It never ever has the illusion of the ability to stand on its own feet and to win in a fair competition. That is why it is ready to use any kind of means without hesitation. And of course it does - under the banners of the most noble ideas." – **Vladimir Bukovsky**

"Communism feeds on aggression, hatred, and the imprisonment of men's minds and souls. This shall not take root in the United States." – **Emanuel Celler**

"I don't like Communism because it hands out wealth through rationing books." – **Omar Torrijos Herrera**

"Capitalism and communism stand at opposite poles. Their essential difference is this: The communist, seeing the rich man and his fine home, says: 'No man should have so much.' The capitalist, seeing the same thing, says: 'All men should have as much.' "– **Phelps Adams**

"I don't really view communism as a bad thing." – **Whoopi Goldberg**

"When I die, my only wish is that Cambodia remain Cambodia and belong to the West. It is over for communism, and I want to stress that." – **Pol Pot**

"There are many people in the world who really don't understand, or say they don't, what is the great issue between the free world and the Communist world. Let them come to Berlin. There are some who say that communism is the wave of the future. Let them come to Berlin. And there are some who say in Europe and elsewhere we can work with the Communists. Let them come to Berlin. And there are even a few who say that it is true that communism is an evil system, but it permits us to make economic progress. Lass' sie nach Berlin kommen. Let them come to Berlin." – **John Fitzgerald Kennedy**, Speech in Berlin

"The substance of the eminent Socialist gentlemen's speech is that making a profit is a sin. It is my belief that the real sin is taking a loss!" – **Winston Churchill**

"Communism has never come to power in a country that was not disrupted by war or corruption or both." – *John Fitzgerald Kennedy*

"Communism is the opiate of the intellectuals with no cure except as a guillotine might be called a cure for dandruff" – **Clare Booth Luce**

*"We need the private sector to create jobs. If the government could create jobs Communism would have worked, but it didn't." – **Tim Scott***

"The real issue behind these people who are gun grabbers, the truth is - based on fact - the reason why is, they want control. They want control of the people. That's what socialism is and communism." – **Luke Scott**

*"I know that I am leaving the winning side for the losing side, but it is better to die on the losing side than to live under Communism." – **Whittaker Chambers***

"Communism destroys democracy. Democracy can also destroy Communism." – **Andre Malraux**

*"I have taken an oath in my heart to oppose communism until the day I die." – **Eldridge Cleaver***

"The real evil of the Russian communist state is not communism. It is the secret police and the concentration camp." – **John Boyd Orr**

*"Nonetheless, one final and inescapable conflict remains before us, the war between democracy and communism. Although each side has equipped itself with fearsome weapons and is pitted against the other in readiness for battle, the core of their conflict is internal and ideological. Which side will triumph in this final ideological conflict? Anyone who believes in the reality of God will surely answer that democracy will win." – **Sun Myung Moon**, Divine Principle, Introduction.*

"With his trademark courage and conviction, President Reagan led us out of the Cold War, spreading his vision of freedom, resulting in the release of millions of people from the yoke of communism." – **John Doolittle**

*"No one should suffer from the great delusion that any form of communism or socialism which promotes the dictatorship of the few instead of the initiative of the millions can produce a happier or more prosperous society." – **Charles E. Wilson***

"Unionization, as opposed to communism, presupposes the relation of employment; it is based upon the wage system and it recognizes fully and unreservedly the institution of private property and the right to investment profit." – **John L. Lewis**

*"After 7,000 biblical years — 6,000 years of restoration history plus the millennium, the time of completion — communism will fall in its 70th year. Here is the meaning of the year 1978. Communism, begun in 1917, could maintain itself approximately 60 years and reach its peak. So 1978 is the border line and afterward communism will decline; in the 70th year it will be altogether ruined. This is true. Therefore, now is the time for people who are studying communism to abandon it." – **Sun Myung Moon**, The Way of Restoration (April, 1972)*

"Don't listen to what the Communists say, but look at what they do."
– **Nguyen Van Thieu**, President of South Vietnam.

"In a higher phase of communist society... only then can the narrow horizon of bourgeois right be fully left behind and society inscribe on its banners: from each according to his ability, to each according to his needs." – **Karl Marx**

"How do you tell a communist? Well, it's someone who reads Marx and Lenin. And how do you tell an anti-Communist? It's someone who understands Marx and Lenin." – **Ronald Reagan**

"At the end of a century that has seen the evils of communism, Nazism and other modern tyrannies, the impulse to centralize power remains amazingly persistent." – *Joseph Sobran*

"[Cold war demonology] is a color word, and I probably should not have used it. It means just sort of interpreting everything in terms of a great communist conspiracy and in terms of communists being supermen who somehow can overcome the great problems of differences between national units, and so on. They are not supermen at all. They are men with feet of clay which extend almost all the way up to their brains." – **Edwin O. Reischauer**, former U.S. ambassador to Japan, testimony at hearing, January 31, 1967.

"For us in Russia communism is a dead dog. For many people in the West, it is still a living lion." – *Alexander Solzhenitsyn*

"The years ahead will be great ones for our country, for the cause of freedom and the spread of civilization. The West will not contain Communism, it will transcend Communism. We will not bother to denounce it, we'll dismiss it as a sad, bizarre chapter in human history whose last pages are even now being written." – **Ronald Reagan**

"I have spent all my life under a Communist regime, and I will tell you that a society without any objective legal scale is a terrible one indeed. But a society with no other scale but the legal one is not quite worthy of man either." – *Alexander Solzhenitsyn*

"In examining any dictatorship, there are two good tests. Firstly, what is the relation between the rulers and the proletariat or common people? Are the rulers members of the proletariat, as they would have you believe? Do they even identify their interests with those of ordinary citizens? The truth seems to be that, no matter where you find them, the so-called proletarian dictatorships are actually controlled by a small elite who ordinarily lose little sleep in worrying about the rights of the common man. Secondly,

have the proletariat any effective say in what the rulers do? In the proletarian dictatorships I am familiar with ordinary people enjoy little or no control over their Government or over their own lives and futures."
– **Muhammad Reza Pahlavi** (1961)

Mission for my Country, London, page 162

"In our country, the lie has become not just a moral category but a pillar of the State." – Alexander Solzhenitsyn

"Communism is the corruption of a dream of justice." – **Adlai E. Stevenson**

"Communism is the death of the soul. It is the organization of total conformity – in short, of tyranny – and it is committed to making tyranny universal." – Adlai E. Stevenson

"Communists always say that Capitalism leaves holes for crime, poverty and a higher society and that it is wrong. Communists do an even worse job at correcting this. Capitalism has a mission to give every person everything they want, and right now we are set out to fulfill that mission. All we lack is a means." – **Cole Stewart**

"It all came from there." – Lech Walesa, pointing to a TV when a reporter asked him why communism fell.

"Communists are of two kinds only. Gadarene Swine whose wits have been taken from them so that they rush headlong down the slope to their own destruction, and ordinary voracious swine who, if you were standing in their sty, had a heart-attack and fell among them, would instantly set upon and devour you."– **Dennis Wheatley**

"The scientific approach uncovers, that Communism does not eliminate the inequality between men, the social injustice, exploitation of man by man and other evils of society – communism merely changes their form and gives birth to new evils, which become eternal fellow-travelers of communism." ... "All in all, Engels talked so much rot of every kind, that now all the world's academies of science should be directed to rectify his mistakes and idiocies."" – Aleksandr Zinovyev

"Today the primary threat to the liberties of the American people comes not from communism, foreign tyrants or dictators. It comes from the tendency on our own shores to centralize power, to trust bureaucracies rather than people." – **George H. Allen**

"In an ironic sense, Karl Marx was right. We are witnessing today a great revolutionary crisis – a crisis where the demands of the economic order are colliding directly with those of the political order. But the crisis is happening not in the free,

*non-Marxist West, but in the home of Marxism-Leninism, the Soviet Union ...
{Communism will be} left on the ash heap of history."* – **Ronald Reagan**

"What is a communist? One who hath yearnings for equal division of
unequal earnings." –Ebenezer Elliott (1781-1849), Epigram.

*"There is not so much difference between the ideologies of capitalism and commu-
nism, you know. The difference is simple. Capitalism is the exploitation of man by
man, and communism is the reverse."* – **John Gardner**, *The man from Barbarossa*

"In October 1917, we parted with the old world, rejecting it once and
for all. We are moving toward a new world, a world of Communism. We
shall never turn off that road." – **Mikhail Gorbachev**

"Any man who is not a communist at the age of twenty is a fool. Any
man who is still a communist at the age of thirty is an even bigger fool."
– **George Bernard Shaw**

"Communism needs democracy like the human body needs oxygen." – **Leon
Trotsky**

"In Germany, [the Nazis] first came for the Communists, and I did not
speak up, because I was not a Communist. Then they came for the Jews,
and I did not speak up, because I was not a Jew. Then they came for the
trade unionists, and I did not speak up, because I was not a trade unionist.
Then they came for the Catholics, and I did not speak up, because I was a
Protestant. Then they came for me – and by that time no one was left to
speak up." – **Martin Niemoller**

*"Some tell me "Preach the pure gospel!" This reminds me that the Communist
secret police also told me to preach Christ, but not to mention communism. Is it really
so, that those who are for what is called "a pure gospel" are inspired by the same
spirit as those of the Communist secret police?"* – **Richard Wurmbrand**, *Tortured
For Christ, p. 75 (1967).*

"Communism is the death of the soul. It is the organization of total
conformity - in short, of tyranny - and it is committed to making tyranny
universal" – **Adlai E. Stevenson**

*"When I was young I had a moment of believing in the Communist doctrine.
I wanted to save the world through Communism. Quite soon I understood that
it doesn't work, but I've never pretended it didn't happen to me."* – **Wislawa
Szymborska**

"Marriage is socialism among two people."... **Barbara Ehrenreich**

*Communism has decided against God, against Christ, against the Bible, and
against all religion.* – **Billy Graham**

"It's easier to fool people than to convince them that they have been fooled"– **Mark Twain**

And lastly, one of my illuminating favorites:

"Those who say religion has nothing to do with politics do not know what religion is." – Mohandas K. Gandhi

Have you had enough quotes already? Perhaps you noticed that some quotes are pro-communist and others anti-communist. We selected from a wealth of quotations from around the world to reflect a world of confusing viewpoints. Our objective is to give the reader a sense of understanding about the various ways in which people live and think. Again, our quality of living depends on how we piece together the fabric of our own society. We must understand those pieces and selectively support those we like so long as they are based on principle. Our core beliefs must be rock solid and consistent with our moral code.

In America, and assuming the reader is American, we know what life has given us. According to Thomas Jefferson "We may consider each generation as a distinct nation …" Each succeeding generation can be seen as a new country. Each generation will choose the rules by which it will live.

The 'tried and true' will always be challenged by those who seek change for the sake of change … or for other nefarious reasons. Those with a thirst for power will subvert any system. Samuel Webster said it best, "Communism is the perfect system, in theory. As are Monarchy, Fascism and Democracy. The only reason they don't work is because of Human nature to pervert the situation into the best one for them. Nothing else."

Most people think in terms of the two party system, republicans and democrats. The tradition role of republicans is to govern as a republic under the rule of law respecting individual rights above that of a government. Republic means republican. Democrats stand for majority rule as in a democracy. Hopefully this simple explanation covers the basic differences and why one hears the argument that America is a republic and not really a democracy.

Now is the time for all good men to come to the aid of their country. Seems I have heard line before? Nowadays it means women too, but that is not how it was taught in typing class.

Anyway, we have talked about several important subjects concerning individualism vs. collectivism. You have been exposed to several pages of quotations about personal responsibility, free enterprise capitalism, socialism, Communism and so on, but as Mom used to say, "The proof of the pudding is in the eating." Until I thought of using this fourteenth century proverb, I often wondered exactly what it meant, so I decided to Google it. I found it has a 14th century origin. Its meaning is perfect for introducing the last chapter: LIFE UNDER COMMUNISM IN EASTERN EUROPE. Translated, the proverb means: "**To fully test something you need to experience it yourself.**

So if you are ready to have the bejabbers scared out of you, read on...

> *"It's a different outlook, and one that I understand. When you are a former member of the Warsaw Pact, when you have lived behind the Berlin Wall, when you have experienced the communist systems that existed in these countries, for them, the West represents hope."*
>
> ... JEAN-PIERRE RAFFARIN

LIFE UNDER COMMUNISM IN EASTERN EUROPE

After World War II, communists took control of eight Eastern European nations. The following Internet excerpts are from the recollections of a child who grew up in Romania during that era who finally managed to emigrate and find success in America.*

"The rise of Communist Russia turned out to be one of the greatest mistakes and disasters humanity has suffered during the past few centuries. When it happened, the Communists were the poor people, not very bright, not the intellectuals. But if you were poor enough – and not very bright – you could come to the Communist Party, become a member and have the illusion of power. It was a very attractive proposition for that type of person.

The governments were very vengeful. They hated rich people. They hated intellectuals. They hated anyone who posed any type of threat to their plans. And they killed many people and put others in concentration camps and jails. Families never heard from their loved ones again.

And while the Communists may have said they wanted everything to be the same for everybody, deep down they were hypocrites. They seized the homes of people they killed or sent to jail and lived in them. They took their cars and drove them around town. In essence, they became the new aristocracy. They robbed people like my family and took all the farm machinery, equipment and anything that was used to work the land with. Then they put it all in the middle of the farm and burned it. They did this (as) a big production, an example made for people to show them that life was going to be hard now."

"And it wasn't long before secret police started popping up everywhere. They would appear on your doorstep and interrogate you. They'd stop you on the street and begin asking questions. They would make you turn against your neighbor. When someone wouldn't cooperate, they'd torture or kill them. These were very scary times."

"My family, like others who weren't immediate converts to the Communist cause, didn't want to voluntarily give away everything they had worked so hard to achieve. But what choice did we really have? The Party leaders were killing people. If we stood up against them, they wouldn't have thought twice before putting bullets in our brains."

"My grandparents' lives in America had changed their spirits. This country (America) has a way of living, feeling, and thinking that no other country on earth has. We know that we are the best and with great power come great responsibility. We own our fate. We decide how we are going to react. Americans are not victims, nor perpetrators. We are helpers and survivors. We stand for honor, duty, and order. Even though, the communists looked and talked like they were organized, behind the puppet curtain was a chaotic mess."

"My parents raised me in a place where the rules were made of deceit. The reason America is such a successful triumph of the human spirit is because people are fair and logic is seen in every aspect of American life. Not so in a Communist country. The people who came to power under Communism did not earn or deserve their titles or positions. They took them. Whenever something is not earned, you do not know how to treat it or how to hold on to it – you don't appreciate it. You misuse it."

"As a student in a Communist Romanian school, I could not have been anymore defiant. Their silly rules did not make any sense like reading only Communist propaganda and making sure we screamed our allegiance to the Communist Party."

"By the time I was in high school, the political situation in Romania had begun to settle down a little because of outside pressure from different countries. It also became easier to live there because the corruption among the secret police and Party members grew to epic proportions. The corruption was out in the open. Communists wanted money from people and they would do things under the table, even if everybody else around knew it was going on.

If you were lucky enough to have some money, any money, you could get whatever you wanted from the Communists who controlled the cities and villages. My parents managed to get some of their property back through bribes."

"I refused to be a young Communist and didn't follow the rules. That's not to say that I went out of my way to make trouble, because I didn't. But I did do things like go to church when you weren't supposed to do that."

"While the Communists didn't close all the churches, if you were seen in a church they stigmatized you. But I loved to go to church. It was a refuge of sorts for me, support for my confusion. I would go alone and hide from the prying eyes of the secret police. And I would pray. I would pray that one day I would go to America and escape this life. I would ask God to listen and answer my prayers."

"When the Communists came and took away our land and possessions, we became closer to the rest of our family. We rarely fought with each other and we helped one another. It made our extended family bonds strong. This is how my mom viewed God, and that is what she instilled in me as a child. Whenever something happened, I always tried to see the lesson even in the worst moments. When you are taught this simple skill as a child, your mind automatically goes to the positive in any event. It's not what happens to you, it's how you react to it that matters the most."

"For several months in the early 1950s, after the Communists took everything away from us, my family lived in small room. We barely had enough food to eat and clothing to put on our backs. We had no money to buy sugar, and my mom used homemade marmalade in my sister's milk. I remember how my parents, after they were stripped of their possessions, weren't even allowed to have jobs. It was punishment by the Communists for their resistance."

"We wore uniforms each day to school that demonstrated our "sameness." The Communists mandated that no one should have any more than anyone else. Nobody was supposed to have more than one home, and if the home's square footage was bigger than the Party felt was appropriate, the rest of the house would be allocated to other Communists. We had friends, many friends, who lived in a house and shared bedrooms with other families and used a common kitchen for everyone."

"In school, the teachers told us that God didn't exist. They explained that we should not go to church because there was nothing there for us. The only thing we should believe in, they said, was Communism and its philosophies. We read from Marx and Engels, and nobody else. We were not allowed to read American authors or any book that said anything positive about America. And we were not allowed to own foreign currency, especially U.S. dollars. If we were caught with foreign money, we were treated the same way that people are treated in America when they are caught with illegal drugs – we were sent to jail."

"Those Communist teachers hated me. ... (And) singled me out for scrutiny every chance they had. Then, at the end of the school day, I would come home and tell my parents about how terrible school was. And every day, my grandfather took me aside. "Stella," he said. "Do not believe these people. Don't do whatever they tell you to do. Do not believe in Communism. It is evil. We believe in other things than they do.""

... Stella Moga, Author of "Stella's Way"

Stella's Way is the life story of **Stella Moga**, a Romanian immigrant who faced many hurdles, including a child's death, to become a successful entrepreneur, wife, mother and grandmother. Her story is a reminder that the American Dream is real.

Learn more about Stella at **http://www.lechaperonrouge.com**

OR **http://stellasway.wordpress.com**

*Learn more at The CONSTITUTIONAL RIGHTS FOUNDATION: http://www.crf-usa.org/bill-of-rights-in-action/bria-19-1-a-life-under-communism-in-eastern-europe

Free enterprise capitalism versus state controlled collectivism is best illustrated by the results of the cold war. Communism failed miserably with the collapse of the USSR in Russia and the Eastern European Republics, circa 1990.

The American Free Enterprise System won by out-producing the centralized, socialist state run monopolies and by the demands for freedom from communist governance by the people living in the Iron Curtain countries.

Another long story made short

Life under despotic communism is no picnic. Strange is that word as I type it here to introduce a recent personal experience. You will see why later – at the end of the story.

My best friend and I were invited to a family gathering at the home of her brother. His wife came to America as an infant during the time of the Hungarian Revolution or uprising of 1956. I was seated for dinner next to parents of that infant who is now a fully grown mother of two college age girls about to begin their careers.

Dinner conversation is oft times quite revealing. And when I asked the gracefully aging parents of that infant about how and when they came to America their story became captivating. As the uprising was unfolding, the young parents gathered up bare essentials, the clothes they were wearing and along with their baby girl somehow made it across the border in the dead of night.

Once out of Hungary, a series of fortunate events enabled that young family to make it through the diplomatic jungle and set sail for America. In asking how they were lucky enough to move past the inevitable show stopping bureaucratic checkpoints, he responded in all seriousness, "It was because we had a pretty baby."

A most difficult moment in their trip to America came as they sailed into the New York Harbor. He said they cried. Thinking they appreciated the idea of freedom in America, I welled up a bit and asked if they cried at the sight of the Statue of Liberty. "No," he said, "It was the sight of the ships' crew throwing leftover food off the ship and into the water."

> *"Politics ought to be the part-time profession of every citizen who would protect the rights and privileges of free people and who would preserve what is good and fruitful in our national heritage."*
>
> ... DWIGHT D. EISENHOWER

FIVE STAR CITIZENS

Citizenship in a freedom loving country is a birthright but one must exercise the basic duties of citizenship in five ways. The birthright of freedom in America is a given, but the right to keep it must earned. Our Founding Fathers expected it of us.

1. Five Star Citizens are FEARLESS!

Many people fear government and if the idea of taking part in governing alarms you – get over it! YOU are the leader of your life! Take charge of it and fear not those who govern because eventually they WILL take advantage of your trust. The first step is to conquer fear and join the best and the bravest among us as a fearless INDIVIDUAL!

Historian Lord Acton (1834-1902) warned that political power is the most serious threat to liberty. His essays and letters abound with memorable insights. For instance: "Liberty is not a means to a higher political end. It is itself the highest political end...liberty is the only object which benefits all alike, and provokes no sincere opposition...The danger is not that a particular class is unfit to govern. Every class is unfit to govern ... Power tends to corrupt, and absolute power corrupts absolutely."

Containing the power hungry personalities amongst us is an individual responsibility. Why? Because there will always be people who seek to gain power and control over the lives of others. When the people permit those who govern to gain too much power, they will always take advantage of the powerless. Do the names Hitler, Stalin, Pol Pot, Castro and Hussein strike any bells? And those are just a few of the extreme examples from recent history.

2. Five Star Citizens know history and keep up with current affairs!

History is the study of change over time. So why is the study of history so important? The only sure thing in life is change. Because, as many have said, history has proven that those who do not pay attention to the lessons of history will repeat the mistakes. So, a sense of history is crucial to good decision making in managing the inevitable changes in societies.

History is also the accumulation of knowledge we call experience and experience is not repeating mistakes. Some claim to have say twenty years experience. Do they? Or do they have one year's experience twenty times? Logic suggests that a good decision today is more likely when one considers the related factors that went into those bad decisions of the past. Knowing the history of one's country is one element of responsible citizenship.

America must avoid making the mistakes that caused other free countries to fail. Americans also need to understand the world's history as did their Founding Fathers when they wrote the Constitution. Those mostly young Founders studied governments throughout recorded history. They drew upon that knowledge when, in just 4400 words, the very best protections for the individual citizen against oppressive government were written into law. Of course, the Bill of Rights was added later to make the whole thing foolproof ... or so we think?

Apathy and ignorance are the silent enemies of liberty. They will ultimately lead to the loss of freedom and such loss usually happens from within. They not only threaten democracy but guarantee its eventual destruction.

The birth of America changed the status of the individual citizen and gave Americans a legacy of freedom to pass on to future generations. It is the responsibility of each citizen to behave in ways that preserve, protect and defend that legacy.

3. Five Star Citizens THINK for themselves!

Informed citizens study all sides of an issue and decide what they want to believe – as individuals. Thinking people refuse to take politically motivated TV commercials too seriously or permit undue influence by the media and special interest groups.

Since the nature of politicians and their supporters is to seek power at your expense, re-structuring the truth to fit their agenda is just another example of 'the end justifies the means'. Thinking for oneself means 'reading between the lines' in the search for truth. As with divorce, there are three sides to every story: His, Hers and The truth! Take the position of a judge and/or juries ... hear both sides, consider the merits of each and seek your own truth.

Internet news is the modern way to learn. We like The Drudge Report website because it links to the very latest news from a variety of reliable sources throughout the world. Also, there are links to a variety of viewpoints from those in position to shape public opinion.

4. Five Star Citizens VOTE in every election!

It is the duty of every citizen to secure rights and freedoms by participating in the affairs of their countries. Low voter turnout takes freedom for granted and is a disgrace to America in the eyes of the world. Do your part to stop the trend – get involved! Civic responsibility is a habit one can feel good about. It is good citizenship. It is your insurance against disaster. Think of it as survival training for you and your descendants.

Some describe America as 'highly polarized.' Poppycock! We see a country where the two party system is working just fine. But, for the half of eligible voters who don't vote, well they have voluntarily given up their right to a legitimate opinion – about anything related to government.

5. Five Star Citizens use their political clout!

Individuals CAN and DO have influence – IF they make themselves heard. Make it a point to write or call elected officials and centers of influence that shape public opinion like talk shows, networks, newspapers and magazines.

Informed communication and follow-up action is powerful. Get on your own soapbox! Be a committee of one ... a lobbyist for freedom. Voting is power. HOWEVER, uninformed voting just for the sake of saying, "I voted today" doesn't cut it. The best voters are those who are well-informed and can argue an issue from all points of view.

–Rod Miller 2002

> *"Responsibility is the price of freedom."*
>
> ... ELBERT HUBBARD

SUMMARY

Individualism and Free Enterprise Capitalism versus centralized state controlled Socialism and Communism needs to be understood and the differences recognized. The statist mindset can be counted on to chip away at freedom. Therefore, it is the duty of each citizen to guard against those who advocate solutions to problems that do not necessarily exist. The socialism idea is attractive and draws from the weakest of minds, but at what cost in terms of individual freedom for every individual.

As free market capitalism is eroded by those who embrace subtle concessions to socialism, the power hungriest of politicians will fill any void. They will, even unwittingly (or on purpose), move further toward full scale communism even though some people may mean well. Sometimes the worst of the worst bury themselves among the easily influenced and perpetuate the socialist/communist agenda because they ARE dedicated communists. Survival of freedom depends on astute citizens who recognize the symptoms of encroachment and vigorously stand in opposition. The choice is simple. Do you want to enjoy individual liberty or be subjected to the will of others?

Let us take a look at BOTH sides, living FREE versus FREE living, with the realization that ultimately, there is no middle ground. Politically, middle ground is temporary and like a vacuum and given the chance, socialism will fill it. Once filled and with support of the masses, power and force will prevail and the next evil ism will come to be. Evil comes with power. Power begets evil. Benevolent dictatorship is a pipedream. The risk is too great to exchange freedom for promises.

The choice depends on how one understands the consequences of giving up on freedom. Winning the hearts and minds of the people determines which system will prevail. Of course, there are other systems that are not purely atheistic communism. Islam is a system of life combining religion and government, but the main event in world politics remains the battle between the unique American way of life introduced to us by the America's Founding Fathers and the Godless communism of Marx and Engels.

The two party system in America, namely the Republicans and Democrats, has managed to blur the political landscape to such a degree that determining just what either of them stands for is sometimes difficult. Perhaps now is the time to face reality, draw a line in the sand and choose sides? Which side best fits our personal beliefs and value system? Henceforth, let us identify ourselves as individuals with rights and liberties OR fall in with groups favoring socialism as a way of life through centralized government control. Let us realign our thinking and make labels have meaning again.

The earlier quotes addressed the concepts of individual freedom, socialism and communism. I especially like the quote cited in the INTRODUCTION:

"In a sense there have always and ever been only two political philosophies: liberty and power. Either people should be free to live their lives as they see fit, as long as they respect the equal rights of others, or some people should be able to use force to make other people act in ways they wouldn't choose." – David Boaz

Mr. Boaz succinctly describes freedom/liberty and power/force in the simplest way.

Multiple readings of this book and its timeless essays can help the reader to assimilate what, at times, can be confusing concepts. It is so easy to hear a new idea and embrace it only to later find it is an old idea with documented failures to its credit.

Differentiating between all sides of an issue can lead to reasonable decisions. We intended to provide snippets of the thinking of prominent proponents of those who advocate for individual freedom versus those who choose government handouts, i.e., 'free living.' We hope we enabled readers to, as suggested earlier, "understand what it is that they disagree with."

Time to choose up sides ... the battle before us is at hand and will continue for all time. There will always be those who seek the power to rule the lives of others. For those who cherish the spirit of freedom, the laws of nature are on your side. The spirit of freedom can never be defeated for those whose very souls have that "burning desire to live unrestrained."

But remember this, once a society chooses the socialist path to communism there is almost no retreating to the former condition without a revolution to throw off the chains of political masters. Violence is sometimes the only possible resolution to political oppression. However, history repeats itself... possibly someday Cuba will once again join the world community as a free society. How?

Well, recently published news featured a story about Cuba and its fifty year long experiment with communism. Everything is free in Cuba, but the government is about to introduce taxes. Living free in Cuba is not so attractive with the average income the peso equivalent of nineteen dollars ($19) per month. The government is bloated with low paid workers and some workers shift away from the government towards individual enterprise. Small plots of land are being made available for farming (Sounds like the Pilgrim story ... is history repeating itself in Cuba?). It looks like Cuba has a chance to re-join the world? Let's hope so. Its people are getting a thirst for the better life and communism is once again a failing proposition. One new restaurant owner, formerly an underpaid government architect, had this to say, "Honestly, I didn't change professions just for the money, although this does pay better," he says. "I love what I'm doing now. And the more you love what you do, the more success you'll have." Truer words were never spoken and the essence of individualism!

Finally, the primary message and story line of this book is: **Capitalism always wins and eventually, socialism always fails. That is the natural way of things and how life is meant to be. Don't fight the Free Enterprise Market Economy. Regulate it to achieve a level playing field if you must, but for the economic good of society ... embrace it!**

AFTERWORD

"The penalty good men pay for indifference to public affairs is to be ruled by evil men." – **Plato**

Earlier we mentioned that everything in life has a price tag. If you want to be a great athlete in your chosen sport, it cannot happen without paying the price. Assuming one is dedicated to a set of goals, it takes practice and the persistence to achieve excellence to the extent of one's capabilities. Anyone with dedication and desire can maximize their potential. Far too many people are content with making the *best* of the conditions of their lives. The best success usually comes to those who seek to make the *most* of their lives.

Apathy, ignorance and indifference to public affairs will most certainly deprive Americans of the continuation of their liberties at some future time. For those who may wish to disagree, please be reminded that history is on my side. Despite warnings, like the quote above from Plato who lived centuries before the coming of Christ, the wisdom of the giants of history such as Thomas Jefferson, Winston Churchill and many others seems to be lost to the masses.

When tyranny and oppression takes root in our lives and/or the lives of our friends, there comes a time when evil must be faced head on and defeated. Rebellions within sovereign nations are common. When our friends are endangered, we 'come to the rescue' for many reasons some of which are not clear. When despotic dictators such as Hitler, Stalin and many others choose aggression as a means to control the lives of other nations, the predictable result is WAR.

Most people wish to live peacefully to enjoy family and friends and live as prosperously as they can within their station in life. The beauty of the American Dream is the upward mobility (opportunity) available to those having the desire to upgrade their "station in life." As I see it, war *can* be the result when citizens choose not to participate in the affairs of their country. When the people abandon their civic responsibility to other individuals and organizations, they lose their individual political clout.

Yes, joining a group gives the group more power. Any group with a large body of advocates has influence, but there is always a danger within any group. It is natural for any member of a group, be it a union, association or other organization, to attract the type of person who thirsts for the power to impose their will. Worst case scenario is when a country permits an all powerful leader to control the destiny of an entire nation.

Simply put, the price tag for freedom is a continuing individual commitment to the principles that made America great. Tinkering with success opens the door to failure.

Freedom is like a monthly house or car payment. Even if your home is 'free and clear' and your car is paid off, you may feel secure, but there are maintenance costs that if neglected will eventually result in the loss of home and car. The price of maintenance to preserve freedom is participation. Every citizen should not be bashful in using their individual political clout in defense of their individual personal freedom.

Loss of assets can be temporary. Loss of freedom is confining. Loss of a life in war is a waste of human potential. Every war takes its toll. All wars have lasting wounds. In particular, The Viet Nam war took friends and family. It did mine.

Fred, my brother Robert C. Miller and the author served together as Marine Corps reservists in the late 1950's. Fred was sent early to Viet Nam and was the first Marine captured by the Viet Cong. The *unconfirmed* time of capture as I recall was in November, 1961. Other accounts suggest Fred and Robert were first reported missing in 1964. They became known as "Salt" and "Pepper" because of skin color. During the recovery of their remains in

1990 Vietnamese officials acknowledged they had been captured alive and killed in captivity. The remains were recovered, returned and interred in a common grave at Arlington National Cemetery.

Buried together in one grave, this tombstone identifies the final resting place of Marine **Sergeant Robert L. Greer** and Marine **Sergeant Fred T. Schreckengost.**

These fine young men and 58,280 others died fighting communism in just this one war. The survivors live with the pain of their memories.

From 1775 to now (2013), the United States of America has experienced a grand total loss or 1,326,612 dead and 1,531,026 wounded in all the wars. Another 38,159 continue to be missing in action. The impact of these losses on their families and friends is incalculable.

Endless freedom is never guaranteed and future wars will be fought.

Nobody I know advocates war for the sake of war. So far, history proves that a universal 'lasting peace' is a pipe dream. Hopefully, this book has presented political and economic views that the reader can embrace – and defend in the extreme if need be.

What Can I Do?

Spreading ideas has never been easier because the power of every person is enhanced by the technology of our times. Of course, everyone, including those with evil intent has access, so to win the hearts and minds of the people depends on the quality of ideas and our ability to communicate them effectively. We hope the validity of the ideas presented in this book have been confirmed in the reader's mind.

How many times have we heard, "My vote doesn't count?" The centuries old message of this proverb sheds light on the importance of every informed person:

For Want of a Nail

For want of a nail the shoe was lost.
For want of a shoe the horse was lost.
For want of a horse the rider was lost.
For want of a rider the message was lost.
For want of a message the battle was lost.
For want of a battle the kingdom was lost.
And all for the want of a horseshoe nail

The spirit of freedom is that burning desire to live unrestrained so use your political clout to protect your individual freedom. YOU are important. Find a way to actively participate!

AFTERTHOUGHT

May I suggest a good personal attitude toward just about any issue or consideration is to do your own due diligence by challenging conventional wisdom. Take a chance. At the risk of being proven wrong, you will be in a win-win position when you consider and understand all the practical possibilities. Understanding and retaining important points and details about any issue adds to your personal knowledgebase.

My point in closing with the following example is to suggest *anything* is worthy of your intellectual curiosity.

For instance, let us consider this 'far out' (pun in process) example: Professor Stephen Hawking, the renowned cosmologist at the Department of Applied Mathematics and Theoretical Physics at The University of Cambridge UK is frequently in the news. His website: **http://www.hawking.org.uk/** will pretty much tell you what you need to know about the remarkable Prof. Hawking.

With all due respect to Prof. Hawking, I am personally at variance with some of his and other intellectual's opinions and theories regarding the "origins of the universe."

Humans tend to accept the idea that everything has a beginning and an end. My personal belief about the 'big picture' is there was no beginning of the universe and there will be no end to it? The UNIVERSE as I see it has no ends and no middle. It has always existed and will forever continue to exist without limitations. This is not to suggest a disbelief in God, but just another way to come to grips with the question about why we are here and how it all came about. I will leave defining God and the universe to the intellectuals, theologians and their followers (Creationism vs. Evolution) to define God in ways that fit their belief system. For me, I retain the right to think independently (out of the box?) and I hope you will too.

So how does this all tie into the spirit of freedom, free enterprise economics, socialism, living free vs. free living and all those essays you read that brought you to this point?

Ponder this thought for a moment if you will? In the grand scheme of things, the essays here are just very tiny pieces of life's puzzle. Most everything in life has to do with how those and other pieces fit together. How the human race puts the puzzle together will determine the speed at which the human race moves forward.

My contention has to do with how socialism waits for others to achieve. In the meantime, the foot draggers plan and scheme trying to figure out how to re-distribute or "spread the wealth" while those who are motivated to achieve move forward in anticipation of rising to the top on their own merits. Achievers expect hangers on to extract a piece of someone else's success but their confidence drives them to 'outrun' those who cannot or will not produce on their own.

Freedom gives rise to opportunity. The spirit of freedom never fully dies within us and must sometimes lay dormant waiting for an opportunity to re-emerge. The Pilgrims coming to the new world, the old world prisoners sent to Australia as well as seeds from fallen plants and trees somehow manage to take root and re-establish themselves given the chance.

A particular favorite thought of mine comes from Kahlil Gibran's *The Prophet*, "Your children are not your children. They are the sons and daughters of Life's longing for itself." And so life marches on. And it will march on beyond the physical limits of this Earth.

We will create and assemble the necessary puzzle pieces to lead us through the universe as planetary colonists.

As a child, I recall how some people claimed the moon was actually made of green cheese. Turns out it wasn't though I feel certain some people believed it. Being a child, I had my doubts, but kept an open mind. Today, plans are in the works to establish a colony on the moon where it looks like we will have to figure out how to get any color cheese on our own.

Then it is on to Mars. The trip already has 80,000 one way ticket requests from those wanting to be among the first settlers. My bet is those planetary colonists will thrive on creativity and ingenuity or perish in the attempt such as the Jamestown Settlement in the Colony of Virginia, the first permanent English Settlement in the Americas. But that will not hinder the human race from striving until it succeeds. With a fully engaged spirit of freedom, they will find ways to live unrestrained until once again, the laggards outnumber them and introduce 'socially responsible' concepts. Then it will be time to move on to other planets and the process will be repeated ad infinitum.

Back to the present for now means thwarting the advance of socialism to buy time until the last bastions of individual freedom are gone and the human race again must find the least resistant path to success. Indeed, the destiny of the human race IS to colonize the universe.

The spirit of freedom is at the heart of all living things and the burning passion to live unrestrained will always seek the path of least resistance to individual success whether it is here on Earth or "out there" as the future unfolds.

Indeed, the destiny of the human race IS to colonize the universe. The spirit of freedom will make it happen.

ABOUT THE AUTHORS

MAXWELL ANDERSON was the well-known playwright. *The Guaranteed Life* was first written as a preface to *Knickerbocker Holiday* in 1938. It was rewritten as a pamphlet in 1950.

SIR ERNEST BENN, a successful businessman in England, was President of the Society of Individualists. *Rights for Robots* is condensed from a 1950 address.

SPRUILLE BRADEN was formerly Ambassador to Argentina. *For a Moral Revolution* is extracted from a 1951 address.

EARL BROWDER was the former head of the Communist party in the United States. *The Communist Idea (Part* II) is extracted from his booklet, *Keynes, Foster and Marx; State Capitalism and Progress,* published by him in 1950.

ASA V. CALL was President of the Pacific Mutual Life Insurance Company. *Insuring Your Insurance* is extracted from a 1949 address.

FRANK CHODOROV was Associate Editor of *Human Affairs*. *Peace or Politics* is extracted from an article in *Analysis,* December, 1950.

RUSSELL J. CLINCHY, a minister in the Congregational Church, was a staff member of the Foundation for Economic Education. *Charity: Biblical and Political* was first published in 1951.

W. M. CURTISS, formerly Professor of Marketing at Cornell University, was a staff member of the Foundation for Economic Education. *Athletes, Taxes, Inflation* was first published in 1950. *Price Supports* were first published in 1949.

C. L. DICKINSON assisted the General Manager of the farmers' Cooperative G.L.F. Exchange. *Dollars Make Poor Eating* is extracted from a 1950 address.

J. OLLIE EDMUNDS was President of John B. Stetson University. *That Something* is a statement issued by him in May, 1951.

CRAWFORD H. GREENEWALT was President of E. I. DuPont de Nemours & Company. *For the Better Economic Life* is extracted from a 1951 address.

JOHN M. HANCOCK was a partner in Lehman Brothers. *The Freedom to Compete* is extracted from his statement before the Senate Trade Policies Committee, November 9, 1948.

F. A. formerly Professor of Marketing at Cornell University, was a staff member of the Foundation for Economic Education. *The Communist Idea (Part III)* was first published in 1950. *Inflation* was first published in *1951.* *Morals and the Welfare State* was first published in 1951.

HENRY HAZLITT was Associate Editor of *Newsweek* and Editor of the *Freeman. Private Enterprise Regained* first appeared as a column in *Newsweek,* June 27, 1949.

BETTY KNOWLES HUNT, housewife and mother, was a free lance writer and columnist. *Show Me Any Other Country* first appeared in the *Bridgeport* (Connecticut) *Post,* February 25, 1947.

BERTRAND DE JOUVENEL was a noted French author and lecturer in history and economics. *No Vacancies* was first published in 1948.

MARY C. LACY was formerly Librarian of the Bureau of Agricultural Economics, (U. S. Dept. of Agriculture). *Food Control during Forty-six Centuries* is extracted from a March, 1922 address before the Agricultural History Society.

JAMES MADISON was the fourth President of the United States. *The Most Dreaded Enemy of Liberty* is from *Letters and Other Writings of James Madison.*

CLARENCE MANION was Dean of the College of Law, Notre Dame University. *Legalized Immorality* is extracted from his book, *The Key to Peace* (Heritage Foundation, 1950). KARL MARX and FREDERICK ENGELS were the authors of *The Communist Manifesto. The Communist Idea (Part* I) is extracted from pages 32-34 of the New York Labor News Company's 1948 edition of that book.

LUDWIG VON MISES, Visiting Professor of Economics at the Graduate School of Business Administration, New York University, was the outstanding representative of the "Austrian school" of economics. *The Individual in Society* is extracted from his book *Human Action* (Yale University Press, 1950).

BEN MOREEL, former Chief of the Bureau of Yards and Docks, as well as Chief of Civil Engineers of the Navy, was Chairman of the Board of Jones & Laughlin Steel Corporation. *Power Corrupts* is extracted from a 1951 address. *Survival of the Species* was first published in 1950.

TOWNER PHELAN was Vice-President of the St. Louis Union Trust Company. *Liberalism Stands for Freedom* was reprinted from the *St. Louis Union Trust Company Letter* of October, 1948.

LEONARD E. READ, formerly Manager of the Los Angeles Chamber of Commerce and Executive Vice-President of the National Industrial Conference Board, was President of the Foundation for Economic Education. *On That Day Began Lies* was first published in 1949. *The Penalty of Surrender* was first published in 1948.

DEAN RUSSELL, Air Force captain, joined the staff of the Foundation for Economic Education in 1947 after completing his formal education.

The Bill of Rights was first published in the fall 1948 issue of *Popular Home Magazine. The First Leftist* was first published in 1951. *Ownership in Common* was first published in 1951. *Wards of the Government* was first published in 1950.

THOMAS J. SHELLY was a teacher of economics and history at Yonkers High School in Yonkers, New York. *A Lesson in Socialism* was first published in 1951.

WILLIAM GRAHAM SUMNER was Professor of Political Science at Yale, 1872-1909. *On Minding One's Own Business* is Chapter VIII of his book, *What Social Classes Owe to Each Other* (Harper & Brothers, 1883; republished by The Caxton Printers, 1952).

JOHN UNKEL was employed on the maintenance staff of the Foundation for Economic Education. *Some Wandering Thoughts,* first published in 1950, was left as a penciled note on the desk of another staff member.

MIKE FRANC has held a number of positions on Capitol Hill, is vice president of Government Relations at The Heritage Foundation.

THOMAS YOUNG, PhD. earned a Bachelor of Science in Applied Physics and a Doctor of Philosophy in Business Economics from The University of Utah. Dr. Young is involved in management consulting and venture capital funding advising clients across the United States, Europe and Asia.

ROD MILLER is Founder and Executive Director of the Spirit of Freedom Foundation (2001) after a career in computing technologies businesses. He manages the Foundation's website: **http://sprt76.org**

Made in the USA
Middletown, DE
17 July 2019